Fully Revised and Updated Edition

QUIZ?TIME

Fully Revised and Updated Edition

QUIZ?TIME

by

Ivar Utial

Assisted by

**Dr. Usha Manohar
Vinay Mohan Sharma**

PUSTAK MAHAL®
Delhi • Bangalore • Mumbai • Patna • Hyderabad

Publishers
Pustak Mahal®, Delhi

J-3/16, Daryaganj, New Delhi-110002
☎ 23276539, 23272783, 23272784 • *Fax:* 011-23260518
E-mail: info@pustakmahal.com • *Website:* www.pustakmahal.com

Sales Centre
10-B, Netaji Subhash Marg, Daryaganj, New Delhi-110002
☎ 23268292, 23268293, 23279900 • *Fax:* 011-23280567
E-mail: rapidexdelhi@indiatimes.com

Branch Offices
Bangalore: ☎ 22234025
E-mail: pmblr@sancharnet.in • pustak@sancharnet.in
Mumbai: ☎ 22010941
E-mail: rapidex@bom5.vsnl.net.in
Patna: ☎ 3294193 • *Telefax:* 0612-2302719
E-mail: rapidexptn@rediffmail.com
Hyderabad: *Telefax:* 040-24737290
E-mail: pustakmahalhyd@yahoo.co.in

Printed at : Param Offsetters, Okhla, New Delhi-110020

Dear Friends,

It affords me immense pleasure to see your ever-increasing thirst for General Knowledge. Your letters – full of curiosity, surprise and the urge for learning – assure me that India will ever be marching on the road to progress, at least, in the field of intellectual quest. Can a country's advancement be ever retarded whose youth is eager to assimilate new things?

Quiz is very much in the air these days. Be it on television or radio, in magazines or newspapers, or in full-length books, it is always 'Quiz Time'. No doubt, quiz is one of the best ways to increase knowledge and understanding of the world we inhabit. So, I too thought of presenting you this book.

Go through 'Quiz-Time', enjoy it and learn from it, and then write to me your candid assessment. You are aware that you are my torchbearer in the field of writing. Through you I learn of my shortcomings and your suggested topics guide me in taking up my future projects. Don't you agree?

O.K. friends! Your letters shall be eagerly awaited.

With love.

Yours,

Ivar Utial

Post Box 2562

New Delhi-110 005

for you!

Contents _____

Contents

SCIENCE

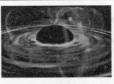
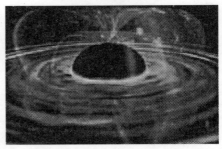

1. There is a bird, an inhabitant of the snows, which cannot fly but is an efficient swimmer. Name the bird. Which creature is the greatest enemy of its eggs?

2. What is the difference between animate and inanimate beings?

3. Which creature (after man, of course) is known for its intelligence?

4. Name the creature whose eyes can focus in two different directions simultaneously.

5. What is the distance covered by the bee scurrying between the beehive and the flowers for collecting a pound of honey?

6. Birds from Siberia and other cold regions migrate to warm places during winter. Why?

7. Which vegetation is known as "Patthar ka Phool"?

8. Explain the terms *stoma* and *stomata* used in Botany.

9. What is the lifespan of the queen-bee? What is the maximum number of eggs she lays in one day?

10. From where does the atmosphere get maximum oxygen?

11. What is a Bathyscaphe and what is it used for?

12. What are Black Holes?

13. Which organisation has developed the Anupam-Pentium supercomputer, India's fastest supercomputer?

14. Name the research ship which made the first nautical survey.

15. When was India's Nautical Research Institute established?

16. Why do plants always bend towards light?

17. How is the height of a horse measured?

18. Mule, donkey and pony are members of the horse family. Which other animal belongs to this family?

19. Which planet is known as the 'Morning Star'?

20. Which is the biggest water-snake?

21. What will be the number of pigeons in a pigeon-colony, born of a pair within three years, if breeding continues at its normal rate?

22. Which are the longest and the shortest bones in the human body?

23. What is an Encephalograph?

24. What is AIDS and how does it spread?

25. For which disease is Bacillus Calmette-Guerin Vaccine used?

26. Of the four blood groups of humans, which group can accept all the other groups?

27. What is the percentage of blood in a healthy human body?

28. What is a Geostationary satellite? Is it really stationary?

29. Name India's first rocket and mention its launching station.

30. What is Sriharikota? Why is it famous?

31. What is OTEC?

32. Which was India's first hydro-electric project?

33. What is 'PURNIMA'? And what is its function?

34. When and where were the first efforts made to generate electricity from hot-water springs?

35. What is meant by horsepower? Who named it so and why?

36. What is Mach Number?

37. What is calendering and what is it used for?

38. What is a transistor? Who invented it?

39. Which gas leaked the most during the Bhopal gas tragedy? But which other gas was the cause of the most deaths?

40. What is Photovoltaic Cell? How does it work?

41. What are the various things used as Superconductors these days?

42. Why do we usually sweat before rains?

43. Coloured cloth looks of deeper hue when wet. Why?

44. Who invented the first steamship?

45. What kind of a satellite is INSAT-1B? Who made it and how was it launched?

46. What is the chemical difference between chalk and limestone?

47. What is a communications satellite and who first conceived it?

48. Which was the first rocket to land on the moon?

49. Name the novelist who had imagined a journey to the moon, which proved to be a fact later.

50. Who was Robert Godard and what is he famous for?

51. What is meant by Escape Velocity?

Q. 44

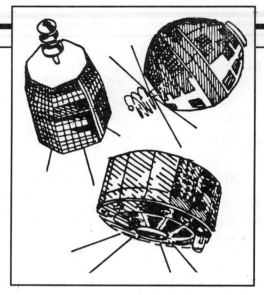

52. What types of rays are known as Cathode rays?

53. What is Superconductivity and how is it acquired?

54. Is there a stone which can float on water? If yes, name it.

55. Who was the Indian scientist who named his famous work on mathematics after his daughter?

56. Who was the first Indian F.R.S. (Fellow of Royal Society)?

57. Who was Dr. Meghnad Saha? With which institution is he associated?

58. Who was Dr. Homi Bhabha? Name the institution he established.

59. How can bats see in the dark?

60. Which is the largest flying bird?

61. What is the difference between salt-water fish and fresh-water fish?

62. Who invented the Logarithm?

63. What is the Fibonacci Sequence?

64. Who was Mahaviracharya and what is his famous work?

65. Name the most famous work of Greek mathematician Euclid?

66. Why is the Barnali Dynasty famous in the field of mathematics?

67. Which is the largest planet in our Solar System?

68. What is Jantar-Mantar and why is it famous?

69. Where has the earth been dug the deepest so far?

70. When and where was the biggest explosion carried out by man?

71. At which place does the wind blow the fastest on earth?

72. What is a weather satellite? Name the first such satellite.

73. What is amalgam?

74. What ingredients are there in carbohydrates?

75. What is the commonly used name of dilute acetic acid?

76. What is brine?

77. In which liquid can ice be kept without melting?

78. Why does a silver spoon turn black when it touches the yolk of an egg?

79. Which metal melts at normal heat?

80. What are gravitational waves?

81. In a cold region like Ladakh, even in bright sunshine, a shady spot is unaffected by the heat and remains cold. Why?

82. Why do glass containers or utensils crack when boiling water is poured into them?

83. When we are munching dry bread, we hear a loud crunching sound with each movement of the jaw, while a person sitting next to us does not hear it. Why is it not audible to him?

84. Can a singer break glass into fragments with the effect of his music?

85. What are chromosomes? How many chromosomes do we have in our body cells?

86. What is Mongolism?

87. What is Haemophilia? How does it affect a patient?

88. Who developed the Nuclear Reactor first?

89. Who is the inventor of the heart-lung machine?

90. At what temperature does gold melt?

91. Who invented the Radar?

92. Who is the inventor of the talkies (cinema with sound)?

93. Who made the first refrigerator?

94. Who invented air-conditioning?

95. Who made the first motor-car?

96. Who invented the electric fan?

97. What is the optical instrument for viewing distant objects with both eyes called?

98. In winters distant sound is more clearly audible than in summers. Why?

99. Who invented the helicopter?

100. What is a galaxy?

101. Name the laboratories in India currently engaged in research in superconductivity.

102. What are semiconductors and where are they used?

103. What is the distance between the two rails of broad-gauge railway line and narrow-gauge railway line?

104. What is Demerara Sugar?

105. Why is it that the number of jewels in a watch is always odd?

106. What is the difference between 'Sterling Silver' and 'German Silver'?

107. Where is Jodral Bank situated and what is it famous for?

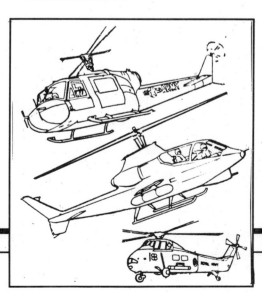

Q. 99

108. Which planet is nearest to the sun (apart from the earth)?

109. Is the Pole Star a definite star?

110. What are Pulsars?

111. How many stars can we see in the star-studded sky without the aid of any telescope?

112. Next to the sun, which star looks the brightest?

113. How much time does sunlight take to reach the earth?

114. The Platypus is a mammal but it has a prominent characteristic which differs from other mammals. What is that?

115. Which bird can fly for the longest duration at a stretch?

116. Which is the largest animal in the world?

117. Which is the fastest growing living being?

118. Name the astronaut to fly in Vostok-I. What was the duration of the flight?

119. When was the Nobel Prize instituted?

120. Who invented the graph-system in mathematics?

121. Why does the North Pole change its direction?

122. Who invented the revolver?

123. Who conceived the Hovercraft?

124. Who invented the sewing machine?

125. Why are bigger bubbles formed with a soap-water solution and not with plain water?

126. What is the Glen Effect which was first discovered by the US scientist John Glen?

127. Who was the first woman astronaut?

128. Neil Armstrong was the first to step on the moon. Who was the second person?

129. Name the insects which make minaret-like mounds that are firm and rock-like?

130. Which farthest star can we see without the help of a telescope?

131. What is anti-matter and where is it found in the cosmos?

132. What is N.M.R.?

133. What is decibel?

134. Why is Niels Bohr famous?

135. Who propounded the Quantum Theory?

136. Why is the sun visible before sunrise in the polar region?

137. Name the colour having maximum refractive index.

138. Why is a small drop of water round?

139. The letters N.L. are added after the name of a Nobel Prize winner. What do they signify?

140. Who invented the rail engine?

141. Which was the year when the Nobel Prize was not awarded? Why?

142. Lemmings, a species of rodent found in Norway, periodically rush towards the sea. Why?

143. Name the fish which is born in the sea but spends its life in lakes and ponds.

144. Why does the salmon come from the sea to rivers?

145. Who were the first men to land in the deepest place on earth? How did they reach there?

146. What is meant by Nautical mile?

147. What is the Nautilus? What made the Nautilus famous?

148. Name the explorer who, at the beginning of this century, came back from an Antarctic expedition but died 17 years thereafter at the Arctic region while searching for a fellow explorer.

149. What is fathom?

150. What is cyclotron?

151. Which is the strongest source of artificial light?

152. What is the lowest temperature recorded so far?

153. What are antimolecules?

154. The Moon has no atmosphere. But is there a satellite having its own atmosphere?

155. What are Supernovae?

156. What is meant by QUASAR?

157. Which is the planet often called the twin-planet of earth because of a marked resemblance to the earth?

158. Name the space-ship in which the first Indian astronaut Rakesh Sharma went into space. Also name the space-ship with which his space-ship was connected.

159. What are Auroras and why are they formed?

Q. 158

160. What is water-glass?

161. Who learns swimming easily and quickly – a fat person or a slim one?

162. If Gangotri is the source of the Ganga, which river emanates from 'Dakshin Gangotri'?

163. Who was the founder-father of Council of Scientific and Industrial Research?

164. When was the Royal Asiatic Society established?

165. Which institute keeps the international weights and measures in custody (kilogram and metres)?

166. Which institute was established in the country for conducting research on virus?

167. When and where was the first modern observatory set up?

168. Where is Occupational Health Research Institute situated and what is its function?

169. When was The Indian Council of Medical Research established?

170. Which institute is named PUSA Institute and where is it situated?

171. What is a penny-farthing?

172. Why does a table-tennis ball dance on a fountain?

173. Why are the sea and the sky blue?

174. Why does the flame of a candle always burn upward?

175. Who was James Watt and why is he famous?

176. What is the boiling and freezing point of heavy water?

177. What is the difference between Celsius and Centigrade?

178. What is 'Lye'?

179. Who invented sunglasses?

180. If blue vitriol is copper sulphate and green vitriol is ferrous sulphate, what is white vitriol?

181. What are the alloys of – Brass, Bronze, Mild Steel, German Silver and White Gold?

182. Is it possible for man to die from lack of water without his feeling thirsty?

183. Sugar contains chemical elements found in charcoal and water. Is this correct?

184. Bones are considered dry but is there any water in our bones?

185. How do rats of the desert area quench their thirst and meet the requirement of body water?

186. Generally the cause of death in a desert is dehydration. How can we reduce the water requirement of our body?

187. Do women have less quantity of body water than men?

188. How much water-content is there in water-melon?

189. Why does a man die of thirst in the sea?

190. What is Ambergris?

191. Why is the Civet Cat so endearingly popular?

192. What is the source of musk?

193. Christopher Columbus and other explorers found the South American natives playing with 'bouncy balls' of hardened juice. What was it?

194. What proportion of water is sweet and fit for drinking, of all the water available on the earth?

195. Is the size of the brain linked in any way to intelligence?

196. Which gas turns into liquid at the lowest temperature?

197. Einstein spent a good part of his later life on one particular problem in Physics which was his last dream. What was it?

198. What is meant by hydrogenated oil?

199. What are the roaring forties?

200. Who tried to extract gold from sea-water in bulk?

201. What are polymetallic nodules?

202. What is our biggest international achievement in ocean research?

203. Who was Dr. Salim Ali and why is he famous?

204. How much solar energy can we get per square metre in a year?

205. Who was the first Indian scientist to be awarded the Nobel Prize for Physics and what was his contribution?

206. When was the X-ray invented and who invented it?

207. What is the scientific name of the machine used for measuring breath?

208. Who was the Indian mathematician whose birth-centenary was celebrated in 1987?

209. Who discovered bacteria?

210. What is the ozone layer and how does it protect us?

211. Is the ozone layer disappearing?

212. What is the difference between an electric dynamo and an electric motor?

Q. 206

213. What is debugging?

214. What is galvanising?

215. What is the speed of electric current?

216. Who was the first Indian doctor to successfully perform heart-bypass surgery?

217. What is C.A.T. and why is it used?

218. What is biopsy?

219. Which mosquitoes carry malarial fever?

220. Who used anaesthesia for the first time?

221. How much water deficiency can the human body easily tolerate?

222. Which scientist discovered the process by which plants convert sugar out of carbon dioxide?

223. Who is the 'Radium Lady'?

224. Name the non-Indian Nobel Prize winning scientist whose theories and research have helped us immensely in bringing about the 'green revolution'.

225. How much solar energy do plants and trees use?

226. Two thin shirts can keep us warmer than a thick shirt in winter. Why?

227. Why are temple bells big in size?

228. Which medium does sound travel faster in — water or air?

229. One mile is 1.609 kilometres. How many miles are there in one kilometre?

230. Name the great Indian engineer who was also a politician and who died at the age of 100 plus.

231. Who was Al-Beruni and why is he famous?

232. Name the famous scientist in the field of Astrophysics.

233. What is the other tensile and strong metal like iron? Who discovered that metal?

234. What is mutation?

235. What is gene-engineering?

236. Who gave us the nomenclature 'Bacteria'?

237. What is the main difference between vegetation and animals?

238. Which is the fastest-growing tree?

239. Why do sparrows take a dust-bath?

240. When was the Nobel Prize for Physics awarded to C. Venkata Raman (C.V. Raman)? When and where was Raman born?

241. Why is radio transmission clearer after sunset?

242. Why is the danger signal red in colour?

243. Why is it easier to swim in the sea than in a river?

244. Why do we feel suffocated on cloudy nights and not so much on clear nights?

245. When we bounce a ball while travelling in a moving train we can catch it again. Why?

246. Why do camphor particles dance when dropped in clear water?

247. Besides chlorophyll, what are the other pigments to give different colours to trees and plants?

248. Where is the biggest bird colony in the world and which are the main birds found there?

249. Why are flowers and fruits so colourful and attractive?

250. When and where was the first zoo in the world established?

251. Which birds cover the longest distance while migrating?

252. How many migratory birds visit India during winters?

253. Who invented the Internal Combustion Engine?

254. Who invented the Washing Machine?

255. Who invented the freezer?

256. Who invented the Steam Engine?

257. Who invented the Adding Machine?

258. Who invented the gas balloon?

259. Who invented the Calculating Machine?

260. Who invented the Electric Motor?

261. Name the six simple machines.

262. Who discovered Insulin?

263. How does a snake hear when it has no ears?

264. What is the full form of L.S.D.? How does it affect our metabolism?

265. Name the most commonly used drug.

266. Does alcohol really stimulate the brain?

267. What was the contribution for which Einstein was awarded the Nobel Prize in Physics?

268. Who gave us the treatment for Rabies?

269. Why do we remember Alexander Fleming?

270. Name the bird of the Dinosaur-age.

271. Name some of the commonly used tranquillisers.

Q. 267

272. What is the well-known product with which the Universal Fastener Company is associated? Who established it?

273. Which is the most used metal?

274. Who is the father of the Mutation Theory?

275. In 1986, along with Halley's comet, scientists spotted another comet. Which was that?

276. Which acid is present in tomato sauce?

277. The first ever experiment in the field of generating electricity with sea-water was made in France. Do we, in India, have areas where this project can be carried out?

278. What is the Shanti Swarup Bhatnagar Award?

279. What is fuel cell? Who invented it and where is it used?

280. We have heard a lot about 'Flying Saucers'. They are also known as UFOs (Unidentified Flying Objects). It was after a well-known sighting in 1947 that this name was given to these objects. What was that incident?

281. Which metal is as hard as diamond?

282. Does desert absorb more heat and solar energy than moist earth?

283. Why is a desert cooler at night than moist places?

284. Camels are of two kinds – those with one hump are called Arabian. The others have two humps. What are they known as?

285. How many cocoons are destroyed for obtaining one pound of silk?

286. Name the animal which is dumb though it has a long tongue.

287. One cubic foot of sweet water weighs 62.4 pounds. What is the weight of one cubic foot of sea-water, iron and cork?

288. What are the branches of mathematics in which Ramanujan did his new research work?

289. How many hectares are there in one acre?

290. Which apparatus is used for measuring the intensity of an earthquake?

291. How do living beings store carbohydrates?

292. Who demonstrated the first experiment of an electric train?

293. Fats are usually light yellow. Why?

294. What are enzymes?

295. How much food can a python consume in one go?

296. Name a marine animal which keeps a big harem.

297. How many eggs does a peahen lay at one time?

298. Is the bald eagle really bald? Why is it named so?

299. Is an overdose of Vitamin 'A' harmful?

300. How many vitamins are needed for a healthy body?

301. How many minerals do we need for good health?

302. What is meant by 14-carat gold?

303. Why is Sushrut famous?

304. Who was Charak?

305. What is the rate of hewing of trees and forests in our country?

306. How many years do Uranus, Neptune and Pluto take to revolve around the sun?

307. Does the sun rotate around its axis like the Earth?

308. Why is a deep-water diver not allowed to come to the surface fast?

309. How much air can we pump into our lungs?

310. How deep can a man dive without the aid of any implement?

311. How do the Eskimos procure their drinking water in the frozen Arctic region?

312. What is Plate Tectonics Theory?

313. What is Heroin?

314. In "X-rays", what does "X" mean?

315. Although the climate is cold at high altitude, sun-burns are very common there. What is the reason?

316. What is the rate of fall in temperature as height is gained?

317. After crossing Jupiter, Saturn, Uranus and others, a space-ship is going towards a far-off planet. Which ship is that?

318. Identify the three dinosaurs in the sketch at the bottom.

319. Where do maximum number of earthquakes occur?

320. Who was the leader of the first Indian Antarctic expedition?

321. What are the various changes that occur for the formation of hills and mountains?

322. Edible oils develop a kind of smell and undergo changes in taste. What is the reason for these changes?

Q. 318

323. How many cells are there in the human body?

324. What is meant by artificial intelligence?

325. What is cybernatics?

326. What is meant by oxygen-point?

327. What is a dye? Is every colour a dyeing agent?

328. Where does space begin?

329. How many litres are there in one gallon water?

330. How many kilograms are there in one quintal and what is 10 quintals known as?

331. When was the telescope first used for the study of stars?

332. How is it ascertained that car batteries need recharging? What apparatus is used for ascertaining this?

333. What is the strength of the current shot by the eel?

334. Is there an acid in grapes?

335. Which gas is used for disinfecting water of bacteria?

336. For measuring temperature at the South Pole which thermometer will be ideal – the one with alcohol or with mercury?

337. What is meant by the Aperture of a camera lens?

338. Letter 'C' denotes the Roman numeral 100. What numbers do the following letters denote – L, M, D?

339. Does sound travel faster through water or in a vacuum?

340. There are two alloys which are commonly used. One of them contains Copper and Tin but not Zinc, another has Copper and Zinc but not Tin. Identify them.

341. What is safety glass?

342. Of the two Wright brothers (of aeroplane fame) who was the elder one? Which of them died first and how?

343. What is the pulse-rate of an average healthy male?

344. What is the name of the person who designed a machine called the Analytical Engine that had the basic features of a modern computer?

345. A young boy lifted the lid off a kettle of boiling water and recognised the power of steam. Who was this future scientist?

346. Which is the heaviest liquid?

347. Plants are green because of Chlorophyll, our blood is red due to Haemoglobin. What are the main elements present in Chlorophyll and Haemoglobin responsible for the said colours?

348. With what speed is the message carried to our brain when any part of our body is hurt?

349. What is the minutest thing that our naked eyes can see?

350. What is the difference between electricity and electronics?

351. What is 'liquid wood'?

352. What is the size of a nanoparticle?

353. What is a light-year?

354. What is the name of our home galaxy?

355. Who made a world record for the longest stay in space?

356. What is a space-station? Name the first space-station.

357. What is Lithosphere?

358. What is Richter Scale?

359. Name the world's largest island.

360. How many bones are there in the human skeleton?

361. How many bones are there in our face?

362. What is the number of teeth in humans called primary, milk, temporary, or deciduous teeth?

363. Protein deficiency causes two major diseases in humans. One is Kwashiorkor. Name the other.

364. How does a mother transmit HIV to her unborn child?

365. Which are the three systems of temperature measurement now in use?

366. What is the name of the Indian doctor who performed 6,00,000 eye operations during the period 1943 to 1990?

367. What is a Gyroscope?

368. Who coined the term 'Horse Power'?

369. What is C-DOT?

370. Which is the largest mineral resource in India?

371. What is the name of the largest asteroid?

372. What is the name of the first scientist to receive the Bharat Ratna?

373. Banganapalle, Neelam, Alphonso. They are varieties of a food item. Name that.

374. What is the name of India's first nuclear research reactor?

375. What is the 'Painted Lady'?

376. Why is August 11, 1999 unique?

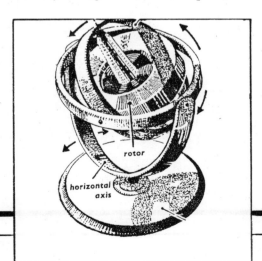

Q. 367

377. What is the life expectancy of a blue whale?

378. How many hours do cats sleep in a day?

379. "Give me a space to stand away from the earth and I shall lift this earth." Who said these words?

380. When did man first land on the moon?

381. The lift was invented solely for the use of a king. Which king?

INVENTIONS AND DISCOVERIES

Invention	Year	Inventor	Country
Adding Machine	1642	Wilhelm Schickard	Germany
Aeroplane	1903	Orville & Wilbur Wright	USA
Airship (Non-Rigid)	1852	Henri Giffard	France
Aerosol Spray	1926	Erik Rotheim	Norway
Airship (Rigid)	1900	G.F. von Zeppelin	Germany
Artificial Heart	1957	Willem Kolff	Netherlands
Atomic Bomb	1945	J. Robert Oppenheimer	USA
Automatic Rifle	1918	John Browning	USA
Bakelite	1907	Leo H. Baekeland	Belgium
Ballistic Missile	1944	Wernher von Braun	Germany
Balloon	1783	Jacques & Joseph Montgolfier	France
Ball-point Pen	1888	John J. Loud	USA
Barometer	1644	Evangelista Torricelli	Italy
Battery (Electric)	1800	Alessandro Volta	Italy
Bicycle	1839-40	Kirkpatrick Macmillan	Britain
Bicycle Tyres (Pneumatic)	1888	John Boyd Dunlop	Britain
Bifocal Lens	1780	Benjamin Franklin	USA
Bolt-action Rifle	1889	P. von Mauser	Germany
Bunsen Burner	1855	R. Willhelm von Bunsen	Germany
Burglar Alarm	1858	Edwin T. Holmes	USA
Car (Steam)	c. 1769	Nicolas Cugnot	France
Car (Petrol)	1888	Karl Benz	Germany
Carburettor	1876	Gottlieb Daimler	Germany
Carpet Sweeper	1876	Melville R. Bissell	USA
Cash Register	1879	James Ritty	USA
Cellophane	1908	Dr. J. Brandenberger	Switzerland
Celluloid	1861	Alexander Parkes	Britain
Cement (Portland)	1824	Joseph Aspdin	Britain
Chronometer	1735	John Harrison	Britain

Invention	Year	Inventor	Country
Cinema	1895	Nicolas & Jean Lumiere	France
Clock (Mechanical)	1725	I-Hsing & Liang Ling-Tsan	China
Clock (Pendulum)	1656	Christian Huygens	Netherlands
Compact Disc Player	1979	Sony, Philips Co.	Japan, Netherlands
Crossword Puzzle	1913	Arthur Wynne	USA
Dental Plate	1817	Anthony A. Plantson	USA
Dental Plate (Rubber)	1855	Charles Goodyear	USA
Diesel Engine	1895	Rudolf Diesel	Germany
Disc Brake	1902	Dr. F. Lanchester	Britain
Dynamo	1832	Hypolite Pixii	France
Electric Flat Iron	1882	H.W. Seeley	USA
Electric Furnace	1861	William Siemens	Britain
Electric Lamp	1879	Thomas Alva Edison	USA
Electric Motor (DC)	1873	Zenobe Gramme	Belgium
Electric Motor (AC)	1888	Nikola Tesla	USA
Electric Washing Machine	1906	Alva J. Fisher	USA
Electro-magnet	1824	William Sturgeon	Britain
Electroplating	1805	Luigi Brugnatelli	Italy
Electronic Computer	1824	Dr. Alan M. Turing	Britain
Facsimile Machine	1843	Alexander Bain	Britain
Film (Moving Outlines)	1885	Louis Prince	France
Film (Talking)	1922	J. Engl, J. Mussolle & H. Vogt	Germany
Film (Musical Sound)	1923	Dr. Le de Forest	USA
Frequency Modulation (FM)	1933	E.H. Armstrong	USA
Frisbee	1948	Fred Morrison	USA
Frozen Food	1924	Clarence Birdseye	USA
Fountain Pen	1884	Lewis E. Waterman	USA
Galvanometer	1834	Andre-Marie Ampere	France
Gas Lighting	1792	William Murdock	Britain
Glass (Stained)	c.1080	Augsburg	Germany

Invention	Year	Inventor	Country
Glassware	c.1500 BC		Egypt & Mesopotamia
Glider	1853	Sir George Cayley	Britain
Gramophone	1878	Thomas Alva Edison	USA
Guided Missile	1942	Wernher von Braun	Germany
Gyro-compass	1911	Elmer A. Sperry	USA
Helicopter	1924	Etienne Oehmichen	France
Holography	1947	Denis Gason	Britain
Hovercraft	1955	Christopher Cockerell	Britain
Hydrogen Bomb	1952	Edward Teller	USA
Iron Working (Carbonised)	c.1200 BC	—	Cyprus & N. Palestine
Jet Engine	1937	Sir Frank Whittle	Britain
Kodak Camera	1888	George Eastman	USA
Laser	1960	T.H. Maimah	USA
Launderette	1934	J.F. Cantrell	USA
Lift (Mechanical)	1852	Elisha G. Otis	USA
Lightning Conductor	1752	Benjamin Franklin	USA
Linoleum	1860	Frederick Walton	Britain
Linotype	1883	O. Margenthaler	USA
Locomotive	1804	Richard Trevithick	Britain
Loom (Power)	1785	E. Cartwright	Britain
Loudspeaker	1900	Horace Short	Britain
Machine Gun	1718	James Puckle	Britain
Magnetic Recording Tape	1928	Fritz Pfleumer	Germany
Maps	c. 3800 BC	—	Sumeria
			(clay tablets of river Euphrates)
Margarine	1869	Hippolyte M. Mouries	France
Match (Safety)	1826	John Walker	Britain
Microphone	1876	Alexander Graham Bell	USA
Microprocessor	1971	Robert Noyce & Gordon Moore	USA
Microscope	1590	Z. Janssen	Netherlands

Invention	Year	Inventor	Country
Microwave Oven	1947	Percy Le Baron Spencer	USA
Motor Cycle	1885	G. Daimler of Cannstatt	Germany
Movie Projector	1893	Thomas Edison	USA
Neon Lamp	1910	Georges Claude	France
Neutron Bomb	1958	Samuel Cohen	USA
Nylon	1937	Dr. Wallace H. Carothers	USA
Optical Fibre	1955	Narinder Kapany	Germany
Paper	A.D. 105	—	China
Parchment	c. 1300 BC	—	Egypt
Parking Meter	1935	Carlton C. Magee	USA
Parallel Computing	1979	Seymour Cray & David Gelerntes	USA
Pasteurisation	1867	Louis Pasteur	France
Pencil	1792	Jacques-Nicolas Conte	France
Photoelectrical Cell	1893	Julius Elster, Hans F. Geitel	Germany
Photography (On Metal)	1826	J.N. Niepce	France
Photography (On Paper)	1835	W.H. Fox Talbot	Britain
Photography (On Film)	1888	John Carbutt	USA
Plasticine	1900	William Harbutt	UK
Pogo Stick	1921	George B. Hansburg	USA
Porcelain	A.D. 851	—	Earliest report from China
Potter's Wheel	c. 6500 BC	—	Asia Minor
Pop-up Toaster	1927	Charles Strite	USA
Printing Press	c. 1455	Johann Gutenberg	Germany
Printing (Rotary)	1846	Richard Hoe	USA
Printing (Web-fed Rotary)	1865	William Bullock	USA
Propeller (Ship)	1837	Francis Smith	Britain
Radar	1922	A.H. Taylor & Leo C. Young	USA
Radio Telegraphy	1864	Dr. Mohlon Loomis	USA
Radio Telegraphy (Transatlantic)	1901	G. Marconi	Italy
Rayon	1883	Sir Joseph Swan	Britain

Invention	Year	Inventor	Country
Razor (Electric)	1931	Col. Jacob Schick	USA
Record (Long-playing)	1948	Dr. Peter Goldmark	USA
Refrigerator	1850	James Harrison, Alexander Catlin	USA
Rollerblades	1980	Scott & Brennan Olsen	USA
Rubber (Latex Foam)	1928	Dunlop Rubber Co.	Britain
Rubber (Tyres)	1846	Thomas Hancock	Britain
Rubber (Vulcanised)	1841	Charles Goodyear	USA
Rubber (Waterproof)	1823	Charles Macintosh	Britain
Rubik Cube	1975	Prof. Erno Rubik	Hungary
Safety Pin	1849	Walter Hunt	USA
Safety Razor	1895	King Camp Gillette	USA
Scotch Tape	1930	Richard Drew	USA
Self-starter	1911	Charles F. Kettering	USA
Ship (Steam)	1775	J.C. Perier	France
Ship (Turbine)	1894	Hon. Sir C. Parsons	Britain
Silk Manufacture	c. 50 BC	—	China
Skateboard	1958	Bill & Mark Richards	USA
Skyscraper	1882	W. Le Baron Jenny	USA
Slide Rule	1621	William Oughtred	Britain
Slinky Spring	1946	Richard James	USA
Spinning Frame	1769	Sir Richard Arkwright	Britain
Spinning Jenny	1764	James Hargreaves	Britain
Spinning Mule	1779	Samuel Crompton	Britain
Steam Engine	1698	Thomas Savery	Britain
Steam Engine (Piston)	1712	Thomas Newcomen	Britain
Steam Engine (Condenser)	1765	James Watt	Britain
Steel (Stainless)	1913	Harry Brearley	Britain
Submarine	1776	David Bushnell	USA
Super Computer	1976	J.H. Van Tassel	USA
Swiss Army Knife	1891	Karl Elsener	Switzerland

Invention	Year	Inventor	Country
Tank	1914	Sir Ernest D. Swington	Britain
Teddy Bear	1903	Margarete Steiff	Germany
Telegraph	1787	M. Lammond	France
Telegraph Code	1837	Samuel F.B. Morse	USA
Telephone (Imperfect)	1849	Antonio Meucci	Italy
Telephone (Perfected)	1876	Alexander Graham Bell	USA
Telescope	1608	Hans Lippershey	Netherlands
Television (Mechanical)	1926	John Logie Baird	Britain
Television (Electronic)	1927	P.T. Farnsworth	USA
Terylene	1941	J.R. Whinfield, J.T. Dickson	Britain
Transformer	1831	Michael Faraday	Britain
Transistor	1948	Shockley, Bardeen & Brittain	USA
Transistor Radio	1955	Sony	Japan
Video Tape	1956	Charles Ginsberg	USA
Velcro (Hook-and-Loop Fastener)	1948	George de Mestral	Switzerland
Washing Machine (elec.)	1907	Hurley Machine Co.	USA
Watch	1462	Bartholomew Manfredi	Italy
Water Closet	1589	Designed by J. Harrington	Britain
Welder (Electric)	1877	Elisha Thomson	USA
Windmill	c.600	Persian Corn Grinding	
Wireless (Telegraphy)	1896	G. Marconi	Italy
Writing	c. 3500 BC	Sumerian Civilisation	
X-ray	1895	Wilhelm K. Roentgen	Germany
Yo-Yo	1929	Donald F. Duncan	USA
Zip Fastener	1891	W.L Judson	USA

MILESTONES IN MEDICINE

Invention	Year	Inventor	Country
Ayurveda	2000-1000 BC	Atreya	India
Western Scientific Therapy	460-370 BC	Hippocrates	Greece
Yoga	200-100 BC	Patanjali	India
Ashtanga Hridaya	c.550 AD	Vagbhata	India
Sidhayoga	c.750	Vrdukunta	India
Anatomia	1316	Mondino	Italy
Chemotherapy	1493-1541	Paracelsus	Switzerland
Blood Transfusion	1625	Jean-Baptiste Denys	France
Circulation of Blood	1628	William Harvey	Britain
Biochemistry	1648	Jean Baptiste van Helmont	Belgium
Bacteria	1683	Leeuwenhock	Netherlands
Neurology	1758-1828	Franz Joseph Gall	Germany
Physiology	1757	Albrecht von Haller	Switzerland
Vaccination	1796	Edward Jenner	Britain
Histology	1771-1802	Marie Bichat	France
Stethoscope	1819	Rene Laennec	France
Embryology	1792-1896	Karl Ernest-Van Baer	Estonia
Morphine	1805	Friedrich Sertumer	Germany
Chloroform as Anaesthetic	1847	James Simpson	Britain
Hypodermic Syringe	1853	Alexander Wood	Britain
Rabies Vaccine	1860	Louis Pasteur	France
Bacteriology	1872	Ferdinand Cohn	Germany
Leprosy Bacillus	1873	Hansen	Norway
Cholera T.B. Germs	1877	Robert Koch	Germany
Malaria Germs	1880	Laveran	France
Diphtheria Germs	1883-84	Klebs & Loffler	Germany
Aspirin	1889	Dreser	Germany
Virology	1892	Ivanovski & Bajernick	USSR, Netherlands
Psychoanalysis	1895	Sigmund Freud	Austria

Invention	Year	Inventor	Country
Serology	1884-1915	Paul Ehrlich	Germany
Anti-toxins (Science of Immunity)	1890	Behring & Kitasato	Germany, Japan
Adrenaline	1894	Schafer and Oliver	Britain
Endocrinology	1902	Bayliss & Starling	Britain
Electrocardiograph	1903	Willem Einthoven	Netherlands
Typhus Vaccine	1909	J. Nicolle	France
Sex Hormones	1910	Eugen Steinach	Austria
Vitamins	1912	Sir F.C. Hopkins	Britain
Vitamin A	1913	McCollum and M. Davis	USA
Vitamin C	1919	Froelich Holst	Norway
Synthetic Antigens	1917	Landsteiner	USA
Thyroxin	1919	Edward Calvin-Kendall	USA
Insulin for Diabetes	1921	Banting & Best	Canada
Vitamin D	1925	McCollum	USA
Penicillin	1928	Alexander Fleming	Britain
Electroencephalogram	1929	Hans Berger	Germany
Cardiac Pacemaker	1932	A.S. Hyman	USA
Vitamin B1	1936	Minot & Murphy	USA
Cortisone	1936	Edward Calvin-Kendall	USA
D.D.T. (Dichloro-Diphenyl-Trichloroethane)	1939	Paul Muller	Germany
Rh-factor	1940	Karl Landsteiner	USA
LSD (Lysergic acid diethylamide)	1943	Hoffman	Switzerland
Streptomycin	1944	Selman Waksmann	USA
Kidney Machine	1944	Kolf	Netherlands
Chloromycetin	1947	Burkholder	USA
Aureomycin	1948	Duggar	USA
Reserpine	1949	Jal Vakil	India
Terramycin	1950	Finlay & Others	USA
Cryosurgery	1953	Henry Swan	USA

Invention	Year	Inventor	Country
Open Heart Surgery	1953	Walton Lillehel	USA
Poliomyelitis Vaccine	1954	Jonas Salk	USA
Poliomyelitis Vaccine (Oral)	1954	Albert Sabin	USA
Oral Contraceptive Pills	1955	Gregory Pincus	USA
Artificial Heart	1957	Willem Kolff	Netherlands
Use of Artificial Heart (for surgery)	1963	Michael de Bakey	USA
Heart Transplant Surgery	1967	Christian Barnard	S. Africa
CAT Scanner	1968	Godfrey Hounsfield	Britain
Resonance Imaging	1971	Raymond Damadian	USA
Recombinant-DNA Technology	1972-73	Paul Berg, H.W. Boyer, S. Cohen	USA
First Test Tube Baby	1978	Steptoe & Edwards	Britain
Positron Emission Tomography	1978	Louis Sokoloff	USA
Gene Therapy on Humans	1980	Martin Clive	USA
Genes Associated with Cancer	1982	Robert Weinberg & others	USA

HISTORY

382. What are Jataka Stories?

383. Hindus have their Gita, Muslims have their Quran. Name the main sacred book of the Parsees.

384. A Roman emperor, who ruled from 54 AD to 68 AD, was notorious for his cruelty and tyranny. Who was he?

385. Who was Kautilya?

386. Name the founder-father of the Brahmo Samaj.

387. Who is the Irishwoman known for her wholehearted support given to India's freedom struggle?

388. When did Chandragupta Vikramaditya reign? Which Chinese traveller visited India during his reign?

389. During the rule of King Harshvardhan (606-647 AD), a Chinese traveller visited India. Who was he?

390. What was the period of the First World War?

391. Which great thinker and philosopher outlined the principles of Communism?

392. What has been the contribution of Pandit Madan Mohan Malviya in the field of journalism?

393. Which country, apart from India, celebrates its Independence Day on 15th August?

394. An Afghan ruler dealt a crushing defeat to Humayun in 1539-40. Who was he?

395. How many times did Jawaharlal Nehru go to jail for his activities during the freedom struggle?

396. In which year was Pondicherry annexed by Independent India?

397. By what name is Mehrunnisa famous in history?

398. What was the age of Joan of Arc when she was burnt alive at the stake? In which year did it take place?

399. When and where was *Jana-gana-mana* sung first?

400. Who ascended the throne after Chandragupta Maurya's death? How was he related to King Ashoka?

401. Name the British Ambassador who came to India during the reign of Jahangir. Also name the King of England then.

402. When was the "Shak" century started?

403. What is the place of birth of Jesus Christ and where was Prophet Mohammed born?

404. What was Hitler's secret service named?

405. Name the battle which marked the end of the Napoleanic era.

406. After Timur the Lame's aggression in 1398, another bloody aggression on Delhi saw mass killings. Who had attacked then?

407. Who was the first woman Governor in Independent India?

408. Who got the Qutub Minar built and when?

409. Which famous traveller from Greece visited India during the reign of Chandra-gupta Maurya and for how many years did he stay here?

410. How many Gurus have been there in Jainism? What are they known as?

411. What was the name of Akbar's Hindu wife?

412. What were the full names of Aurangzeb and Shahjahan?

413. To which country did King Henry VI belong? What is the unusual fact he is known for?

414. What is the International Calendar known as?

415. How many viceroys were appointed to India between 1858 and 1947?

416. How many Governor-Generals came to India appointed by the East India Company?

417. Where do these famous words appear – "If there be a paradise on earth it is here, it is here, it is here"?

418. When did Queen Elizabeth I ascend the throne of England?

419. Where did Mohammed Tughlaq shift his capital from Delhi?

420. What has been the significance of 24th January 1966 for Mrs. Indira Gandhi?

421. Name the US President who never shook hands with anybody during his office tenure, thinking it below his Presidential dignity.

422. Who was the founder of the Arya Samaj?

423. In which year was Netaji Subhash Chandra Bose imprisoned in Mandalay jail? Also mention the year when he suddenly disappeared from his house in Calcutta.

424. Who wrote *Mein Kampf* (My Struggle)?

425. Which country presented the famous Statue of Liberty to the USA?

426. Name the empress who ruled the longest.

Q. 423

427. What was the period of the Second World War?

428. Which ruler is associated with the Sanchi Stupa?

429. Where is the 'samadhi' of Kasturba Gandhi located?

430. The 16th President of the USA has been particularly popular and famous. Who was he and what was his profession before entering politics?

431. Who was the first European traveller to reach India via Africa by sea?

432. How old was Akbar when he ascended the throne?

433. Who founded the Indian National Congress?

434. When was the Battle of Plassey fought, and between whom?

435. What is the Child-Marriage Law known as?

436. Which important building was constructed in India between 1631 and 1652?

437. When were Maharashtra and Gujarat formed as two separate States?

438. After the disintegration of the Soviet Union, when did independent Russia come into existence?

439. Which emperor ruled for the shortest duration?

440. What are the four 'Ashramas' into which man's lifespan is divided according to the Vedas?

441. Which German post is equivalent to the post of the Indian Prime Minister?

442. How many Princely States were there in India at the time of Independence?

443. After Dr. Zakir Hussain's death, the Presidential office was held by a Supreme Court judge for some time. Who was he?

444. When did the Dalai Lama seek asylum in India?

445. Who was the first Indian to enter the ICS (Indian Civil Service)?

446. Dr. Annie Besant, Sarojini Naidu and Nelly Sengupta held an important post during different spans before Independence. What was this post known as?

447. What was the name of Shivaji's father? Who were the two persons in Shivaji's life who influenced him the most?

448. Were Julius Caesar and Nero related?

449. From where did Marco Polo start his long tour to the East and to which destination?

450. What is the term of office of the US President?

451. Who was the last Mughal Emperor? When was he born and where did he die?

452. Who was Amerigo Vespucci and what is he famous for?

453. Where and how did Humayun die?

454. What was the name of Razia Begum's father?

455. When was Mrs. Vijayalakshmi Pandit elected the President of the UN General Assembly?

456. Who was the Prime Minister of England when India attained freedom?

457. What is the present name of Mesopotamia?

458. Who was India's second Prime Minister?

459. Where was the Indo-Pak Summit held in 1966? What loss did India suffer after the event?

460. Which was the first state to be formed on language basis after the re-organisation of states? When was it formed?

461. When was the shifting of the capital from Calcutta to Delhi announced first?

462. When was Haryana formed?

463. Name the British king who abdicated his throne in order to marry a common woman.

464. When were the first General Elections held in India?

465. Who was the first-ever woman Prime Minister in the world?

466. When was the Great Wall of China built?

467. Which place is known as *Kala Pani*?

468. Who took over as the Chairman of the Communist Party of China after Mao Zedong's death?

469. What were the names of Gautam Buddha's father and mother? When did his mother expire?

470. When was Shivaji born? How old was he at the time of his death?

471. In which year did Mahmud of Ghazni loot the Somnath Temple?

472. What is the date inscribed on the book held by the Statue of Liberty in New York?

473. When and where was Lord Buddha born?

474. Washington DC is the capital of USA. When was it made the capital and what does the abbreviation DC stand for?

Q. 469

475. What is Narendra Nath Dutt known as all over the world? What institution did he establish?

476. Name the battles fought on the battlefield of Panipat.

477. Laxmi, Devdas Gandhi's wife, has the good fortune of being the daughter-in-law of Mahatma Gandhi and the daughter of a great man. Who was he?

478. Who was the first Indian to be a member of the British House of Commons? (He had also presided over the Congress session thrice.)

479. Name the three extremist leaders of the Congress.

480. Name the Governor-General of India between 1898 and 1905.

481. When was the first Round Table Conference held and what was the status of the British Prime Minister during the Conference?

482. When did the mass massacre at Jalianwala Bagh take place?

483. Give the date and venue of the first session of the Congress. Who presided over it? Initially, this session was to be held in another city. Which city was it and why was the session shifted?

484. How did the news of Napolean's defeat reach England?

485. What was the total expenditure incurred on World War II?

486. Who were Shah Jehan's parents? Who were the two important persons he got assassinated to rule the kingdom?

487. What was Swami Dayanand's real name? Where and when was he born?

488. Who was the first navigator to go round the world?

489. Why is Nalanda famous?

490. When were the Khajuraho temples built?

491. Which part of India was called Kalinga?

492. When were modern universities established? And when were the universities of Delhi and Benares established?

493. Who started the Bhoodan Yagya?

494. State Subhash Chandra Bose's date of birth and his parents' names.

495. When did Lok Nayak Jayaprakash Narayan escape from Hazaribagh jail by scaling the walls? How many other prisoners were there with him?

496. What is the real name of Meeraben, Gandhiji's follower? When and where was she born?

497. Where is Taxila, the great ancient centre of learning, located?

498. When was the Indian Penal Code enacted and when did it come into force?

499. Who made the Eiffel Tower of France and when was it constructed?

500. When was the tricolour adopted as India's National Flag?

501. When was Tipu Sultan born and what was his mother's name (his father was Hyder Ali)?

502. Miss Margaret Nobel met an Indian in London and was influenced by him to such an extent that she came all the way to India and became his follower. Who was she?

503. Who established the 'Servants of India Society'?

504. On 14th June, 1929, during the freedom movement, a great revolutionary was imprisoned for the Lahore Conspiracy Case, and was kept in the Lahore jail. He went on hunger-strike against the inhuman treatment meted out to political prisoners. Who was the patriot? And for how many days did his hunger-strike last?

505. Where is Akbar's tomb situated?

506. What was Laxmi Bai's maiden name? Who called her 'Chhabili'?

Q. 506

IMPORTANT DATES IN INDIAN HISTORY

A.D.

1001 First invasion of India by Mahmud of Ghazni.

1025 Destruction of Somnath Temple by Mahmud of Ghazni.

1205 Accession of Qutub-ud-Din to the throne of Delhi.

1210 Death of Qutub-ud-Din.

1221 Invasion of Mongols under Changez Khan.

1236 Accession of Razia Sultana to the throne of Delhi.

1240 Death of Razia Sultana.

1287 Death of Balban.

1296 Accession of Ala-ud-Din Khilji.

1316 Death of Ala-ud-Din Khilji.

1325 Accession of Muhammad-bin-Tughlaq.

1336 Foundation of Vijayanagar Empire in South India.

1398 Invasion of Timur Lang.

1469 Birth of Guru Nanak.

1498 First voyage of Vasco da Gama; discovery of sea route to India via the Cape of Good Hope.

1509 Accession of Krishnadeva Raya.

1526 First Battle of Panipat.

1542 Birth of Akbar at Amarkot.

1545 Death of Sher Shah.

1556 Second Battle of Panipat.

1576 Battle of Haldighati.

1597 Death of Rana Pratap.

1600 Establishment of East India Company.

A.D.

1605 Death of Akbar.

1606 Execution of Guru Arjun Dev.

1611 Jahangir marries Nur Jahan.

1616 Sir Thomas Roe visits Jahangir.

1627 Birth of Shivaji.

1628 Shah Jehan becomes Emperor.

1631 Death of Mumtaz Mahal.

1634 The English were permitted to trade in Bengal.

1659 Battle of Samugarh; Aurangzeb's accession to the throne.

1664 Shivaji crowns himself.

1666 Shivaji visits the Mughal court of Agra; his imprisonment and escape.

1675 Execution of Teg Bahadur, the ninth Guru of Sikhs.

1680 Death of Shivaji.

1707 Death of Aurangzeb.

1708 Death of Guru Gobind Singh.

1739 Nadir Shah invades India.

1757 Battle of Plassey.

1761 Third Battle of Panipat.

1830 Raja Ram Mohan Roy visits England.

1833 Death of Raja Ram Mohan Roy.

1839 Death of Maharaja Ranjit Singh.

1857 Indian Mutiny.

1861 Birth of Rabindranath Tagore.

1869 Birth of Gandhiji.

BATTLES AND WARS IN INDIA

Battle of Hydaspes — In 361 BC when Alexander the great had to turn back from Hydaspes (Beas) after his troops refused to march into India against the Nanda Empire.

Battle of Kalinga — It was fought in 361 BC between Ashoka the great and the king of Kalinga.

1st Battle of Tarain (1191 AD) — Prithvi Raj defeated Muhammad Ghori.

2nd Battle of Tarain (1192 AD) — Muhammad Ghori defeated Prithvi Raj.

First Battle of Panipat (1526) — Babur defeated Ibrahim Lodi. This laid the foundation of Mughal rule in India.

Second Battle of Panipat (1556) — Akbar defeated Hemu. It ended Afghan rule.

Battle of Talikota (1565) — The united alliance of Bijapur, Bidar, Ahmednagar and Golkunda under Hussain Nizam Shah defeated Ram Raja of Vijaynagar.

Battle of Haldighati (1576) — Akbar defeated Rana Pratap.

Battle of Plassey (1757) — The British under Lord Clive defeated Sirajuddaulah. It laid the foundation of British rule in India.

Third Battle of Panipat (1761) — Ahmed Shah Abdali defeated the Marathas.

Battle of Buxer (1764) — The British under Sir Hector Munro defeated the Muslim army under three Mohammedan leaders: Mir Qasim, Shuja-ud-daulah and Shah Alam II. The battle made the British supreme in India.

The First Sikh War (1845) — The Sikh Army crossed the Sutlej in 1845 at which the East India Company declared war. The British occupied Lahore and forced the Sikhs to accept humiliating terms of peace.

The Second Sikh War (1849) — A drawn battle was fought between the English and the Sikhs at Chelianwala.

Indo-China War (1962) — Chinese forces attacked India on October 20, 1962. Great losses to India.

Indo-Pak War (1965) — An indecisive war between India and Pakistan. It led to the 'Tashkent Pact' between the two countries.

Indo-Pak War (1971) — Indian forces in joint command with Bangladesh army accepted the surrender of the Pak army in Bangladesh. As a result, Bangladesh was liberated.

Kargil War (1999) — Indian forces scored a grand victory over the Pakistani army and Pak-supported mercenaries in a conflict in the Kargil sector of Jammu & Kashmir. The operation was named 'Operation Vijay.'

GEOGRAPHY

507. Is Australia an island or a continent?

508. What and where is the Great Barrier Reef and what is its length?

509. Name the biggest island in the world.

510. On the bank of which river is the important Chinese town Nanking situated?

511. To which country do the Dutch belong? Name the capital of this country.

512. Which are Sri Lanka's two main ethnic groups?

513. Name the lakes at the highest and the lowest altitudes.

514. Name the capital of Dadra and Nagar Haveli.

515. How many canals flow through Venice, the city of canals?

516. Name the capital of Zambia.

517. Tashkent is the capital of which country?

518. What is the time difference between Indian Standard Time and Greenwich Mean Time?

519. Which instrument is used to measure wind speed?

520. Vietnam is situated on the eastern side of Kampuchea. Name the two countries bordering its north.

521. Which is the highest mountain in Africa?

522. What is Kanyakumari known as in English?

523. The new state of Uttaranchal has been carved out of which state?

524. What is the diameter and circumference of the Earth?

525. Which is the capital of Vietnam?

526. There is a city on the bank of river Danube which was formed by joining two towns. In 1872, these towns were accepted as a combined city.

From the clue given above name the country and its capital.

527. Which is the longest day in India?

528. Russia is located in two continents. Which other country is situated in two continents?

529. What is rubber known as in its crude form, which is sticky and liquid?

530. Name the two states of the U.S.A. which are far off and cut off from the mainland. When were they granted statehood?

531. Espana is the native name of which country?

532. Name the country which came into existence after wresting independence from Indonesia in May 2002.

533. Darwin is the name of a person. What else is known as Darwin?

534. In which continent is Sierra Leone located? What does the name mean?

535. Who is known as the founder-father of the Iron Industry in India?

536. Which Indian state is surrounded by a neighbouring country from three sides?

537. What is the length of the English Channel?

538. In which year was the city of New Delhi officially inaugurated by the British Government?

539. Which two seas does the Suez Canal join? When was it opened and who is credited with building it?

540. Name the capital of Assam.

541. One hectare is how many acres?

542. What do the Japanese call their country?

543. On which river is the Bhakra Nangal Dam constructed?

544. Which is the highest mountain peak in India?

545. What is the Mac Mohan line?

546. Name the rivers on the banks of which Patna, Lucknow, Kota and Surat are situated.

547. What special quality the cactus illustrated alongside is famous for?

548. There is a place near Aurangabad, Maharashtra, which is famous for its Buddhist art of 200 BC to 600 AD. Name the place.

549. Name the largest city of Africa.

550. Name the capital of Chhattisgarh.

551. In which state is the Bharatpur Bird Sanctuary situated?

552. Where are the deserts of Gobi and Thar?

553. Where do we find places named Delhi, Madras and Calcutta, apart from India?

554. While travelling from the East to the West and crossing each longitude, how much time has to be adjusted?

555. Which city is the capital of Jharkhand?

556. What are Walloons?

557. What is meant by the Midnight Sun, and where is it seen?

558. When was Delhi declared a Union Territory?

559. How many different movements are there of the Earth?

560. Chandigarh is the capital of which state?

561. What is Mohs scale and what is it us d for?

Q. 547

562. What is meant by minerals?

563. What particular portion of the Earth was known as Gondwanaland?

564. What existed 50-60 million years ago at the place where the Himalayas are situated today?

565. What is the Deccan trap and where is it situated?

566. What is the name of the line which separates India from Pakistan?

567. Mention the name and the area (covered) of the largest desert in the world.

568. Which is the biggest island in the Mediterranean Sea?

569. Which is the second largest country in the world, areawise?

570. Name the capital city of Croatia.

571. Name the largest cork producing country.

572. Name the largest crater in the world.

573. Name the capital of Australia.

574. What was the previous name of Leningrad?

575. How much area of the Earth is cultivable?

576. Which two countries of the world produce 80% of the world's rubber?

577. Name the largest sea and the largest ocean of the world.

578. Which state of the USA has Honolulu as its capital?

579. Name the fastest growing tree (apart from the bamboo, which is not a tree botanically).

580. In which states of India are the following iron and steel industry cities located— Bhilai, Rourkela, Durgapur. Which countries helped in establishing them?

581. What is the length, breadth and depth of the Suez Canal?

582. Name the five States bordering Andhra Pradesh.

583. What are the various types of coal? How are they differentiated?

584. Who discovered Australia?

585. Which river passes through the Thar desert?

586. Which is the biggest delta in the world?

587. Name the second and third highest mountain peaks in the world after Everest.

588. Name the Royal and Administrative capital of Saudi Arabia.

589. Which is the largest lake in Africa that stands second in the world as a sweet water lake?

590. What was Thailand's previous name?

591. Where are copper mines in India located?

592. Name the largest lake in the world and in India.

593. What was Corbett National Park previously known as? When was the present name given to it?

594. Andaman and Nicobar islands are an archipelago (cluster of several islands). How many of them make Andaman and how many of them make Nicobar?

595. Which is the State with the highest percentage of literacy in India? And which is the State with the lowest?

596. When was Haryana formed as a State and what was its number among the States existing at that time?

597. Which Indian State was called NEFA and when was a new name bestowed on it?

598. When was the Panama Canal completed? What is its length, breadth and depth?

599. Japan is known as the country of islands. How many islands are there in Japan and which are the most important ones among them?

600. Name the three important rivers of China that meet the Pacific Ocean.

601. Name the Administrative, Legislative and Judicial capital of South Africa.

602. Which is the oldest republic in the world and has the same name for the country and its capital?

603. Name the countries standing serially at numbers 1, 2 and 3 in coal production.

604. When is Rabi crop sown and when is it harvested?

605. What are the main crops of Kharif, and when are they sown and harvested?

606. In which year did the devastating earthquake of Quetta take place?

607. What is the border between Pakistan and Afghanistan called?

608. Which is the smallest country in the world and what is its area?

609. On the bank of which river are the three important cities, viz. Vienna, Budapest and Belgrade, situated?

610. Which is the largest coffee producing country in the world?

611. Which is the largest State of India, areawise?

612. Name the biggest teakwood exporting country.

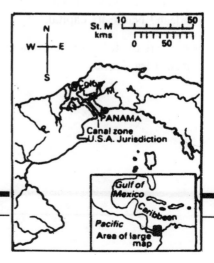

Q. 598

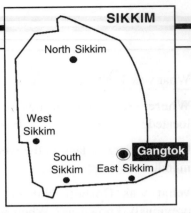

SIKKIM

613. What is the commonly used language of Argentina?

614. On which river is the Gandhi Sagar dam near Kota built?

615. Name the capital of Iceland.

616. Name the largest jute-producing country in the world.

617. Montreal, the famous city of Canada, is situated on the confluence of two rivers. One of them is river Ottawa. Name the other.

618. Name the old capital of Orissa (prior to Bhubaneshwar).

619. Which is the second language spoken by the largest number of people, after Hindi, in India?

620. New York City is situated on the mouth of a river. Which river is it?

621. Which is the largest country in the world?

622. Which are the four countries bordering Israel?

623. Which state was carved out of Uttar Pradesh? Name its capital.

624. Where are the following currencies used – Rial, Lira, Franc, Yen?

625. What are the lines drawn on charts and maps through points of equal temperatures known as?

626. Which is the country surrounded by France, Italy, Austria and Germany?

627. Which place in India is known for its diamond mines?

628. Everest is the highest point on the Earth. Which is the lowest?

629. Which city is known as the city of mosques, having more than 2000?

630. Aquaba Gulf is situated between two countries. Which are they?

631. In which year did Sikkim become the 22nd State of the Indian Union?

632. Which are the three new states that came into existence in November 2000 in India?

633. What are the new names of Calcutta, Bombay and Madras?

GEOGRAPHICAL DISCOVERIES

Amundsen Raold	–	Discovered South Pole on December 14, 1911.
Armstrong, Neil A.	–	(U.S.A.) First Person to set foot on the moon on July 20, 1969.
Cabot Sebastian	–	Discovered Newfoundland in 1497.
Columbus Christopher	–	Discovered America in 1492 and South America in 1498.
Copernicus Nicolas	–	Discovered solar system in 1540.
Edmund Hillary	–	Conquered Mt. Everest on May 29, 1953, along with Sherpa Tenzing.
Ferdinand de Lesseps	–	Conceived the plan for the Suez Canal on which work was completed in 1869.
Henry Hudson	–	Discovered Hudson Bay in 1610.
Kepler Johannes	–	Discovered the Laws of Planetary Motion in 1609.
Magellan Ferdinand	–	Sailed round the world in 1519.
Marco Polo	–	A Venetian traveller who explored China (in 1272), India and south-eastern countries.
Peary Robert	–	Discovered North Pole in 1909.
Mrs. Junko Tabei	–	She was the first-ever woman to climb Mt. Everest on May 16, 1975.
Tasman Abel J.	–	Dutch navigator, discovered Tasmania Island (1642) and New Zealand.
Vasco Da Gama	–	The Portuguese sailor rounded the Cape of Good Hope and discovered the sea route to India and reached Calicut (now Kozhikode) in 1498.

GEOGRAPHICAL NAMES

Bengal's Sorrow	Damodar River	Hermit Kingdom	Korea
Blue Mountain	Nilgiri Hills	Herring Pond	Atlantic Ocean
Bride of the Adriatic	Venice, Italy	Holy Land	Jerusalem
Britain of the South	New Zealand	Island Continent	Australia
China's Sorrow	Hawang Ho	Island of Cloves	Zanzibar
China's Sorrow	Hwang Ho	Island of Pearls	Bahrain
City of Dreaming Spires	Oxford, England	Key to Mediterranean	Gibraltar
City of Eternal Springs	Quito (S. America)	Land of Cakes	Scotland
City of Golden Gates	San Francisco, USA	Land of Five Rivers	Punjab
City of Golden Temples	Amritsar, India	Land of Golden Fleece	Australia
City of Magnificent Distances	Washington D.C. USA	Land of Kangaroo	Australia
		Land of Lilies	Canada
City of Palaces	Kolkata	Land of Maple Leaf	Canada
City of Seven Hills	Rome	Land of Morning Calm	Korea
City of Skyscrapers	New York	Land of Perpetual Greenery	Natal (South Africa)
Cockpit of Europe	Belgium		
Dark Continent	Africa	Land of the Golden Pagoda	Burma
Emerald Island	Ireland	Land of the Midnight Sun	Norway
Empire City	New York	Land of the Rising Sun	Japan
Eternal City	Rome	Land of the Thousand Lakes	Finland
Forbidden City	Lhasa	Land of Thousand Elephants	Laos
Garden City of India	Bangalore	Land of Thunderbolt	Bhutan
Garden of England	Kent, England	Land of White Elephants	Thailand
Garden Province of S. Africa	Natal	Land of Windmills	The Netherlands
Gate of Tears	Bab-el-mondab	Manchester of the Orient	Osaka (Japan)
Gateway of India	Bombay (Mumbai)	Never Never Land	Outbacks of North Australia
George Cross Islands	Malta		
Gift of the Nile	Egypt	Pearl of Antilles	Cuba
Granite City	Aberdeen (Scotland)	Pearl of the Orient	Hong Kong
Great White Way	Broadway, New York, USA	Pearl of the Pacific	Guyayaquil Port of Ecuador

Pillars of Hercules	Straits of Gibraltar	Sugar Bowl of the World	Cuba
Pink City	Jaipur	Switzerland of the East	Kashmir
Playground of Europe	Switzerland	Venice of the East	Kochi, India
Power Keg of Europe	Balkans	Venice of the North	Stockholm
Quaker City	Philadelphia, USA	White City	Belgrade, Yugoslavia
Queen of the Arabian Sea	Kochi, India	Whitman's Grave	Guinea (West Coast Africa)
Quest of the Adriatic	Venice		
Roof of the World	The Pamirs in Central Asia	Windy City	Chicago
Sick Man of Europe	Turkey	World's Bread Basket	Prairies of North America
Sorrow of Bengal	River Damodar, West Bengal		
Spice Garden of India	Kerala	World's Loneliest Island	Tristan da Cunha (mid Atlantic)

FAMOUS SITES (INDIA)

Site	Location	Site	Location
Ajanta	Aurangabad	Amarnath Cave	Kashmir
Amber Palace	Jaipur (Raj.)	Anand Bhawan	Allahabad
Birla Planetarium	Kolkata	Black Pagoda	Konark (Orissa)
Bodhisatva	Ajanta Caves	Brihdeshwar Temple	Tanjore
Brindaban Gardens	Mysore	Buland Darwaza	Fatehpur Sikri
Chenna Kesava Temple	Belur	Char Minar	Hyderabad
Chilka Lake	E. Coast of India near Bhubaneshwar	Dal Lake	Srinagar
Dilwara Temples	Mt. Abu (Raj.)	Elephanta Caves	Mumbai
Ellora Caves	Aurangabad	Gateway of India	Mumbai
Golden Temple	Amritsar	Hanging Gardens	Mumbai
Gol Gumbaz	Bijapur	Howrah Bridge	Kolkata
Hawa Mahal	Jaipur	Jagannath Temple	Puri
Island Palace	Udaipur	Jai Stambha (Tower of Victory)	Chittorgarh
Jahaz Mahal	Mandu	Jantar Mantar	New Delhi
Jog (Gersoppa) Falls	Karnataka	Kailash Temple	Ellora
Khajuraho	Chhatarpur	Kanya Kumari Temple	Cape Comorin

Site	Location	Site	Location
Konark	Puri	Lingaraj Temple	Bhubaneshwar
Laxmi Vilas Palace	Baroda	Mahakaleshwar	Ujjain
Lal Bagh Garden	Bangalore	Marble Rock	Jabalpur
Malabar Hills	Bombay (Mumbai)	Mt. Girnar	Junagarh
Minakshi Temple	Madurai	Nishat Bagh	Srinagar
Natraja	Madras	Pichola Lake	Udaipur
Panch Mahal	Fatehpur Sikri	Raj Ghat	Delhi
Qutub Minar	Delhi	Sanchi Stupa	Sanchi (Bhopal)
Red Fort	Delhi	Shalimar Bagh	Srinagar
Sarnath	Varanasi	Shantivan	Delhi
Statue of Gomateshwar	Karnataka	Sun Temple	Konark
Taj Mahal	Agra	Tirupati Balaji Temple	Tirupati
Tower of Silence	Mumbai	Veer Bhumi	Delhi
Victoria Garden	Mumbai	Victoria Memorial	Calcutta
Shakti Sthal	Delhi	Vijay Ghat	Delhi

WONDERS OF THE WORLD

Ancient

1. Hanging Gardens of Babylon 2. Temple of Diana al Ephesus (Rome) 3. Statue of Jupiter at Olympia 4. Mausoleum of Mausolus (Ruler of Halicarnassus) 5. Pyramids of Egypt 6. Light House at Alexandria 7. Colossus of Rhodes, 912 ft. statue of Helos, the Sun God, stands at one side of the harbour.

Medieval World

1. Colosseum of Rome 2. Great Wall of China 3. Porcelain Tower of Nanking 4. Stonehenge, England 5. Mosque at St. Sophia (Constantinople) 6. Catacombs of Alexandria 7. Leaning Tower of Pisa 8. Taj Mahal (Agra).

Modern World

1. Taj Mahal (India) 2. Chichen Itza (Mexico) 3. Christ the Redeemer (Brazil) 4. Great Wall of China 5. Machu Picchu (Peru) 6. Petra (Jordan) 7. Colosseum of Rome (Italy)

IMPORTANT TOWNS ON RIVER BANKS

INDIA

Town	River	Town	River
Agra	Yamuna	Kanpur	Ganga
Ahmedabad	Sabarmati	Kolkata	Hooghly
Allahabad	Confluence of Ganga and Jamuna and the mythical Saraswati	Kota	Chambal
		Lucknow	Gomti
		Ludhiana	Sutlej
Ayodhya	Saryu	Mathura	Jamuna
Badrinath	Alaknanda	Nasik	Godavari
Cuttack	Mahanadi	Pandharpur	Bhima
Delhi	Jamuna	Patna	Ganga
Dibrugarh	Brahmaputra	Sambalpur	Mahanadi
Ferozepur	Sutlej	Srinagar	Jhelum
Guwahati	Brahmaputra	Surat	Tapti
Haridwar	Ganga	Tiruchirapalli	Cauvery
Hyderabad	Musi	Ujjain	Shipra
Jabalpur	Narmada	Varanasi	Ganga
Jamshedpur	Subarnarekha	Vijayawada	Krishna

PAKISTAN

Town	River	Town	River
Karachi	Indus	Lahore	Ravi

BANGLADESH · MYANMAR

Town	River	Town	River
Chittagong	Majyani	Yangon	Irrawady

CHINA

Town	River	Town	River
Shanghai	Yang-tse-Kiang	Nanking	Yang-tse-Kiang
Canton	Si-Kiang	Chungking	Yang-tse-Kiang

AFRICA AND WEST ASIA

Town	River	Town	River
Kabul (Afghanistan)	Kabul	Basra (Iraq)	Euphrates and Tigris
Cairo (Egypt)	Nile	Ankara (Turkey)	Kazil
Baghdad (Iraq)	Tigris	Khartoum (Sudan)	Confluence of White and Blue Nile

EUROPE AND AMERICA

Town	River	Town	River
Lisbon (Portugal)	Tagus	New Orleans (USA)	Mississippi
Berlin (Germany)	Spree	Cologne (Germany)	Rhine
Belgrade (Yugoslavia)	Danube	Vienna (Austria)	Danube
Paris (France)	Seine	Warsaw (Poland)	Vistula
Danzing (Germany)	Vistula	Hamburg (Germany)	Elbe
Budapest (Hungary)	Danube	Dresden (Germany)	Elbe
London (Britain)	Thames	Rome (Italy)	Tiber
Glasgow (Britain)	Clyde	Bristol (Britain)	Avon
Liverpool (Britain)	Mersey	New Castle (Britain)	Tyne
Quebec (Canada)	St. Lawrence	Ottawa (Canada)	Ottawa
Montreal (Canada)	St. Lawrence	New York (USA)	Hudson
Philadelphia (USA)	Delaware	Washington (USA)	Potomac

LITERATURE

634. Name the four Vedas. Which is the oldest of them all?

635. Who is the author of *Bapu aur Mahatma*? Which prize did the writer win for it?

636. How many chapters are there in *Ramcharit Manas*? In what form are they arranged?

637. Who is the composer of *Vikramank Dev Charit*?

638. Name the famous work of Malik Mohammad Jayasi?

639. Who wrote *Arya Bhattam*?

640. Who is the author of *Shahnama*?

641. Who wrote *Ashtadhyayai*?

642. What was Ras Khan's original name?

643. Name the world-famous Dutch painter who committed suicide at the age of 37.

644. Who wrote *Harshcharit* and *Kadambari*?

645. What is the name of astronomer Mihir's famous book?

646. When and where was the Vaishnav Saint Chaitanya born? What was his wife's name?

647. Name the Greek thinker who said – "There will be no end to the troubles of states, or indeed, my dear Glaucon, of humanity itself, till philosophers become kings in this world, or till those we now call kings and rulers really and truly become philosophers."

648. Who composed *Vairagya Sandeepani*, *Janaki Mangal* and *Ramagya Prashna*?

649. Who wrote *Priya Pravas*? Give the poet's full name.

650. A politician, recipient of the Bharat Ratna, also earned fame with his work *The Philosophy of Rabindranath Tagore*. Who was he?

651. Who is the author of *Gita Rahasya*, a philosophical treatise on the *Gita*?

652. In which field have Bendre and Hebbar made a contribution?

653. Which of Maithili Sharan Gupt's works brought him fame?

654. Which is the most famous work of Kalhan and what does it describe?

655. Name the famed composer of *Geet Govindam*.

656. For which of his works did Rabindranath Tagore receive the Nobel Prize? In which year did he win it?

657. Who instituted the Mangala Prasad Paritoshik, which is awarded for the best literary work?

658. Who is the author of *Gunahon Ke Devta* and *Suraj Ka Satvan Ghoda*?

659. Name the literary figure who earned fame with his book *Ashadh Ka Ek Din*.

660. Who wrote *As You Like It* and *All Is Well That Ends Well*?

661. Who is the author of *Under the Greenwood Tree*?

662. Who was George Eliot? What was his real name?

663. Is *Oliver Twist* the title of some book or the name of a writer?

664. Where was Amrita Shergil, the renowned artist, born? Who were her parents?

665. Which children's magazine in Hindi has the largest circulation? Who is its editor?

666. Name the monthly magazine published by the Central Social Welfare Board. Who is its editor?

667. How many brothers and sisters did Gyaneshwar have? What is the name of his famous work in Marathi?

668. There are two well-known books in English entitled *Paradise Lost* and *Paradise Regained*. Are these written by one author or are these by two different authors? Were they published simultaneously?

669. Who is the creator of the famous character Sherlock Holmes?

670. Who said, "Veni, Vidi, Vici"?

671. Who composed *Leelavati*?

672. What is the real name of Mark Twain, the American writer?

673. Who wrote *Raghuvansha, Abhigyan Shakuntalam, Ritusamhar, Kumar Sambhav, Malvikagni Mitra, Vikramorvashim, Meghdoot*? Separate the plays and verse compositions out of these.

674. Venus is the Roman Goddess of love and beauty. Name her parallel in Greek mythology.

675. What is Hans Christian Andersen famous for? To which country did he belong?

Q. 672

676. In Greek it is known as Pseudonym, in French, Nom de Plume. What is its English version?

677. What was the pen name of Cecil Day Lewis, the well-known poet and detective fiction writer?

678. Who wrote *A Memory of Solfevino* and when?

679. A writer, who wrote *Chandra Kanta* and *Chandra Kanta Santati,* started working on another book, but unfortunately could complete only six chapters before his death. Who was this writer and what is the name of his incomplete work?

680. There is a magazine for children entitled *Children's World.* Which institution publishes it? Who had established it and when?

681. What is AIFACS? Where is it situated and when was it started?

682. What is Gyan Peeth Award?

683. Who wrote *Panchatantra*?

684. For which of his works did Ernest Hemingway receive the Nobel Prize?

685. *Gubare Khatir* is a well-known work of a freedom fighter who was also a minister in the first ministry constituted after independence. Who is this person?

686. Name the British Prime Minister to have won the Nobel Prize for literature. Name the year in which he won it.

687. What were the real names of the litterateur who wrote under the pseudonym 'Mukti Bodh', 'Ugra' and 'Firaq'?

688. *Revenue Stamp* (or Rasidi Ticket) is the autobiography of a renowned author. Who is s/he?

689. Who received the Jnanpeeth award first after it was instituted?

690. What was Ghalib's real name? How did he reach the Delhi Darbar?

691. Who wrote the song *Sare Jahan Se Achchha Hindustan Hamara...*?

692. What is the popular name of the world-famous novelist and Nobel Laureate Mrs. Richard J. Walsh?

693. What is the title of Pt. Nehru's biography written by Krishna Hathi Singh?

694. Which Indian newspaper has the largest circulation?

695. Who is Georges Simenon?

696. Who wrote *A Passage to India*?

697. Out of the *nine gems* in Akbar's court, one of them wrote *Akbarnama*. Who was he?

698. Who wrote *Alice in Wonderland* and *Through the Looking Glass*?

699. Name the books which established Maxim Gorky as a world-class writer?

700. A French writer wrote a book with Kolkata as its backdrop. A large part of the royalty of the sale proceeds was donated for improvement of slums. What is the name of this book?

701. Who designed the comic strip *Dennis the Menace*?

702. Who is the author of *Faust*?

703. Name the author of *The Three Musketeers* and *Black Tulip*.

704. The author of *Kanupriya* and *Andha Yug* also edited, for long, a popular Hindi magazine. Who is this litterateur?

705. In which year did Vasudev Sharan Aggarwal receive the Sahitya Akademi award?

706. One poet wrote the following – *Surtiya, Nartiya, Nagtiya, Aas chahat sab koy.*

Another poet completed the couplet by adding this line – *Goad liye, Hulsi firre, Tulsi sau sut hoy.*

Who were these two poets?

707. Gulsher Khan is popularly known by his nom de plume in the field of Hindi literature. What is this name? One of his novels was serialised on TV. What is it entitled?

708. Which is Shakespeare's last play?

709. What is the name of Shivani, the well-known fiction writer in Hindi?

710. Who were the three famous poets of England who died in 1821, 1822 and 1824 respectively?

711. *Twinkle twinkle little star...* is an unusually popular nursery rhyme. Who wrote it?

712. Who is the author of *Crime and Punishment*?

713. A world-renowned American novelist committed suicide on July 2, 1961, by shooting himself with a gun. Who was this writer?

714. What is Virginia Woolf's maiden name?

715. How did the expression O.K. begin?

716. In which work was *Vande Mataram* first published?

Q.708

717. A British short-story writer, poet, and novelist born in India in 1865, became famous with his book *The Jungle Book*, *Seven Seas* and *Kim*. Name him.

718. Who created James Bond?

719. *Decameron* has a prominent place in literature. Who is its author?

720. *The Emperor's New Clothes* and *The Little Mermaid* are written by a world-renowned writer for children. Who is he?

721. What is *Esperanto*?

722. Who wrote the plays *Sakharam Binder*, *Ghasi Ram Kotwal*, *Shanata*, *Court Chalu Ahe*?

723. The Brontes were a family of English writers. Name these three sisters.

724. An Indian woman writer in English wrote *Storm in Chandigarh*, *The Freedom Movement in India and Rich Like Us*. Name her?

725. Who became popular with *Madhushala*?

726. Which Dogri poetess has written *Meri Kavita, Mere Geet*?

727. Which Punjabi author has written *Ek Chadar Maili Si*?

728. Gulshan Nanda is known for his popular appeal in fiction. How many novels has he written? Name his first and last books.

729. There are approximately 5,000 languages and dialects in the world. How many of them are in India?

730. Which novel is considered the best novel of Jane Austen?

731. Name the English daily published from Delhi having the largest circulation. When was it established?

732. Name the works for which Ramdhari Singh 'Dinkar' received the Sahitya Akademi and Jnanpeeth Awards.

733. Who is the author of *Maila Anchal*? Also name the story on which *Teesri Kasam* was based.

734. Name Maithili Sharan Gupt's first collection of poems. When was it published?

735. In 1884, an essayist started a literary journal which he edited for ten years. Who was the literary figure?

736. Gandhiji started editing the English version of *Nav Jeevan* along with its Hindi edition. What was the English edition known as?

737. What was the full name of Vinoba who was also the author of *Bhoodan Yagya*, *Geet Pravachan* and *Vinoba ke Vichar*?

738. A poet, who declared boldly *Masi kagad chhuyo nahin, kalam gahi nahin haath*, was also an acknowledged poet of Hindi. Name him.

739. Of the many Muslim saint-poets, who contributed immensely to the Hindi devotional literature of Krishna-cult, there was one known as Saiyad Ibrahim. What is his popular name?

740. Who is the composer of *Saket*, *Panchvati*, *Jayadrath Vadh* and *Bharat Bharati*?

741. A well-known poet said, *"Siva ko bakhano, ya bakhano chhatrasaal ko."* A name to be reckoned with in the field of war literature in Hindi. Who was he?

742. What was the full name of the Persian poet Omar Khayyam (1049-1132)?

743. To which country did William Wordsworth belong? How was he related to Dorothy, with whom he was living?

744. "Our sweetest songs are those that tell of our saddest thoughts." Who wrote these lines and in which poem?

745. Who is the author of the story on which Mrinal Sen based his film *Khandahar*?

746. Name the British poet Robert Browning married.

747. In 1822, a gifted young poet died by drowning. Who was he?

748. Who wrote *The Pilgrim's Progress*?

749. When was *Daily Telegraph* first published?

750. What is meant by RSVP, which we often see printed on invitation cards?

751. In Terracotta sculpture, the main medium is earth or soil, signified by the word "terra". What does the word "cotta" mean?

Q.745

752. Name the famous French novelist who won the Nobel Prize in 1957.

753. Who is the first Indian author to win the Booker Prize?

754. In order to popularise science amongst teenagers, Shri Ram Mehra & Co., Agra, started a Science journal in 1960 in Hindi. What was its name and who was its editor then?

755. From where is *Kalyan*, the religious journal, published?

756. What was the real name of the British satirist Saki?

757. Who was the American novelist who had a passion for bull-fighting, shikar and fishing?

758. Who is the lyricist of *Karvan Guzar Gaya, Gubar Dekhte Rahe*?

759. *Magadh* is written by a litterateur who was as much active in the field of politics as in literature. Name him.

760. In the field of education we are well aware of the name Montessori. Who started it?

761. Name the famous Indian novelist who was also cartoonist R.K. Laxman's brother.

762. Who gave the slogan "Freedom is my birthright and I shall have it"?

763. What is "Pravda"? Name the country it is associated with?

764. Which honour has been bestowed on Dr. Mulk Raj Anand?

765. Which film-critic is the author of the following books – 75 *Years of Indian Cinema, The History of Indian Movies, A Pictorial History of Indian Cinema*?

766. Who wrote *Uncle Tom's Cabin*, a work which broke the all-time sales record?

767. Ved Rahi was awarded the Sahitya Akademi Award in 1983 for his collection of short stories, *Aale*. In which language is it written?

768. George Orwell wrote *Animal Farm*. What was Orwell's real name?

769. Who transcribed the *Ramayana* into Tamil?

770. Name the collection of verses with which new poetry entered Hindi literature. Who was its editor?

771. When and where was the first newspaper published in India?

772. Name the National level unions of Journalists. Which of these was established first?

773. What is E.A.S. Prasanna's autobiography entitled?

774. Who was the Irish playwright and novelist who was awarded the Nobel Prize in 1969?

775. Which English author and lexicographer was known for his wit?

776. Who is the poet of *Vidhwa*, *Bhikshuk*, and *Woh Todti Patthar*?

777. Who is the famous Urdu authoress who enacted a small role in the film *Junoon*?

778. *Indira Gandhi Writes* is a collection of letters written by Mrs. Gandhi in reply to letters received from children the world over. Which celebrated female journalist has edited it?

779. Who wrote *Godan*? What was the author's real name?

780. Who wrote *The Life of Samuel Johnson*?

781. What is the literal meaning of the Greek word "Photography"?

782. Who has written *Tamas*, the controversial TV serial? Who directed it?

783. Name the American writer famous for his books on self-improvement and positive thinking.

WELL-KNOWN BOOKS

A Bend in the River: *V.S. Naipaul*

A Brief History of Time: *Stephen Hawking*

A China Passage: *John Kenneth Galbraith*

A Clockwork Orange: *Anthony Burgess*

A Critique of Pure Reason: *Immanuel Kant*

A Doll's House: *Henrik Ibsen*

A Farewell to Arms: *Ernest Hemingway*

A Guide for the Perplexed: *E.F. Schumacher*

A Handful of Dust: *Evelyn Waugh*

A House for Mr. Biswas: *V.S. Naipaul*

A Million Mutinies Now: *V.S. Naipaul*

A Midsummer Night's Dream: *William Shakespeare*

A Passage to England: *Nirad C. Chaudhuri*

A Passage to India: *E.M. Forster*

A Prisoner's Scrapbook: *L.K. Advani*

A River Sutra: *Gita Mehta*

A Sense of Time: *H.S. Vatsyayan*

A Strange and Sublime Address: *Amit Choudhary*

A Suitable Boy: *Vikram Seth*

A Tale of Two Cities: *Charles Dickens*

A Thousand Days: *Arthur M. Schlesinger*

A Thousand Suns: *Dominique Lapierre*

A Village by the Sea: *Anita Desai*

A Voice for Freedom: *Nayantara Sehgal*

A Week with Gandhi: *Louis Fischer*

A Woman's Life: *Guy de Maupassant*

Absolute Power: *David Baldacci*

Accident: *Danielle Steel*

Adam Belle: *George Eliot*

Adonis: *P.B. Shelley*

Adventures of Tom Sawyer: *Mark Twain*

Advice and Consent: *Allen Drury*

After All These Years: *Susan Issacs*

After Amnesia: *Ganesh N. Devy*

After Raag: *Amit Choudhary*

Ageless Body, Timeless Mind: *Deepak Chopra*

Agni Veena: *Kazi Nazrul Islaam*

Aina-E-Akbari: *Abul Fazal*

Airport: *Arthur Hailey*

Akbarnama: *Abul Fazal*

Alaska Unbound: *James Michener*

Alexander Quartet: *Lawrence Durrel*

Alice in Wonderland: *Lewis Carroll*

All Quiet on the Western Front: *Erick Maria Remarque*

All the King's Men: *Robert Penn Warren*

All the President's Men: *Carl Bernstein & Bob Woodward*

All Things Bright and Beautiful: *James Herriot*

All's Well that Ends Well: *William Shakespeare*

Amar Kosh: *Amar Singh*

An American Tragedy: *Theodore Dreiser*

An Autobiography: *Jawaharlal Nehru*

An Equal Music: *Vikram Seth*

An Idealist View of Life: *Dr. S. Radhakrishnan*

Anandmath: *Bankim Chandra Chatterjee*

Ancient Evenings: *Norman Mailer*

And Quiet Flows the Don: *Mikhail Sholokhov*

Androcles and the Lion: *George Bernard Shaw*

Angles in America: *Tony Kusher*

Animal Farm: *George Orwell*

Anna Karenina: *Leo Tolstoy*

Antony and Cleopatra: *William Shakespeare*

Ape and Essence: *Aldous Huxley*

Apocalypse Watch: *Robert Ludlum*

Apple Cart: *George Bernard Shaw*

Appointment in Samarra: *John O'Hara*

Area of Darkness: *V.S. Naipaul*

Around the World in Eighty Days: *Jules Verne*

Arrowsmith: *Sinclair Lewis*

As You Like It: *William Shakespeare*

Asia and Western Dominance: *K.M. Panikkar*

Asian Drama: *Gunnar Myrdal*

August 1914: *Alexander Solzhenitsyn*

Autobiography of an Unknown Indian:
    Nirad C. Chaudhuri

Babbit: *Sinclair Lewis*

Baby and Child: *Penelope Leach*

Back to Methuselah: *George Bernard Shaw*

Bandicoot Run: *Manohar Malgaonkar*

Beating the Street: *Peter Lynch*

Beginning of the Beginning: *Osho*

Beloved: *Toni Morrison*

Ben Hur: *Lewis Wallace*

Between the Lines: *Kuldeep Nayar*

Beyond Modernisation, Beyond Self:
    Sisirkumar Ghose

Beyond the Horizon: *Eugene O'Neill*

Bhagvad Gita: *S. Radhakrishnan*

Bharat Bharati: *Maithili Sharan Gupt*

Biographia Literaria: *Samuel Taylor Coleridge*

Black Holes and Baby Universes: *Stephen Hawking*

Black Notice: *Patricia Cornwell*

Blind Ambitions: *John Dean*

Bliss was it in that Dawn: *Minoo Masani*

Blood, Brain and Beer: *David Ogilvy*

Born Free: *Joy Adamson*

Brave New World: *Aldous Huxley*

Bread, Beauty and Revolution: *Khwaja Ahmad Abbas*

Breakthrough: *Gen. Moshe Dayan*

Broken Wing: *Sarojini Naidu*

Brothers Karamazow: *Feodor Dostoevsky*

Business @ The Speed of Thought: *Bill Gates*

Butterfield 8: *John O'Hara*

By God's Decree: *Kapil Dev*

By Love Possessed: *James Gould Cozzens*

Byzantium: *W.B. Yeats*

Caesar and Cleopatra: *George Bernard Shaw*

Canada: *George Bernard Shaw*

Candide: *Voltaire*

Care of the Soul: *Thomas Moore*

Catch-22: *Joseph Heller*

Catcher in the Rye: *J.D. Salinger*

Centennial: *James A. Michener*

Chandalika: *Rabindranath Tagore*

Chemmeen: *Thakazhi Sivasankara Pillai*

Cheny Orchard: *Anton Chekov*

Chesapeake: *James A. Michener*

Chidambara: *Sumitranandan Pant*

Childe Harold's Pilgrimage: *Lord Byron*

Children of Gebalawi: *Naguib Mahfouz*

Chithirappaavai: *P.V. Akilandam*

Chitra: *Rabindranath Tagore*

Choma's Drum: *K. Shivaram Karanth*

Chronicle of a Death Foretold: *Gabriel Garcia Marquez*

Circle of Reason: *Amitav Ghosh*

City of Joy: *Dominique Lapierre*

City of Djinns: *William Dalrymple*

Clear Light of Day: *Anita Desai*

Climate of Treason: *Andrew Boyle*

Colonel Sun: *Kingsley Amis*

Comedy of Errors: *William Shakespeare*

Common Sense: *Thomas Paine*

Communist Manifesto: *Karl Marx*

Confessions of a Lover: *Mulk Raj Anand*

Confessions: *J.J. Rousseau*

Confidential Clerk: *T.S. Eliot*

Conquest of Self: *Mahatma Gandhi*

Conversations with God-1: *Neale Donald Walsh*

Coolie: *Mulk Raj Anand*

Count of Monte Cristo: *Alexander Dumas*

Coverly Papers: *Joseph Addison*

Creation: *Gore Vidal*

Crescent Moon: *Rabindranath Tagore*

Crime and Punishment: *Feodor Dostoevsky*

Crisis into Chaos: *E.M.S. Namboodiripad*

Critical Mass: *William E. Burrows, Robert Windrem*

Cry My Beloved Country: *Alan Paton*

Darkness at Noon: *Arthur Koestler*

Das Kapital: *Karl Marx*

David Copperfield: *Charles Dickens*

Days of Grace: *Arthur Ashe & Arnold Rampersad*

Days of My Years: *H.P. Nanda*

Death in Venice: *Thomas Mann*

Death of a City: *Amrita Pritam*

Death of a Patriot: *R.E. Harrington*

Debacle: *Emile Zola*

Decameron: *Giovanni Boccaccio*

Decline and Fall of the Roman Empire: *Edward Gibbon*

Descent of Man: *Charles Darwin*

Deserted Village: *Oliver Goldsmith*

Devdas: *Sharat Chandra Chatterjee*

Diana V. Charles: *James Whitaker*

Diana: The True Story: *Andrew Morton*

Dilemma of Our Time: *Harold Joseph Laski*

Diplomacy: *Henry Kissinger*

Disclosure: *Michael Crichton*

Discovery of India: *Jawaharlal Nehru*

Distant Drums: *Manohar Malgaonkar*

Divine Comedy: *Alighieri Dante*

Divine Life: *Swami Sivananda*

Doctor Zhivago: *Boris Pasternak*

Doctor's Dilemma: *George Bernard Shaw*

Don Juan: *Lord Byron*

Don Quixote: *Miguel de Cervantes*

Dr. Jekyll and Mr. Hyde: *Robert Louis Stevenson*

Durgesh Nandini: *Bankim Chandra Chatterjee*

Down Under: *Bill Bryson*

Dust to Dust: *Tami Hoag*

Dynamics of Social Change: *Chandra Shekhar*

Earth in the Balance: Forging a New Common Purpose: *Al Gore*

Earth: *Emile Zola*

Elegy written in a Country Churchyard: *Thomas Gray*

Eminent Victorians: *Lytton Strachey*

Emma: *Jane Austen*

Ends and Means: *Aldous Huxley*

English August: *Upamanyu Chatterjee*

Envoy to Nehru: *Escotr Reid*

Essays from Poor to the Rich: *John Kenneth Galbraith*

Essays of Elia: *Charles Lamb*

Essays on Gita: *Sri Aurobindo Ghosh*

Eternal Himalayas: *Major H.P.S. Ahluwalia*

Ethics for the New Millennium: *Dalai Lama*

Expanding Universe: *Arthur Stanley Eddington*

Faces of Everest: *Major H.P.S. Ahluwalia*

Family Reunion: *T.S. Eliot*

Far from the Madding Crowd: *Thomas Hardy*

Farewell the Trumpets: *James Morris*

Farewell to Arms: *Ernest Hemingway*

Father and Sons: *Ivan Turgenev*

Faust: *J.W. Von Goethe*

First Circle: *Alexander Solzhenitsyn*

Food, Nutrition and Poverty in India: *V.K.R.V. Rao*

For Whom the Bell Tolls: *Ernest Hemingway*

Forsyth Saga: *John Glasworthy*

Forty-nine Days: *Amrita Pritam*

Freedom at Midnight: *Larry Collins and Dominique Lapierre*

French Revolution: *Thomas Carlyle*

Friends and Foes: *Sheikh Mujibur Rahman*

From Here to Eternity: *James Jones*

Ganadevata: *Tara Shankar Bandopadhyaya*

Gandhi and Stalin: *Louis Fisher*

Gardener: *Rabindranath Tagore*

Gathering Storm: *Winston Churchill*

Geet Govind: *Jaidev*

Ghasiram Kotwal: *Vijay Tendulkar*

Gitanjali: *Rabindranath Tagore*

Glimpses of World History: *Jawaharlal Nehru*

Godan: *Prem Chand*

Golden Threshold: *Sarojini Naidu*

Gone With The Wind: *Margaret Mitchell*

Good Earth: *Pearl S. Buck*

Good Times, Bad Times: *Harold Evans*

Goodbye, Mr. Chips: *James Hilton*

Grammar of Politics: *Harold Joseph Laski*

Granny Dan: *Danielle Steel*

Great Expectations: *Charles Dickens*

Great Gatsby: *F. Scott Fitzgerald*

Great Tragedy: *Z.A. Bhutto*

Guide: *R.K. Narayan*

Gulag Archipelago: *Alexander Solzhenitsyn*

Gulliver's Travels: *Jonathan Swift*

Hamlet: *William Shakespeare*

Harvest: *Manjula Padmanabhan*

Harry Potter and the Goblet of Fire: *J.K. Rowling*

Heat and Dust: *Ruth Prawer Jhabwala*

Heir Apparent: *Dr. Karan Singh*

Heritage: *Anthony West*

Heroes and Hero Worship: *Thomas Carlyle*

Himalayan Blunder: *Brigadier J.P. Dalvi*

Hindu View of Life: *Dr. S. Radhakrishnan*

Hinduism: *Nirad C. Chaudhuri*

History of India: *Romila Thapar*

How To Know God: *Deepak Chopra*

Hullabaloo in a Guava Orchard: *Kiran Desai*

Hunchback of Notre Dame: *Victor Hugo*

Hungry Stones: *Rabindranath Tagore*

I am not an Island: *K.A. Abbas*

I follow the Mahatma: *K.M. Munshi*

Idols: *Sunil Gavaskar*

If I am Assassinated: *Z.A. Bhutto*

If Only: *Geri Halliwell*

In Evil Hour: *Gabriel Garcia Marques*

In Memoriam: *Alfred Lord Tennyson*

In Retrospect: The Tragedy and Lessons of Vietnam: *Robert McNamara.*

In Search of Gandhi: *Richard Attenborough*

India Changes: *Taya Zinkin*

India Discovered: *John Keay*

India Divided: *Rajendra Prasad*

India Unbound: *Gurcharan Das*

India of Our Dreams: *M.V. Kamath*

India Remembered: *Percival & Margaret Spear*

India Wins Freedom: *Abul Kalam Azad*

India's Priceless Heritage: *N.A. Palkhivala*

Indian Philosophy: *Dr. S. Radhakrishnan*

Inscrutable Americans: *Anurag Mathur*

Inside Asia, Inside Europe, Inside Africa, etc.: *John Gunther*

Interpreter of Maladies: *Jhumpa Lahiri*

Intimacy: *Jean-Paul Sartre*

Invisible Man: *H.G. Wells*

Is Paris Burning: *Larry Collins & Dominique Lapierre*

Isabella: *John Keats*

Islamic Bomb: *Stev Weissman & Herbert Krouney*

Ivanhoe: *Sir Walter Scott*

Jai Somnath: *K.M. Munshi*

Jane Eyre: *Charlotte Bronte*

Jean Christopher: *Romain Rolland*

Jewel: *Danielle Steel*

Julius Caesar: *William Shakespeare*

Jungle Book: *Rudyard Kipling*

Junglee Girl: *Ginu Kamani*

Jurassic Park: *Michael Crichton*

Kagaz Te Kanwas: *Amrita Pritam*

Kamasutra: *Vatsyayana*

Kane and Abel: *Jeffrey Archer*

Kanthapura: *Raja Rao*

Kapala Kundala: *Bankim Chandra Chatterjee*

Kashmir: A Tragedy of Errors: *Tavleen Singh*

Kayar: *Thakazhi Sivasankara Pillai*

Kenilworth: *Sir Walter Scott*

Kidnapped: *Robert Louis Stevenson*

Kim: *Rudyard Kipling*

King Lear: *William Shakespeare*

Kitni Nawon Me Kitni Bar: *S.H. Vatsyayan*

Kubla Khan: *Samuel Taylor Coleridge*

La Peste: *Albert Camus*

Lady Chatterley's Lover: *D.H. Lawrence*

Lajja: *Taslima Nasreen*

Last Burden: *Upamanyu Chatterjee*

Last Things: *C.P. Snow*

Le Contract (Social Contract): *J.J. Rousseau*

Lead Kindly Light: *Vincent Shean*

Leaders: *Richard Nixon*

Leaves of Grass: *Walt Whitman*

Lee Iacocca: *Lee Iacocca*

Les Miserables: *Victor Hugo*

Leviathan: *Thomas Hobbes*

Life Divine: *Sri Aurobindo*

Life is Elsewhere: *Milan Kundera*

Life of Samuel Johnson: *James Boswell*

Lightning: *Danielle Steel*

Lolita: *Vladimir Nabakov*

Like Water for Chocolate: *Laura Esquivel*

Loneliness of the Long Distance Runner: *Allan Silltoe*

Long Day's Journey into Night: *Eugene O'Neill*

Long Walk to Freedom: *Nelson Mandela*

Lord of the Flies: *William Golding*

Love Story: *Erich Segal*

Macbeth: *William Shakespeare*

Magic Mountain: *Thomas Mann*

Mahatma Gandhi and his Apostles: *Ved Mehta*

Mahatma Gandhi: *Romain Rolland*

Main Street: *Sinclair Lewis*

Malgudi Days: *R.K. Narayan*

Man and Superman: *George Bernard Shaw*

Man of Property: *John Gasworthy*

Man, Beast and Virtue: *Luigi Pirandello*

Man-eaters of Kumaon: *Jim Corbett*

Managing for the Future: *Peter Drucker*

Managing for Results: *Peter Drucker*

Mankind and Mother Earth: *Arnold Tonybee*

Many Worlds: *K.P.S. Menon*

Marriage and Morals: *Bertrand Russell*

Maurice: *E.M. Forster*

Mayor of Casterbridge: *Thomas Hardy*

Mein Kampf: *Adolf Hitler*

Memories of Hope: *Gen. Charles de Gaulle*

Men are from Mars, Women are from Venus: *John Gray*

Middle March: *George Eliot*

Midnight's Children: *Salman Rushdie*

Mill on the Floss: *George Eliot*

Moby Dick: *Hermann Melville*

Moonwalk: *Michael Jackson*

Mother India: *Katherine Mayo*

Mother: *Maxim Gorky*

Much Ado About Nothing: *William Shakespeare*

Murder in the Cathedral: *T.S. Eliot*

My Days: *R.K. Narayan*

My India: *S. Nihal Singh*

My Life and Times: *V.V. Giri*

My Music, My Life: *Pt. Ravi Shankar*

My Own Boswell: *M. Hidayatullah*

My Presidential Years: *R. Venkatraman*

My Son's Father: *Dom Moraes*

My Struggles: *E.K. Nayanar*

My Truth: *Indira Gandhi*

Nana: *Emile Zola*

Never at Home: *Dom Moraes*

New Dimensions of India's Foreign Policy:
  A.B. Vajpayee

Nice Guys Finish Second: *B.K. Nehru*

Nemesis: *Agatha Christie*

Nineteen-eighty Four: *George Orwell*

Nisheeth: *Uma Shankar Joshi*

No Full Stops in India: *Mark Tully*

Nostromo: *Joseph Conrad*

O'Jerusalem: *Larry Collins & Dominique
  Lapierre*

Odakkuzhal: *G. Shankara Kurup*

Of Human Bondage: *W. Somerset Maugham*

Oliver Twist: *Charles Dickens*

Oliver's Story: *Erich Segal*

Omerta: *Mario Puzo*

On The Threshold of Hope: *Pope John Paul II*

One Day in the Life of Ivan Denisovich:
  Alexander Solzhenitsyn

One World and India: *Arnold Tonybee*

One World: *Wendell Wilkie*

Operation Bluestar: The True Story: *Lt. Gen.
  K.S. Brar*

Operation Shylock: *Philip Roth*

Othello: *William Shakespeare*

Our Films Their Films: *Satyajit Ray*

Paddy Clark, Ha Ha Ha: *Rodney Doyle*

Painter of Signs: *R.K. Narayan*

Pakistan Cut to Size: *D.R. Mankekar*

Pakistan: The Gathering Storm: *Benazir Bhutto*

Pale Blue Dot: *Carl Sagan*

Panchatantra: *Vishnu Sharma*

Paradise Lost: *John Milton*

Pather Panchali: *Bibhuti Bhushan*

Peter Pan: *J.M. Barrie*

Plain Speaking: *N. Chandrababu Naidu*

Pleading Guilty: *Scott Turow*

Portrait of India: *Ved Mehta*

Post Office: *Rabindranath Tagore*

Prathama Pratishruti: *Ashapurna Devi*

Prelude: *William Wordsworth*

Preoccupations: *Seamus Heaney*

Pride and Prejudice: *Jane Austen*

Prince: *Niccolo Machiavelli*

Principia Mathematica: *Bertrand Russell*

Prison Diary: *Jayaprakash Narayan*

Pygnalion: *George Bernard Shaw*

Rabbit, Run: *John Updike*

Rangbhoomi: *Prem Chand*

Rape of Bangladesh: *Anthony Mascarenhas*

Ravan & Eddie: *Kiran Nagarkar*

Rebel, The: *Albert Camus*

Rebirth: *Leonid Brezhnev*

Red Badge of Courage: *Stephen Crane*

Red Star Over China: *Edgar Snow*

Reflections on the French Revolution: *Edmund Burke*

Remembering Babylon: *David Malouf*

Rendezvous with Rana: *Arthur C. Clarke*

Revolution from Within: *Gloria Steinem*

Riding the Storm: *Harold MacMillan*

Rise and Fall of the Third Reich: *William L. Shirer*

Robinson Crusoe: *Daniel Defoe*

Romeo and Juliet: *William Shakespeare*

Room at the Top: *John Braine*

Roses in December: *M.C. Chagla*

Rubaiyat-i-Omar Khayyam: *Edward Fitzgerald*

Runaway Jury: *John Grisham*

Roots: *Alex Haley*

Saket: *Maithili Sharan Gupt*

Sanctuary: *William Faulkner*

Satyarth Prakash: *Swami Dayanand*

Scarlet Letter: *Nathaniel Hawthorne*

Seven Lamps of Architecture: *John Robinson*

Seven Summers: *Mulk Raj Anand*

Shadow from Ladakh: *Bhabani Bhattacharya*

Shahnama: *Firdausi*

Shape of Things to Come: *H.G. Wells*

She Stoops to Conquer: *Oliver Goldsmith*

Siddhartha: *Hermann Hess*

Six Characters in Search of an Author: *Lugi Pirandello*

Slaughter House Five: *Kurt Vanuegut*

Snakes and Ladders: Essays on India: *Gita Mehta*

Snow Country: *Yasunari Kawabata*

Social Change in Modern India: *M.N. Srinivas*

Sohrab and Rustam: *Mathew Arnold*

Sons and Lovers: *D.H. Lawrence*

Sophie's Choice: *William Styron*

Stopping by Woods: *Robert Frost*

Story of My Life: *Moshe Dayan*

Strangers and Brothers: *C.P. Snow*

Strife: *John Galsworthy*

Sun Stone: *Octavio Paz*

Sunny Days: *Sunil Gavaskar*

Swami and Friends: *R.K. Narayan*

Talisman: *Sir Walter Scott*

Tarzon of the Apes: *Edgar Rice Burroughs*

Tempest: *William Shakespeare*

Tender Insight: *James Redfield*

Thank You, Jeeves: *P.G. Wodehouse*

The Bubble: *Mulk Raj Anand*

The Final Days: *Bob Woodward and Carl Bernstein*

The Invisibles: *Zia Jaffrey*

The Scam: Who Won, Who Lost, Who Got Away: *Debashis Basu and Sucheta Dalal*

The Adventures of Sherlock Holmes: *Arthur Conan Doyle*

The Affluent Society: *John Kenneth Galbraith*

The Age of Reason: *Jean-Paul Sartre*

The Agenda: *Bob Woodward*

The Agony and the Ecstasy: *Irving Stone*

The Ambassadors: *Henry James*

The Arrangement: *Elia Kazan*

The Banyan Tree: *Hugh Tinker*

The Best and the Brightest: *David Halberstam*

The Big Fisherman: *Lloyd Douglas*

The Bride's Book of Beauty: *Mulk Raj Anand*

The Bridges of Madison County: *R.J. Waller*

The Cancer Ward: *Alexander Solzhenitsyn*

The Call of the Wild: *Jack London*

The Canterbury Tales: *Geoffrey Chaucer*

The Captive of the Caucasus: *Alexander Pushkin*

The Cardinal: *Henry Morton Robinson*

The Castle: *Franz Kafka*

The Cat and Shakespeare: *Raja Rao*

The Changing World of the Executive: *Peter Drucker*

The Class: *Erich Segal*

The Clown: *Heinrich Boll*

The Confessions of an Opium Eater: *Thomas Dequincey*

The Coup: *John Updike*

The Court Dancer: *Rabindranath Tagore*

The Dark Room: *R.K. Narayan*

The Day of the Locust: *Nathaniel West*

The Death of Vishnu: *Manil Suri*

The Degeneration of India: *T.N. Seshan*

The End of a Beautiful Era: *Joseph Brodsky*

The End of History and the Last Man: *Francis Fukuyama*

The Executioner's Song: *Norman Mailer*

The Eye of the Storm: *Patrick White*

The Far Pavilions: *M.M. Kaye*

The Faraway Music: *Svetlana Allilueva*

The Fifth Horseman: *Larry Collins and Dominique Lapierre*

The Fire Next Time: *James Baldwin*

The Forbidden Sea: *Tara Ali Baig*

The Fourth Estate: *Jeffrey Archer*

The French Lieutenant's Woman: *John Fowles*

The Ginger Man: *J.P. Donleavy*

The Glass Palace: *Amitav Ghosh*

The God of Small Things: *Arundhati Roy*

The Godfather: *Mario Puzo*

The Golden Gate: *Vikram Seth*

The Grapes and the Wind: *Pablo Neruda*

The Grapes of Water: *John Steinbeck*

The Great Challenge: *Louis Fischer*

The Great Indian Novel: *Sashi Tharoor*

The Heart is a Lonely Hunter: *Carson McCullers*

The Horse Whisperer: *Nicholas Evans*

The Green Knight: *Iris Murdoch*

The Heart of the Matter: *Graham Greene*

The Hot Zone: *Richard Prelurid*

The House of the Spirits: *Isabel Allende*

The Humbold Gift: *Saul Bellow*

The Idiot: *Feodor Dostoevsky*

The Importance of Being Earnest: *Oscar Wilde*

The Interpreters: *Wode Soyinka*

The Joke: *Milan Kundera*

The Judge: *Steve Martini*

The Judgement: *Kuldeep Nayyar*

The Juror: *George Davis Green*

The Keeper of the Keys: *Milan Kundera*

The Legends of Khasak: *O.V. Vijayan*

The Lost World: *Michael Crichton*

The Making of a Midsummer Night's Dream: *David Selbourne*

The Mandarin: *S. Beauvoir*

The Masters: *C.P. Snow*

The Men Who Killed Gandhi: *Manohar Malgaonkar*

The Merchant of Venice: *William Shakespeare*

The Middle Ground: *Margaret Drabble*

The Miser: *Molere*

The Moon and Suspense: *W. Somerset Maugham*

The Moor's Last Sigh: *Salman Rushdie*

The Naked Face: *Sidney Sheldon*

The Night Manager: *John Le Carre*

The Origin of Species: *Charles Darwin*

The Other Side of Midnight: *Sidney Sheldon*

The Painted Veil: *W. Somerset Maugham*

The Pickwick Papers: *Charles Dickens*

The Pilgrim's Progress: *John Bunyan*

The Power and the Glory: *Graham Greene*

The Power of Positive Thinking: *Norman Vincent Peale*

The Power That Be: *David Hallberstam*

The Private Life of Chairman Mao: *Dr. Li Zhisui*

The R Document: *Irving Wallace*

The Rain King: *Saul Bellow*

The Rape of the Lock: *Alexander Pope*

The Remorseful Day: *Colin Dexter*

The Return of the Native: *Thomas Hardy*

The Rights of Man: *Thomas Paine*

The Road Ahead: *Bill Gates*

The Robe: *Lloyd C. Douglas*

The Runway Jury: *John Grisham*

The Satanic Verses: *Salman Rushdie*

The Scope Illusion: *Robert Ludlum*

The Second World War: *Winston Churchill*

The Seven Spiritual Laws of Success: *Deepak Chopra*

The Sheltering Sky: *Paul Bowles*

The Shoes of the Fisherman: *Morris L. West*

The Social Contract: *Rousseau*

The Songs of India: *Sarojini Naidu*

The Sound and the Fury: *William Faulkner*

The Spirit of the Age: *William Hazlitt*

The Story of My Experiments with Truth: *Mahatma Gandhi*

The Strange and Sublime Address: *Amit Chaudhuri*

The Struggle in My Life: *Nelson Mandela*

The Sword and the Sickle: *Mulk Raj Anand*

The Testament: *John Grisham*

The Third Wave: *Alvin Toffler*

The Total Zone: *Martina Navratilova*

The Tree of Man: *Patrick White*

The Trial: *Franz Kafka*

The Trotter-Nama: *Allan Sealy*

The Unfinished Man: *Nizzim Ezekiel*

The Vendor of Sweets: *R.K. Narayan*

The Vicar of Wakefield: Oliver Goldsmith

The Victim: *Saul Bellow*

The Volcano Lover: *Susan Sontag*

The Waste Land: *T.S. Eliot*

The Way of all Flesh: *Samuel Butler*

The Way of the Wizard: *Deepak Chopra*

The Wealth of Nations: *Adam Smith*

The Whiz Kids: *John Byrne*

The World According to Garp: *John Irving*

The Thirteenth Sun: *Amrita Pritam*

Theory of War: *John Brady*

Things Fall Apart: *Chinua Achebe*

Thorn Birds: *Colleen McCullough*

Thousand Cranes: *Yasunari Kawabata*

Three Horsemen of the New Apocalypse: *Nirad C. Chaudhuri*

Thus Spake Zarathustra: *Friedrich Wilhelm Nietzsche*

Timeline: *Michael Crichton*

Time Machine: *H.G. Wells*

Tin Drum: *Gunther Grass*

Tinker, Tailor, Soldier: *John Le Carre*

To Cut a Long Story Short: *Jeffrey Archer*

Tom Jones: *Henry Fielding*

To the Lighthouse: *Virginia Woolf*

Train to Pakistan: *Khushwant Singh*

Treasure Island: *Robert Louis Stevenson*

Trinity: *Leon Uris*

Tropic of Cancer: *Henry Miller*

Tryst with Destiny: *S. Gopalan*

Twelfth Night: *William Shakespeare*

Two Leaves and a Bud: *Mulk Raj Anand*

Ulysses: *James Joyce*

Uncle Tom's Cabin: *Harriet Beecher Stowe*

Under the Net: *Iris Murdoch*

Unto the Last: *John Ruskin*

Untold Story: *General B.M. Kaul*

Utopia: *Thomas More*

Valley of the Dolls: *Jacqueline Susann*

Vanity Fair: *William Thackeray*

Video Nights in Kathmandu: *Pico Iyer*

Waiting for Godot: *Samuel Becket*

Waiting for the Mahatma: *R.K. Narayan*

Wake Up India: *Annie Besant*

War of Indian Independence: *Vir Savarkar*

We the Nation, The Lost Decades: *N.A. Palkhivala*

Westward Ho: *Charles Kingsley*

Wings of Fire: *A.P.J. Abdul Kalam*

Winter Solstice: *Rosamunde Pikher*

Witness to an Era: *Frank Moraes*

Women in Love: *D.H. Lawrence*

World Within Worlds: *Stephen Spender*

Wuthering Heights: *Emily Bronte*

Yayati: *V.S. Khandekar*

Year of the Upheaval: *Henry Kissinger*

Yesterday and Today: *K.P.S. Menon*

You Can Win: *Shiv Khera*

Zlata's Dairy—A Child's Life in Sarajevo: *Zlata Filipovic*

SPORTS

784. When and where was the first Test match played?

785. When was cricket officially played in India for the first time?

786. When did India become a member of ICC (International Cricket Council)?

787. Which is the second oldest cricket club after MCC?

788. When were the rules and regulations for cricket framed?

789. There has been some change or the other in the original forms of everything used for playing cricket since its inception, except one thing. Which is that?

790. When was Indian Cricket Control Board established? Who was its first President?

791. When was Ranjit Singh, India's grand old man of cricket, born and when did he expire?

792. When did the Indian cricket team first tour England and in which year did the English cricket team first visit India?

793. Who scored the first century in Test cricket?

794. Who was the first cricket player of England to score the first Test century?

795. When was the Ranji Trophy instituted? Who won the first Ranji Tournament?

796. What is our National Cricket Trophy known as?

797. Who is the one and only cricketer to bowl an underarm ball in Test cricket?

798. When and against whom did India play its first Test match?

799. When did India win the first Test against England and under whose captaincy?

800. Who captained the Indian cricket team for the maximum number of matches?

801. Name the only Indian sportsman who not only captained the Indian cricket team, but also represented India at the Olympics in hockey.

802. What are the Test achievements of Sir Don Bradman?

803. Name the Trophy presented to the runners-up in the Ranji Trophy matches.

804. Generally, a cricketer is selected for Test cricket after his performance in the Ranji Trophy. Who is the player to have been selected for Test cricket without participating even in a single Ranji match?

805. Who is the first Arjuna Award winning cricketer?

806. When was the Moinuddullah Gold Cup cricket tournament started?

807. When and where was a cricket match telecast in India for the first time?

808. In which year did India win the Gold in the Asian Football Championship?

809. Who was the first Indian cricketer to have been honoured by Wisden?

810. Which Indian cricketer has scored the maximum runs in an innings in a Test match?

811. Which Indian cricketers have scored maiden Test centuries?

812. Who has the honour of first scoring three consecutive centuries in three Tests?

813. Which city in India has three Test grounds?

814. If a fielder catches a ball while fielding, with the help of his cap, will the batsman be declared out?

815. When a batsman hits the opposite stump and takes a start for a run, would he be considered run out?

816. What is meant by 'time out' in cricket?

817. When was the 'World Cup Tournament' in cricket started?

818. What is the name of the trophy awarded to the winners of Men's National Hockey Championship?

819. What is meant by 'Out Mankad-style' in cricket?

820. Which is the oldest Football Tournament? When and where did it start?

821. What is meant by the term 'The Big Three' in Indian Football?

822. Which Indian team was the first Durand Cup winner?

823. When was Football first included in the Olympics?

824. Who is the Indian cricketer to have scored maximum Double Centuries in Test cricket?

825. Who were the captains of the Indian Football teams when we won the Gold Medals in Asian Football?

826. What is the Jules Rimet Cup?

827. Who is accredited for scoring the first-ever goal in the World Cup Tournament?

828. Who was the oldest captain — age-wise — to have helped his country win a Football tournament?

829. Which player is considered to be the wizard of football?

Q. 823

830. In which competition did one contestant win all the events?

831. Who has achieved the only hat trick in World Cup Football?

832. Which country has the credit of having started the Asian Games? When were these games instituted?

833. What is the distance a Marathon race covers?

834. When was Hockey included in the Asian Games?

835. Who won the first Gold Medal for Hockey? Who won the Gold in the tenth Asiad at Seoul in 1986?

836. Which city in Asia has the credit of having hosted the Asian Games thrice?

837. Who is nicknamed 'the flying Sikh'?

838. Name the first bowler who has taken 500 wickets in Test cricket?

839. What is Levy Pinto known for in the Asian Games?

840. When were the modern Olympics started?

841. Who is credited for having started the modern Olympics?

842. Since when is India officially participating in the Olympics?

843. How many gold medals has India won in the Olympics so far in Hockey?

844. In the history of the Wimbledon Tennis Tournament, only one player has won the event after being a Wild Card Entry. Who is s/he?

845. Who has the honour of having received the first Arjuna Award?

846. Name the game(s) with which the following players are associated:
(i) Magan Singh (ii) Yajuvendra Singh (iii) Dibyendu Barua (iv) Niyoti Rai (v) Prakash Padukone.

847. Which Indian has the credit of winning the All England Badminton Championship for the first time and in which year?

848. G.R. Viswanath scored 13 centuries in his Test career. What had been the special feature of these centuries?

849. Name the game(s) the following trophies are associated with:
(i) C.K. Naidu Trophy (ii) Mohan Kumar Mangalam Trophy (iii) Sir Arthur Walker Trophy (iv) Subroto Cup (v) Davis Cup (vi) Uber Cup/Thomas Cup.

850. Who is considered the Indian wizard of Hockey?

851. Who are the two Indian women swimmers to have swum across the English Channel?

852. He is the second Indian after Prakash Padukone who has won the All England Badminton Championship. Who is he?

853. What is meant by Grand Slam?

854. Name the Indian Men's Doubles Tennis players who have reached all four Grand Slam finals in the same year.

855. Which has been the best performance of India at Wimbledon?

856. When was the Davis Cup started? Since when is India participating in it?

857. When was the women's event started at the Wimbledon Tennis Championship and who won the event?

858. Name the countries and games the following players are associated with:
(i) Frank Pushkus (ii) Alexie Metrevellie (iii) Rudy Hartono (iv) Hasan Sardar, Ismailuddin (v) Jahangir Khan (vi) Len Hutton.

859. Name the Indian player who has hit six sixers in one over.

860. Name the game the following players are associated with:

(i) Shriram Singh (ii) Vijay Hazare (iii) Vijay Amritraj.

861. Whom did Muhammed Ali a.k.a. Cassius Clay defeat when he won the World Heavyweight Title in 1964?

862. When was the Wimbledon Tennis Championship first played?

863. In which game is the referee known as 'President'?

864. Name the first person to have crossed the English Channel to and fro swimming non-stop.

865. Name the places where the Olympics were held in 1904, 1920, 1932 and 1952 respectively.

866. How and why is Badminton named so?

867. India had won the Hockey Gold in Olympics successively six times but lost it in 1960. To whom did we lose?

868. What is football player Pele's full name?

869. Mention the number of players of one team participating in a game in the following:
(i) Basketball (ii) Ice Hockey (iii) Water Polo (iv) Polo.

870. During the Olympics, which team has the privilege of entering first in the stadium?

871. What is the colour scheme in the five rings of the Olympic emblem?

872. Who was the first Indian Wimbledon player?

Q. 868

873. Name the first Indian to reach the men's singles quarter-finals at Wimbledon?

874. Who is known as the *Haryana Hurricane*?

875. Name the countries against which Sir Donald Bradman had scored his 29 centuries. (Incidentally, this record was broken by Sunil Gavaskar.)

876. In which game does a player move backward and wins?

877. In which game are the words Ace, Deuce, Service, Game and Set used?

878. In the 1932 Los Angeles Olympics, how many goals did India score in various hockey matches?

879. Which Indian player created a world record in the Old Trafford Test match?

880. Who won the 'Grand Slam' in tennis for the first time?

881. On which dates did Sunil Gavaskar complete his 1,000 and 5,000 runs?

882. Which batsman gets the credit for having scored the first century in one-day internationals?

883. Name the woman who not only won the Asian Tennis Championship but figures in the headlines many a time under the Administrative Services.

884. Name the first to bowl and first to bat in Test cricket.

885. When was Basketball (men and women) included in the Olympics?

886. Who has won the World Professional Snooker Title the maximum number of times?

887. Who is the well-known cricket umpire to be decorated with a National honour in 1986?

888. Who is the first Indian woman to scale Everest?

889. When was Syed Modi, the famous Badminton player, born? How many times has he won the National Badminton Championship? When was he murdered?

890. Which cricketer has scored the maximum runs in one-day internationals?

891. In how many events did P.T. Usha bag medals in the 1986 Seoul Asiad?

892. Name the first Indian cricketer who achieved a hat trick in Test cricket.

893. Which Indian cricketer took all 10 wickets in a Test innings? When did he do so?

894. Which Indian cricketer achieved a hat trick in one-day internationals?

896. With which game is the name of Bapu Nadkarni associated? And what is his full name?

897. She had won a Bronze medal at the Sydney Olympics 2000 for India. What is her name?

898. What is Bradman's highest score as captain of Australia?

895. Who is the first cricketer in Test history to score a century against eight Test playing nations?

TEST CRICKET
Top Ten Highest Individual Innings for India

Batsman	Runs	V/s	Test	Venue	Series
V.V.S. Laxman	281	Australia	2nd	Kolkata	2000-01
S. Tendulkar	248*	Bangladesh	1st	Dhaka	2004
S.M. Gavaskar	236*	West Indies	6th	Chennai	1983-84
V. Mankad	231	New Zealand	5th	Chennai	1955-56
V.G. Kambli	227	Zimbabwe	1st	Delhi	1992-93
V.G. Kambli	224	England	3rd	Mumbai	1992-93
V. Mankad	223	New Zealand	2nd	Mumbai	1955-56
P.R. Umrigar	223	New Zealand	1st	Hyderabad	1955-56
G.R. Viswanath	222	England	5th	Chennai	1981-82
S.M. Gavaskar	221	England	4th	The Oval	1979-80
S.M. Gavaskar	220	West Indies	5th	Port of Spain	1970-71

* Not out

Bowlers Claiming Six or More Wickets in Three Consecutive Test Innings

❑ **C.V. Grimmett (Aus)** : 6/92 vs. South Africa (2nd innings), Melbourne 1931-32; 7/116 and 7/83 vs. South Africa, Adelaide 1931-32.

❑ **C.V. Grimmett (Aus)** : 7/40 vs. South Africa (2nd innings), Johannesburg 1935-36; 7/100 and 6/73 vs. South Africa, Durban 1935-36.

❑ **G.A. Lohmann (Eng)** : 7/38 and 8/7 vs. South Africa, Port Elizabeth 1895-96; 9/28 vs. South Africa (1st innings), Johannesburg 1895-96.

❑ **J.C. Laker (Eng)** : 6/55 vs. Australia (2nd innings), Leeds 1956; 9/37 and 10/53 vs. Australia, Manchester 1956.

❑ **L. Sivaramakrishan (Ind)** : 6/64 and 6/117 vs. England, Mumbai 1984-85; 6/99 vs. England (Ist innings), Delhi 1984-85.

❑ **Imran Khan (Pak)** : 8/58 and 6/58 vs. Sri Lanka, Lahore 1981-82; 7/52 vs. England (1st innings), Birmingham 1982.

❑ **Harbhajan Singh (Ind)** : 7/123 and 6/73 vs. Australia, Kolkata 2000-01; 7/133 and 8/8 vs. Australia, Chennai 2000-01.

WORLD CUP CRICKET

Year	Winners	Runners up	Venue
1975	West Indies	Australia	England
1979	West Indies	England	England
1983	India	West Indies	England
1987	Australia	England	India & Pakistan
1992	Pakistan	England	Australia, New Zealand
1996	Sri Lanka	Australia	India, Pakistan & Sri Lanka
1999	Australia	Pakistan	England
2003	Australia	India	South Africa
2007	Australia	Sri Lanka	West Indies

FILMS

899. Name the first film made in India.

900. Which was America's first talkie film (feature film with sound)?

901. In *Anarkali* (starring Bina Rai and Pradeep Kumar) Bina Rai's voice was dubbed. Who did the dubbing?

902. What is the full name of lyricist Pradeep?

903. Name the artist who has had the distinction of being the first heroine in Indian films.

904. Who made the first Indian movie camera?

905. Which Indian film was made in two languages for the first time?

906. When and where was the first Cinema Hall built in India?

907. Who was the world-famous comedian to show the marvel of his art in *City Lights* and *The Gold Rush*?

908. Who received the first Dadasaheb Phalke award?

909. What was the full name of actor-singer K.L. Saigal?

910. Who has the distinction of being the first to have his or her face on the TV screen, when TV was first introduced in India?

911. Who was the first Indian woman to act in Indian movies as a heroine?

912. Who has the distinction of being known as the first music director in films?

913. Who was the maker of the first Indian silent movie and when was it made?

914. When was the Camera Crane used for the first time in India?

915. Name the first ballet film directed by Uday Shankar. When was it made?

916. When and where was India's first International Film Festival organised?

917. What was Nargis Dutt's real name?

918. When was Satyajit Ray awarded the Padmashree and when was his first film completed?

919. Which was Nutan's first film?

920. Actor Raj Kumar is known for his unique style of acting. When did he enter the film world? What is his date of birth?

921. Indian filmdom has three famous actors who were born within three years of one another. Who are they?

922. When and where was the first Film Festival organised in India?

923. Name the first 70 mm technicolour film made in India.

924. What was the name of the first cinema-scope film?

925. One of the daughters of Master Dina Nath, a renowned personality on Marathi stage, entered the film world with the movie *Aap ki Seva Mein*. Who is she?

926. What is the normal rate of movement of frames (pictures) per second, moving in front of the cinema film projector?

927. There is a successful and popular actor of Hindi films who has been associated with the army, politics and All India Radio (being an erstwhile announcer). Name him.

928. Prior to *Alam Ara* was there any talkie filmed in India?

929. When and where was the first film shown in India?

930. Name the only woman ghazal singer who can be placed along with Anup Jalota, Pankaj Udhas and Ashok Khosla, on the ladder of popularity.

931. Name the hero, the heroine and the director of *Cleopatra*.

932. Identify the child actress who acted as Mini in *Masoom*, a film famous for its song *Lakdi ki Kathi, Kathi pe Ghoda*.

933. Name the musician who brought playback singer Nitin Mukesh into the film world by giving him a chance to sing for his films.

934. Himanshu Rai's wife, who became the owner of Bombay Talkies after his death, remarried a foreigner. Whom did she marry?

935. Which child actress received the President's medal for a remarkable performance in *Angan ki Kali*?

936. An actor got a unique chance to act in his first-ever film with an actress of the calibre of Devika Rani. Although younger to her in age, he performed as the hero against her. Name the actor and the film.

937. Which was the first full-length technicolour film made in India?

938. Which film holds the record for running at the same theatre for six uninterrupted years? Name the theatre.

939. Name the Indian film with the maximum number of songs in it.

940. Where is Hollywood situated and what is it famous for?

941. Arthur Miller's second wife was a world-renowned actress. Who was she?

Q. 932

942. A Hindi feature film had songs written by the great poet Sumitra Nandan Pant. Which was that film?

943. Name the Indian artist who received the Golden Bear Award at the International Film Festival in Berlin in 1967 for his film *Through the Eye of a Painter.*

944. A woman cyclist won the All India Cycling Competition in 1955 and thereafter entered the field of cinema as a comedian. Who is she?

945. When and where was the first talking movie of the world shown?

946. Who made *Mickey Mouse*, the popular cartoon film?

947. Name the character-actor who had the distinction of winning the World Cycling Championship.

948. Which was the first Indian film screened in the USSR (now Russia)?

949. Name the only Sanskrit movie to win the prestigious Swarna Kamal Award.

950. When was the *Children's Film Society of India* established? Name the first film made by this society. When was it made?

951. What is Jayant's real name? Also name his son who achieved instant fame as a villain.

952. Which were the first films directed by Basu Bhattacharya and Basu Chatterjee?

953. In what field has renowned AIR newsreader Devaki Nandan Pandey's son earned name and fame?

954. *Jana Gana Mana*, written by Gurudev Rabindranath Tagore, was picturised in a movie. But it was later removed because it was adopted as our National Anthem. Which movie was it?

955. Which Indian movie received the Karlovy Vary Award in 1956?

956. Name the first movies to be made in the following languages – Malayalam, Marathi, Assamese, Bengali, Punjabi and Sindhi.

957. When was Amitabh Bachchan born? Name the movie with which he made his debut in films.

958. At the 4th International Children's Film Festival held in Bangalore on 14th November 1985, a movie entitled *Dhumketu* was screened. The writer of this script is also a famous scientist. Who is this writer-cum-scientist?

959. What is the full name of B.R. Chopra?

960. Who is the story-writer of Raj Kapoor's famous films *Shri 420* and *Awara*?

961. Name the famous Urdu lyricist who wrote lyrics for *Gaman* and *Umraojan*?

962. When was the cartoon film *Mickey Mouse* shown first?

963. A President of the USA, he was also the Governor of California, but prior to his entry into politics, he was associated with Hollywood. Name him.

964. When did TV transmission start in India?

965. Where is the world's largest cinema hall situated? What is its seating capacity?

966. Name the well-known actress who got her collection of poems, entitled *Lamha-Lamha*, published.

967. Who directed the 1958 feature film *Dhul ka Phul*?

968. On whose novel is the TV serial *Raag Darbari* based?

969. Name the world-renowned Swedish actress who, after having acted in hits like *Anna Christie*, 1930, *Grand Hotel*, 1932, and *Queen Christina*, 1933, retired from acting in 1941.

970. In which film did Begum Akhtar act as a heroine?

971. Which actress wrote a travelogue entitled *China Diary*?

972. One of Sarojini Naidu's nephews has acted in 75 films in 50 years. Who is he?

973. In which movie did Rabindranath Tagore act?

974. The film *Siddhartha* is based on a novel of the same title. Name the author of the novel and the hero and the heroine of the film.

975. Which of V. Shantaram's films achieved the distinction of winning three International awards?

976. The film *Guide* is based on R.K. Narayan's novel entitled *The Guide*. Earlier also one of R.K. Narayan's novels was filmed with Motilal as its hero. The title of the film was the same as the title of the novel. Which film is this?

977. In which movie did Prithviraj Kapoor, affectionately called Papaji in filmdom, appear as the hero for the first time?

978. Who is the well-known director who achieved remarkable success in making a TV serial *Bharat Ek Khoj* on Pandit Nehru's *Discovery of India*?

Q. 975

979. Name the first Silver Jubilee movie.

980. Which movie did Sohrab Modi make, based upon one of the famous novels of Gujarati novelist and freedom fighter K.M. Munshi?

981. *Chitrapat* published in 1932 was the first Hindi film magazine. Who was its publisher-editor?

982. Who was the hero of the Tarzan film *King of the Jungle*? He was also associated with the Olympics.

983. Name the music director who composed music for 150 popular movies including *Devdas*, *Vidyapati*, *Street Singer* and other hits. This music director initiated K.L. Saigal into filmdom.

984. Who are the four Mangeshkar sisters?

RECIPIENTS OF THE DADASAHEB PHALKE AWARD (1969-2006)

❑ Devika Rani Roerich	1969	❑ Ashok Kumar	1988
❑ B.N. Sircar	1970	❑ Lata Mangeshkar	1989
❑ Prithviraj Kapoor	1971	❑ A. Nageshwar Rao	1990
❑ Pankaj Mullick	1972	❑ Bhalji Pendharkar	1991
❑ Sulochana (Ruby Myers)	1973	❑ Bhupen Hazarika	1992
❑ B.N. Reddy	1974	❑ Majrooh Sultanpuri	1993
❑ Dhiren Ganguly	1975	❑ Dilip Kumar (Yusuf Khan)	1994
❑ Kanan Devi	1976	❑ Dr. Raj Kumar (Kannada Film Actor)	1995
❑ Nitin Bose	1977	❑ Sivaji Ganesan (Tamil Film Actor)	1996
❑ P.C. Boral	1978	❑ Kavi Pradeep	1997
❑ Sohrab Modi	1979	❑ B.R. Chopra	1998
❑ P. Jairaj	1980	❑ Hrishikesh Mukherjee	1999
❑ Naushad Ali	1981	❑ Asha Bhonsle	2000
❑ L.V. Prasad	1982	❑ Yash Chopra	2001
❑ Durga Khote	1983	❑ Dev Anand	2002
❑ Satyajit Ray	1984	❑ Mrinal Sen	2003
❑ V. Shantaram	1985	❑ Adoor Gopalakrishnan	2004
❑ B. Nagi Reddy	1986	❑ Shyam Benegal	2005
❑ Raj Kapoor	1987	❑ Tapan Sinha	2006

ENVIRONMENT

985. What is ecology?

986. Who coined the term 'ecology' and when?

987. What is ecosystem?

988. What is meant by ecological balance?

989. Name the four elements of an eco-system.

990. What are omnivores?

991. What is a food web?

992. What are saprophytes?

993. What is a biome?

994. What is the biosphere?

995. Name the major biomes of the world.

996. What is the binomial system of nomen-clature?

997. What is adaptation?

998. What is biotope?

999. What are terricolous creatures?

1000. What are arboreal animals?

1001. What is camouflage?

1002. What is aestivation?

1003. What are benthos?

1004. What are planktons?

1005. When did man appear on earth?

1006. Who is known as the father of the modern theory of evolution?

1007. Which is the largest solar power plant in the world?

1008. What is nuclear power?

1009. What is troposphere?

1010. What is stratosphere?

1011. What is mesosphere?

1012. What is thermosphere?

1013. What is exosphere?

1014. What are amphibians?

1015. What is the Third World?

1016. Name the world's highest navigable lake.

1017. Which is the largest oil-field in the world?

1018. Name the world's first nuclear power station.

1019. Where is the world's largest nuclear power station situated?

1020. What is smog?

1021. What are aerosols?

1022. Which is the most air-polluted city in the world?

1023. What is pH scale?

1024. What was the disaster of 1986 in the Rhine River?

1025. Name the biggest slum area in the world.

1026. What is crop rotation?

1027. Which lady was awarded the Nobel Prize twice in the field of radioactivity?

1028. When was the first atom bomb dropped on Hiroshima?

1029. When and where was the second atom bomb dropped?

1030. What is a neutron bomb?

1031. What is zero decibel?

1032. Which is the most polluted orbit in space?

1033. What is the aim of the Kyoto Treaty?

1034. What is acid rain?

1035. Which non-biodegradable substance is most damaging the environment?

1036. Which country is primarily against the Kyoto Treaty?

1037. Why is plastic non-biodegradable?

1038. What does LNG denote?

1039. What is coal?

1040. What is ozone?

1041. Where is the ozone layer present in the atmosphere?

1042. How is the ozone layer useful for the earth?

1043. What is the main factor responsible for ozone layer depletion?

1044. What is the Montreal Protocol?

1045. What are mangrove swamps called in America?

1046. What causes silicosis?

1047. What is Black Death?

1048. What are hygroscope, anemometer and hygrometer?

1049. What is a nephelometer?

1050. What is a gravimeter?

1051. What is a Geiger counter?

1052. What is a florometer?

1053. How can we know the age of a tree?

1054. What is a tensiometer?

1055. What are meteorological satellites used for?

1056. What is a radiometer?

1057. What is a tide gauge?

1058. What is a barometer? Who invented. it?

1059. What is a rain gauge?

1060. What is a radiosonde?

1061. Which computers are used in meteorological studies?

1062. What is a pyrometer?

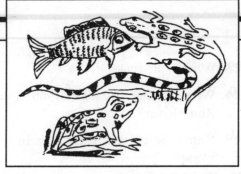

1063. What is a psychrometer?

1064. What is a rawin?

1065. What is a tiltmeter?

1066. What is a sonar?

1067. What is a solarimeter?

1068. What is a seismograph?

1069. What is a Lidar?

1070. What is the full form of CNG?

1071. What is reverse osmosis?

1072. Where is Nek Chand's Rock Garden?

1073. What is known as 'Pleistocene Over-kill'?

1074. Which animals have been threatened to extinction by hunting?

1075. For which wild animal is the Gir Sanctuary famous?

1076. Besides Kaziranga National Park, Assam, where else can you see rhinos?

1077. Where is the lion-tailed macaque found?

1078. Where does the wood for cricket bats come from?

1079. What was discovered by the satellite Nimbus-7?

1080. Which satellite discovered the Van Allenbelts?

1081. Apart from coal, name two other fossil fuels.

1082. Which fish is known as the king of fish?

1083. From which animal is Thyroxine obtained?

1084. What are cold-blooded animals?

1085. Which day is known as World Environment Day?

1086. Although nuclear power is a cheap, clean and long-term source of energy, what is the major danger it poses?

1087. What is global warming?

1088. What is the danger posed by global warming?

1089. What is Ecomark?

1090. Which colour is used as a sign of conservation and the environment?

1091. Who was Dr. Salim Ali?

1092. Which was India's first wildlife sanctuary?

1093. Name the most active environmentalists in India.

1094. When did the Chipko Movement start?

1095. What is the Enron Deal?

1096. What is the Narmada Project?

1097. What is the Bhakra Nangal Project?

1098. When was India's first remote sensing satellite launched?

1099. What is the Chernobyl disaster?

1100. Which is the world's largest oil refinery?

1101. Which bank extends financial help to environmental programmes?

1102. Which was the first National Park in the world?

1103. Which was the first zoo to display animals to the public?

1104. What is ornithology?

1105. What is etiology?

1106. What is florology?

1107. What is cryology?

1108. When did the Bhopal gas leak occur?

1109. Which are the largest mangroves in India?

1110. Where is the largest concentration of man-eating tigers found?

1111. Which book gives a list of endangered species?

1112. Who wrote the book *The Origin of Species*?

1113. Which is the famous journal of UNESCO related to the environment?

1114. What is the J. Paul Getty Award meant for?

1115. Who won the World Food Prize in 1989?

1116. Where is Chilka Lake situated?

1117. What is atmosphere?

1118. What is dry ice?

1119. In which year was the Indian Forest Act passed?

1120. In which year was the Wildlife (Protection) Act passed?

1121. What is the Bishnoi Movement?

1122. What is the Silent Valley Movement?

1123. What is the Narmada Bachao Andolan?

1124. What is the Baliyapal Movement?

1125. What are the main radioactive elements in a nuclear fallout?

1126. What are Biosphere Reserves?

1127. How many Biosphere Reserves does India currently have?

PRINCIPAL GAME SANCTUARIES AND NATIONAL PARKS IN INDIA

Name	State
1. Achanakmar Sanctuary, Bilaspur	Chhattisgarh
2. Achanakmar Sanctuary, Bilaspur	Chhattisgarh
3. Bandhavgarh National Park	Shahdol (Madhya Pradesh)
4. Bandhipur National Park, Mysore	Karnataka
5. Bannarghatta National Park	Mumbai (Maharashtra)
6. Bhimbandh Wildlife Sanctuary, Monghyr	Bihar
7. Borivili National Park, Mumbai	Maharashtra
8. Chandraprabha Sanctuary, Varanasi	Uttar Pradesh
9. Corbett National Park, Nainital	Uttaranchal
10. Cottigao Game Sanctuary, Goa	Goa
11. Dachigam Sanctuary, Srinagar	J & K
12. Dandeli Sanctuary, Dharwar	Karnataka
13. Darraha Wildlife Sanctuary, Kota	Rajasthan
14. Dudhwa National Park, Lakhimpur Kheri	U.P.
15. Eravikulam Rajmallay National Park	Idduki (Kerala)
16. Gandhi Sagar Sanctuary, Mandsaur	Madhya Pradesh
17. Ghana Bird Sanctuary, Bharatpur	Rajasthan
18. Ghatpraba Bird Sanctuary	Bharatpur (Rajasthan)
19. Gir National Park, Junagarh	Gujarat
20. Guindy National Park	Chennai (Tamil Nadu)
21. Hazaribagh Sanctuary, Hazaribagh	Jharkhand
22. Intangki Sanctuary, Kohima	Nagaland
23. Jaldapara Sanctuary, Jalpaiguri	West Bengal
24. Kanha National Park, Mandla & Balaghat	Madhya Pradesh
25. Kaziranga National Park, Jorhat	Assam
26. Khang Chandzenda National Park, Gangtok	Sikkim
27. Kutree Game Sanctuary	Bastar (Chhattisgarh)
28. Manas Sanctuary, Barpeta	Assam

Contd...

Name	State
29. Melapattu Bird Sanctuary	Ahmedabad (Gujarat)
30. Mudumalai Sanctuary, Nilgiris	Tamil Nadu
31. Mukambika Sanctuary, South Canara	Karnataka
32. Nagerhole National Park, Coorg	Karnataka
33. Nawegaon National Park, Bhandara	Maharashtra
34. Palamau Tiger Sanctuary	Daltonganj (Jharkhand)
35. Parambikulam Sanctuary, Palghat	Kerala
36. Pench National Park, Nagpur	Maharashtra
37. Periyar Sanctuary, Idukki	Kerala
38. Ranganthitoo Bird Sanctuary	Sawai Madhopur (Rajasthan)
39. Ranthambhore Tiger Project, Sawai Madhopur	Rajasthan
40. Rohla National Park, Kulu	Himachal Pradesh
41. Sariska Sanctuary, Alwar	Rajasthan
42. Shivpuri National Park	Shivpuri (Madhya Pradesh)
43. Shivpuri National Park, Shivpuri	Madhya Pradesh
44. Similipal Sanctuary, Mayurbhanj	Orissa
45. Similipal Tiger Sanctuary	Mayurbhanj (Orissa)
46. Sultanpur Lake Bird Sanctuary	Gurgaon (Haryana)
47. Sunderbans Tiger Reserve, 24 Parganas	West Bengal
48. Tadoba National Park, Chandrapur	Maharashtra
49. Tungabhadra Sanctuary, Bellary	Karnataka
50. Valvadar National Park, Bhavnagar	Gujarat
51. Waynad Sanctuary, Cannanore, Kozhikode	Kerala

AWARDS
AND
HONOURS

NATIONAL HONOURS (Awarded in 2008)

Padma Vibhushan: Narayana Murthy (information technology), E. Sreedharan (Delhi Metro), L.N.Mittal & Ratan Tata (industry), Justice (Dr.) A.S.Anand & Pranab Mukherjee (public affairs), P.N.Dhar (civil service), P.R.S.Oberoi (trade), Asha Bhonsle (music), Edmund Hillary (mountaineering), Sachin Tendulkar (sports).

Padma Bhushan: Shiv Nadar (information technology), Inderjit Kaur (social work), P.Susheela (arts), Yuli Mikhailovich Vorontsky of Moscow & Mian Bashir Ahmed (public affairs), Shrilal Shukla (literature & education), Amar Nath Sehgal (arts), Dr. (Mrs.) Shyama Chona (education).

Padma Shri

For Arts:

Gangadhar Pradhan, Pandit Gokulotsavji Maharaj, Hans Raj Hans, Dr. (Mrs.) Helen Giri, Jatin Goswami, Jawahar Wattal, John Martin Nelson, Jonnalagadda Gurappa Chetty, Kekoo M. Gandhy, Madhuri Dixit, Mangala Prasad Mohanty, M. Night Shyamalam, Meenakshi Chitharanjan, Moozikkulam Kochukuttan Chakyar, P.K.Narayanana Nambiar, Sabitri Heisnam, Sentila T. Yanger, Dr. Sirkazhi Sivachidambaram, Tom Alter, Prof. Yella Venkateshwara Rao, Pratap Pawar (UK), Mikhailovich Pechinkov (Russia).

For Journalism:

Barkha Dutt, Rajdeep Sardesai, Vinod Dua, Ishwar Chandra Narayana Tyagi.

For Literature & Education:

Prof. Amitabh Matto, Balasubramanian Sivanthi Adithan, Bholabhai Patel, Dr. (Mrs.) Bina Agarwal, Prof. (Dr.) K.S. Nisar Ahmed, Dr. (Mrs.) M. Leelavathy, Dr. Nirupam Bajpai, Dr. Srinivas Udgata, Prof. Sukhdeo Thorat, Surya Kanta Hazarika, Dr. Vellayani Arjunan, Mohammed Yousuf Taing.

For Mango Plantation & Grafting

Haji Kaleem Ullah Khan

Medicine

Dr. Mohsin Wali, Dr. Jayanta Kumar Sinha, Prof. (Dr.) Arjunan Rajsekaran, Prof. (Dr.) C.U. Velmurugendran, Dr. Deepak Sehgal, Prof. (Dr.) Dinesh K. Bhargava, Dr. Indu Bhushan Sinha, Dr. Keiki R. Mehta, Dr. Mohan Chandra Pant, Dr. (Mrs.) Malvika Sabharwal, Dr. Rakesh Kumar Jain, Dr. Raman Kapur, Dr. Randhir Sud, Dr. Shyam Narayan Arya, Prof. (Dr.) Surendra Singh Yadav, Dr.Tatyarao Pundlikrao Lahane, Dr. Tony Fernandez.

Public Affairs

Collette Mathur (Switzerland).

Science & Engineering

Dr. Bhavarlalji Jain, Prof. Kasturi Lal Chopra, Dr. Joseph H. Hulse (Canada), Dr. Sant Singh Virmani (USA).

Social Work

Kailash Chandra Agrawal, Sister Karuna Mary Braganza, Dr. (Mrs.) Kshama Metre, Dr. Kutikuppala Surya Rao, Madan Mohan

Sabharwal, Dr. (Mrs.) Sheela Barthakur, V.R. Gowrishankar, Vikramjit Singh Sahney, Yousaf Ali Musaliamveetil Abdul Kader of UAE, Bibi (Dr.) Inderjit Kaur.

Sport

Baichung Bhutia, Bula Chowdhury Chakraborty.

Trade & Industry

Dr. Amit Mitra.

SCIENCE & TECHNOLOGY
International

The Alexander von Humbolt Foundation Award, 2008: Professor Seyed Ehteshan Hasnain (Indian) 60000 Euros (Rs. 37 lakhs)

Eduard Dolezal Award, 2000 (Society for Photogrammetry and Remote Sensing): Prof. U.R. Rao. 15,000 Austrian Schillings.

Charles F. Kettering Prize (General Motors Cancer Research Foundation, New York): Mansukh Warri (Indian-American) at Monroe Wall. $2,50,000.

Wolf Prize (Israel) 2008: Jointly awarded to John A. Pickett Rothamsted Research Harpenden, Hertfordshire, United Kingdom James H. TumlinsonPennsylvania State University University Park, Pennsylvania, USA W. Joe Lewis Agricultural Research Service, US Department of Agriculture Tifton, Georgia, USAfor their remarkable discoveries of mechanisms governing plant-insect and plant-plant interactions.

L'Oreal-Unesco Award (2001): Dr. Indira Nath.

Hughes Medal (Royal Society of London): Prof. C.N.R. Rao.

Vuk Kvrhovac Award: Dr. Sharad Pendsey (diabetes consultant).

National

Shanti Swarup Bhatnagar Awards - 2008: Dr. G.P.S. Raghav (Chandigarh), Dr. L.S. Shashidhara (Hyderabad), Dr. Pradip Thalappil (Chennai), Dr. Jarugu Narasimha Moorthy (Kanpur), Dr. P.N. Vinayachandran (Bangalore), Dr. Ranjan Kumar Mallik (Delhi), Dr. Jaikumar Radhakrishnan (Mumbai), Dr. Ravinder Goswami (Delhi), Dr. Raghunathan Srianand (Pune), Dr. Srikant Sastry (Bangalore).

IIT Kharagpur's Nina Saxena Technology Award - 2008: Dr. Subhash P. Andey, Dr. Prakash S. Kelkar, Dr. Madan V. Nanoti, all scientists with the Geo-Environment Management Division NEERI were presented the award for their contribution in the field of Healthcare.

Fibre Optic Person for 1998: P.R. Venkateswaran of ISRO. Rs. 50,000.

Hari Om Ashram Awards, 1998: Dr. A.P.J. Abdul Kalam and R. Chidambaram. Rs. 1,00,000.

Outstanding Geologist National Award (Geological Mining and Metallurgical Institute of India): Dr. M. Santhosh, Centre for Earth Science Studies, Thiruvananthapuram. Rs. 25,000.

Gujar Modi Science Award, 2008: Padma Shri Dr. T.V.Ramakrishnan.

13th H.K. Firodia Award, 2008: Award I of Rs 2 lakhs to Dr. C.S. Seshadri, Director, Chennai Mathematical Institute, Chennai for his work in the field of algebraic geometry and invariant theory. Award II of Rs 1 lakh to Dr. Raghavendra Gadagkar, Professor at Centre for Ecological Sciences, Indian Institute of Science, Bangalore, for his work on animal behaviour and molecular biology.

Devi Ahilya Award: R. Chidambaram. Rs. 1,00,000.

O P Bhasin Awards, 2004: Dr. S. E. Hasnain

LITERATURE
International

Pan-Amazon.com short story award: Mira Nair. $10,000 (later withdrawn).

Richest fiction prize (Dublin): British writer Nicola Barker for her novel *Wide Open*. $1,15,000.

National

Col. James Todd Award (Maharana Mewar Foundation)

Years	Winners
1997-98	Mark Tully (London, UK)
1998-99	Domnique Lapierre (France)
1999-00	Sir V S Naipaul (London, UK)
2000-01	Dr. Chitranjan S. Ranawat (USA)
2001-02	Luigi Zanzi (Italy)
2002-03	M.M. Kaye (London, UK)
2003-04	Lord Richard Attenborough (London, UK)
2004-05	Abbas Sadriwala (Florida, USA)
2005-06	Mohammed Dada Bhai (Bahrain)
2006-07	Prof. Lloyd I. Rudolph & Susanne Hoeber Rudolph (USA)
2007-08	William Dalrymple (Scotland)

Vallathol Award, 2008: Puthussery Ramachandran.

MUSIC & ARTS
International

Rock and Roll Hall of Fame 2008: John Mellencamp, Leonard Cohen and Madonna honoured.

World Music Awards 2007: Outstanding contribution to R & B: Patti Labelle, Outstanding Contribution to Music: Celine Dion, Entertainer of the year:Rihanna, Best Selling DJ: David Guetta, Best Selling Internet Artist: Akon, Best Selling Latin Group: Maná, Best Selling New Artist: Mika, Best Selling Pop Female Artist: Rihanna, Best Selling Pop Male Artist: Justin Timberlake, Best Selling Pop Rock Female Artist: Avril Lavigne, Best Selling Pop Rock Male Artist: Mika, Best Selling Rap Hip Hop Artist: 50 Cent, Best Selling R&B Female Artist: Ciara, Best Selling R&B Male Artist: Akon.

Polar Music Prize 2008: Pink Floyd and Renee Fleming.

62nd Tony Awards 2008: Play – August: Osage County by Tracy Letts, Musical – In the Heights, Revival of a Play – Boeing Boeing by Marc Camoletti, Revival of a Musical – Rodgers & Hammerstein's South Pacific, Leading Actor in a Play – Mark Rylance, Boeing Boeing, Leading Actress in a Play – Deanna Dunagan, August: Osage County, Leading Actor in a Musical – Paulo Szot, Rodgers & Hammerstein's South Pacific, Leading Actress in a Musical – Patti LuPone, Gypsy, Featured Actor in a Play – Jim Norton, The Seafarer, Featured Actress in a Play – Rondi Reed, August: Osage County, Featured Actor in a Musical – Boyd Gaines, Gypsy, Featured Actress in a Musical – Laura Benanti, Gypsy, Book of a Musical – Passing Strange, Stew, Original Score (Music and/or Lyrics) Written for the Theatre – In the Heights, Music & Lyrics: Lin-Manuel Miranda, Direction of a Play – Anna D. Shapiro, August: Osage County, Direction of a Musical – Bartlett Sher, Rodgers and Hammerstein's South Pacific, Choreography – Andy Blankenbuehler, In The Heights, Orchestrations – Alex Lacamoire & Bill Sherman, In the Heights, Scenic Design of a Play – Todd Rosenthal, August: Osage County, Scenic Design of a Musical – Michael Yeargan, Rodgers and Hammerstein's South Pacific, Costume Design of a Play – Katrina Lindsay, Les Liaisons Dangereuses, Costume Design of a Musical – Catherine Zuber, Rodgers & Hammerstein's South Pacific, Lighting Design of a Play – Kevin Adams, The 39 Steps, Lighting Design of a Musical – Donald Holder, Rodgers & Hammerstein's South Pacific, Sound Design of a Play – Mic Pool, The 39 Steps, Sound Design of a Musical – Scott Lehrer, Rodgers & Hammerstein's South Pacific, Regional Theatre Tony Award – Chicago Shakespeare Theater, Special Tony Award – Robert Russell Bennett, for achievements in orchestration, Lifetime Achievement in the Theatre – Stephen Sondheim.

8th Latin Grammy Awards 2008: Recording of the Year :La Llave De Mi Corazon – Juan Luis Guerra, Album of the Year:La Llave De Mi Corazon – Juan Luis Guerra, Song of the Year:La Llave De Mi Corazon – Juan Luis Guerra, Songwriter (Juan Luis Guerra), Best New Artist:Jesse & Joy, Best Female Pop Album:Yo Canto – Laura Pausini, Best Male Pop Vocal Album:Mtv Unplugged – Ricky Martin, Best Pop Album by a Duo or Group with Vocals:El Mundo Se Equivoca – La Quinta Estacion, Best Urban Music Album:Residente O Visitante – Calle 13, Best Urban Song:Pal Norte – Calle 13 Featuring Orishas, Best Rock Album:El Mundo Cabe En Una Cancion – Fito Paez, Best Rock Album by a Duo or Group with Vocal:Kamikaze – Rabanes, Best Rock Song:La Excepcion – Gustavo Cerati, Best Alternative Music Album:Oye – Aterciopelados, Best Alternative Song:Me Llaman Calle – Manu Chao, songwriter (Manu Chao), Best Salsa Album:Arroz Con Habichuela – El Gran Combo De Puerto Rico.

Brit Awards 2008: Male solo artist: Mark Ronson, Female solo artist: Kate Nash, British Group: Arctic Monkeys, British Album: Arctic Monkeys-Favourite Worst Nightmare, Outstanding contribution to music: Sir Paul McCartney.

50ᵗʰ Grammy Awards 2008: This year's big winner wasAmy Winehouse, who won a total of five awards out of her sixnominations. Herbie Hancock's river: The Joni Letters won Album of the Year, marking the first time in 43 years that a jazz album received the award.

National

Swati Puraskaram (Kerala Govt.) 2007: Pandit Jasraj, Hindustani vocalist.

Lifetime Millennium Distinction Award (Subbarani Reddy Kalapeetham): Pandit Ravi Shankar. Rs. 2,00,000.

Rashtra Vaibhav Awards (Maharashtra Kala Niketan): The Mangeshkar family (Lata, Asha, Usha, Meena, Hridayanath).

Rajiv Gandhi Memorial Award, 2008: Saif Ali Khan, Lara Dutta, Darsheel Safary, Dilip Singh Rana (The great Khali), Malkit Singh, Mehul Choksi, Anna Hazare, Baichung Bhutia, Vir Sanghvi, Baba Kalyani.

Jeevan Gaurav Puraskar, 2002: Asha Bhonsle (Singer).

Guru Kelucharan Mohapatra Award (2008): Kumudini Devi (theatre artiste).

Punyabhushan Puraskar (2008): Former Council For Science and Industrial Research Director Dr R A Mashelkar has been chosen for his contribution to the field of science and technology.

RAMON MAGSAYSAY AWARDS (2007- 08)

Govt. Service –

2007   Jovito R. Salonga (Philippines)

2008   Grace Padaca (Philippines)

Public Service –

2007   Kim Sun-Tae (Korea)

2008   Therdchai Jivacate (Thailand) & Center for Agriculture and Rural Development Mutually Reinforcing Instituitions

Community Service –

2007   Mahabir Pun (Nepal)

2008   Prakash Amte & Mandakini Amte (India)

Journalism –

2007   Palagummi Sainath (India)

2008   Akio Ashi (Japan)

International Understanding –

2007   Tang Xiyang (China)

2008   Ahmad Syafi Maarif (Indonesia)

Emergent Leadership –

2007   Chen Guangcheng (China)

2008   Ananda Galappatti (Sri Lanka)

NEHRU AWARD FOR INTERNATIONAL UNDERSTANDING

The Nehru Award was instituted in 1965 by the Government of India in honour of Pt. Jawaharlal Nehru who passed away in 1964. The Nehru Award now carries an amount of

Rs. 15,00,000 and a citation. Recipients of this award are—

(1) U. Thant (1965), (2) Martin Luther King (1966) (posthumous), (3) Khan Abdul Gaffar Khan (1967), (4) Yehudi Menuhin (1968), (5) Mother Teresa (1969), (6) Kenneth Kaunda (1970), (7) Marshal Tito (1971), (8) Andre Malraux (1972), (9) Julius Nyerere (1973), (10) Raul Prebisch (1974), (11) Jonas Salk (1975), (12) Guiseppe Tucci (1976), (13) Tulsi Meharji Shreshtha (1977), (14) Nichidatsu Fuji (1978), (15) Nelson R. Mandela (1979), (16) Mrs. Barbara Ward (1980), (17) Prof. Gunnar Myrdal and Mrs. Alva Myrdal (1981), (18) Dr. Leopold Sedgar Senghor (1982), (19) Dr. Bruno Kreisky (1983), (20) Mrs. Indira Gandhi (1984) (posthumous), (21) Olaf Palme (1985) (posthumous), (22) Perez de Cuellar (1987), (23) Yasser Arafat (1988), (24) Robert Mugabe (1989), (25) Helmut Kohl (1990), (26) Aruna Asaf Ali (1991), (27) Maurice F. Strong (1992), (28) Aung San Suu Kyi (1993), (29) Mr. Mahathir-bin-Mohammed(1994), (30) Mohammed Hosni Mubarak (1995), (31) Goh Chok Tong (2003), (32) Sultan Qaboos Bin Said al Said (2004), (33) Wangari Maathai (2005), (34) Luiz Inacio Lula da Silva (2006), (35) Olafur Ragnar Grimsson (2007).

*Prize not awarded in 1986

*Prize not awarded in 1996-2003

Presidential Medal of Freedom – America's highest civilian award was conferred on Aung San Suu Kyi of Myanmar by President Bill Clinton on Dec. 7, 2000.

World 2005 Millennium Award – Sheikh Hasina, Former Bangladesh Prime Minister.

Gandhi Peace Prize 2007 – Aman Wadhwa

Dayton Peace Prize (2000) – President Bill Clinton gets this honour in recognition of his role in bringing warring sides in the Bosnian conflict to a historic peace deal on November 21, 1995.

Kalinga Prize – This prestigious prize awarded for popularisation of science, has been instituted by the United Nations Educational Scientific and Cultural Organisation (UNESCO).

1987	Dr. Marcel Roche
1989	Dr. Saad Ahmad Shaban (Egypt)
1990	Misabuddin Shami (Pakistan)
1991	Dr. N.K. Sehgal (India) and Dr. R. Iftimoci (Romania)
1992	Dr. Jorge Flores Valdez (Mexico)
1993	Dr. Peter Okebukola (Nigeria)
1994	Dr. Nikolai Drozdov (Russia)
1995	Juliata Naumi Fieero Gosman (Mexico)
1996	Jayant Vishnu Narlikar (India) and Dr. Jiri Grygar (Czech Republic)
1997	Prof. Daurag Rajan Bal Subramaniyam (India)
1998	Prof. Ennio Condotli and Ms. Regina Paz Lopez
1999	Prof. Marian Ewurama Addy (Ghana) and Emil Gebrielian (Armenia)
2000	Prof. Ernst W. Hamburger (Brazil)
2001	Stefano Fantoni (Italy)
2002	Marisela Salvatierra (Venezuela)
2003	Pervez Amirali Hoodboy (Pakistan)
2004	Jean Audouze (France)
2005	Jeter Bertoletti (Brazil)

INDIRA GANDHI AWARD FOR PEACE, DISARMAMENT AND DEVELOPMENT

1990   Sam Nujoma (Namibia).

1991   Rajiv Gandhi (posthumous).

1992   Saburo Okito (Former Japanese Foreign Minister).

1993   Dr. Vaclav Havel (Czech President).

1994   Archbishop Trevor Hadliston.

1995   General Olusegun Okasanjo (Nigeria).

1996   Medicines Sans Frontiers (Voluntary Organisation–Paris, France).

1997   Jimmy Carter (Former President of America).

1998   Mohd. Yunus (President, Bank of Dhaka).

1999   Dr. M.S. Swaminathan.

2001   Prof. Sadako Ogata (UN High Commissioner).

2002   Norodom Sihanouk (King of Cambodia).

2004   Maha Chakri Sirindhorn (Thai Princess)

2005   Hamid Karzai (Afghan President)

2006   Prof. Wangari Maathai (Kenya)

2007   Bill and Melinda Gates Foundation

The award, administered by the Indira Gandhi Memorial Trust, carries with it Rs. 25 lakhs.

OTHER NATIONAL AWARDS

Arjuna Awards – These awards were started in 1961 and are given to the best sportsmen and sportswomen in the country and carries an amount of Rs. 3 lakhs.

Arjuna Awards (2007) – Chitra K. Soman (Athletics), Anuo Sridhar (Badminton), Tombi Devi (Judo), Bajranj Lal Thakur (Rowing), Avneet Kaur Sidhu (Shooting), Alka Tomar (Wrestling), Prabhjot Singh (Hockey), Arjun Atwal (Golf), Donavalli Harika (Chess), Verghese Johnson (Boxing).

Saraswati Samman – (Carrying cash awards of Rs. 3 lakhs, instituted by K.K. Birla Foundation in 1992 for outstanding contribution to literature in any language included in Eighth Schedule.) The first recipient – Dr. Harivansh Rai Bachchan. The second recipient of the award was Oriya poet Rama Kant Rath in 1993. For 1993 and 1994, the award was given to Vijay Tendulkar and Harbhajan Singh respectively. For 1995, it was given to Smt. N. Balmani Amma. For 1996 it was given to Shamsurrahman Farukhi. For 1997, it was given to Manubhai Pancholi. For 1998, it was given to Shankh Ghosh. The award for 1999 went to Tamil playwright and litterateur Dr. Indira Parthasarathi. For 2000, it was given to Manoj Das, bilingual Oriya writer. For 2001, it was given to Dr Dalip Kaur Tiwana, Punjabi novelist. For 2002, it was given to Himmat Singh Gill. For 2003, it was given to Govind Chandra Pande for his collection of 163 Sanskrit poems titled 'Bhagirathi'. For 2004, it was given to Sunil Gangopadhyaye for his novel 'Prothom Alo'. For 2005, it was given to Ayappa Paniker as the pioneer for modern Malayalam poetry. For 2006, it was given to Jagannath Prasad Das for his collection of poems 'Parikrama' written in Oriya. For 2007, it was given to Naiyar Masud for his collection of short stories *'Taoos Chaman Ki Myna'* (The Myna from Peacock Garden) written in Urdu.

Dronacharya Award (2007) – Sanjeev Kumar Singh (Archery), Jagdish Singh (Boxing), G.E.Sreedharan (Volley Ball), Jagminder Singh (Wrestling).

Rajiv Gandhi Khel Ratna Award (2007) – Mahendra Singh Dhoni (Cricket).

Rajiv Gandhi National Sadbhavana Award (2007) – Prof. N. Radhakrishnan

Vyas Samman – Carrying cash award of Rs. 2.5 lakhs, instituted by K.K. Birla Foundation – 1992 for outstanding contribution to Hindi Literature. First award was given to Dr. Ram Vilas Sharma.

1992 – Prof. Shiv Prasad Singh

1993 – Girija Kumar Mathur

1994 – Dharamvir Bharati

1995 – Kunwar Narayan

1996 – Prof. Ram Swaroop Chaturvedi

1997 – Kedarnath Singh

1998 – Govind Mishra

1999 – Srilal Shukla

2000 – Giriraj Kishore

2002 – Kailash Bajpai

2003 – Chitra Mudgal

2004 – Mridula (Jain) Garg

2005 – Chandrakanta

2006 – Prof. Parmanand Srivastava

2007 – Krishna Sobti

Honest Man of the Year Award 1999 – The eminent Indian journalist and author Khushwant Singh was selected for this award. The earlier recipients of this award are: T.N. Seshan, Dr. Manmohan Singh and Atal Behari Vajpayee.

Bhartiya Jnanpith Award – Instituted by a literary organisation in India for outstanding contribution to Indian literature, it carries a prize of Rs. 2.5 lakhs.

1965 G. Sankara Kurup, for 'Odakkuzhal' (Flute) in Malayalam.

1966 Tarashankar Bandopadhaya, for 'Gandevta' in Bengali.

1967 Kuppali Venkatappagowda Puttappa, for 'Sri Ramayana Darshanam' in Kannada.

1967 Uma Shankar Joshi, for 'Nishitha' in Gujarati.

1968 Sumitranandan Pant, for 'Chidambara' in Hindi.

1969 Prof. Raghupati Sahai 'Firaq' Gorakh-puri, for his book 'Gul-e-Naghma' in Urdu.

1970 Dr. Satyanarayan, a Telugu writer, for his book 'Sreemad Ramayan Kalpa-vriksham' in Telugu.

1971 Vishnu Dey for his book 'Smriti Satta Bhavishyat' in Bengali.

1972 Ramdhari Singh 'Dinkar' for 'Urvashi' in Hindi.

1973 Shared by (i) Dr. Dattatreya Ram-chandra Bendre, a Kannada poet and (ii) Gopinath Mohanty, an Oriya novelist for 'Mati Matal'.

1974 Vishnu Sakharam Khandelkar, for 'Yayati' in Marathi.

1975 Mr. P. V. Akilandam, the popular Tamil writer for his novel 'Chittiraappavi'.

1976 Ashapoorna Devi for 'Prathama Pratishruti' in Bengali.

1977 Dr. Shivram Karanth for Kannada-'Mukajjya-Kanasugalu'.

1978 H.S. Vatsayan 'Ageya' for Hindi collection of poems 'Kitni Nawon Main Kitni Bar'.

1979 Assamese poet and novelist Dr. Virendra Kumar Bhattacharya for his novel 'Mritunjaya'.

1980 Malayalam travelogue writer S.K. Pottekkat.

1981 Amrita Pritam, the romantic Punjabi writer, for 'Kagaz te Kanvas'.

1982 Hindi poetess Mahadevi Verma for her collection 'Yama'.

1983 Kannada novelist Masti Venkatesh Iyengar for his novel 'Chikaveera Rajendra'.

1984 Thakazhi Shiv Shanker Pillai (Malayalam writer).

1985 Pannalal Patel, for 'Maanvi ni Bhavai' in Gujarati.

1986 Sachidanand Routroy (Oriya writer).

1987 V.V. Shirwadkar, for 'Natsamrat' in Marathi.

1988 C. Narayan Reddy (Telugu writer).

1989 Ms. Qurratulain Hyder (Urdu writer).

1990 V.K. Gokak, for 'Bharat Sindhu Rashmi' in Kannada.

1991 Subhash Mukhopadhyay (Bengali).

1992 Naresh Mehta (Hindi literature).

1993 Dr. Sitakant Mahapatra (Oriya poet).

1994 Prof. U.R. Anantmurti (Kannada).

1995 M.T. Vasudevan Nair.

1996 Mahasweta Devi (Bengali writer).

1997 Ali Sardar Jafri (Urdu writer).

1998 Girish Karnad, for 'Tughlak' in Kannada.

1999 Nirmal Verma (Hindi fiction writer) and Gurdayal Singh (Punjabi novelist).

2000 Indira Goswami (Assamese writer).

2001 Rajendra Keshav Lal Shah (Gujarati).

2002 D. Jayakanthan (Tamil).

2003 Vinda Karandikar (Marathi).

2004 Rahman Rahi (Kashmiri poet).

Tansen Samman (2007) – Dr Pandit Gokulotsavji Maharaj for outstanding contribution in the field of Hindustani classical music.

1st Ustad Bismillah Khan Award for Excellence 2008 – Amitabh Bachchan, Nafisa Ali (humanity) Sudershan Patnaik (sand artiste), Kapil Dev (cricketer), Kiran Bedi (IPS officer), Farouque Sheikh (culture), Rajya Sabha MP Amar Singh (harmony), Bhupinder Singh Hooda (CM Haryana), Bindeshwar Pathak (social service), Jyotsna Suri (entrepreneurship), Rajendra Prasanna (music), Ashok Chauhan (education).

K.K. Birla Award (2007) – Swami Rambhadracharya for his epic poem, *Shribhargavaraghaviyyam*, (Vachaspati award), Yashwant Vyas for his satirical novel in Hindi on communal violence, *Comrade Godse* (Bihari award), Prof. R.S. Tripathi for his work *Baudh Darshan Prasthan* (Shankar award).

17th G.D. Birla Award (2007) – Prof. Santanu Bhattacharya for his contribution in the fields of chemical biology and molecular design.

Indira Gandhi Award for National Integration – M.S. Subbulakshmi (1989), Rajiv Gandhi (1990), Param Dham Ashram, Pawnar (1991), Acharya Shri Tulsi (1992), Bishambhar Pandey (1993), Beant Singh and Natwar Thakkar (1994), Gandhi Institute of Public Affairs—Karnataka (1995), Vishwa Bharat Shantiniketan (1996), Dr. A.P.J. Abdul Kalam (1997), Dr. Shankar Dayal Sharma (1998), Prof. Satish Dhawan (1999), HY Sharada Prasad (2001), Ram-Rahim Nagar Slum Dwellers Association (Ahmedabad), Aaman Pathik – Peace Volunteer Group (Ahmedabad), Ram Sinh Solanki and Shri Sunil Tamaiche (jointly), Acharya Mahaprajna(2002), Shri Shyam Benegal(2003), Mahashweta Devi(2004), Javed Akhtar(2005), J S Bandukwala & Ram Puniyani (jointly) (2006), Kasturba Gandhi National Memorial Trust, Indore (2007).

JAMNALAL BAJAJ AWARDS (2007)

For Constructive Work in Society – Yashpal Mittal

For Emphasis on the Use of Science and Technology for Rural Development – Anand Karve

For Uplift of Women and Children (also known as Janki Devi Award) – Ashoka Gupta

Kalidas Award – The Kalidas Samman, instituted by the Madhya Pradesh Government is given for excellence in Performing Arts. Awards—1997-98: Pt. Jasraj, 1998-99: Girish Karnad, D.K. Pattamal, Kalanidhi Narayanan and Arpita Singh, 1999-2000: Pandit Hari Prasad Chaurasia, Pt. Satyadev Dube, K.P. Kitappa and Francis Newton Souza. 2004-05: Kanak Rele.

Nehru Literacy Award – An award instituted by the Indian Adult Education Association in 1968 for outstanding contribution to the promotion of Adult Literacy in India.

1968 Dr. (Mrs.) Wealthy Fisher, founder of Literacy House, Lucknow.

1969 Mrs. Kusum Sayani, Vice-President, Bombay City Social Education Committee.

1970 Mysore State Adult Education Association.

1971 Satyen Mitra, Bengal.

1972 Smt. Durga Bai Deshmukh.

1973 Ranjit M. Chet Singh.

1974 T. S. Avinashlingam Chettiar.

1975 Dr. Mohan Singh Mehta.

1976 T.A. Koshy, Project Director, Council for Social Development, New Delhi.

1977 A.R. Deshpande, former advisor on social education to the Government of India.

1978 G.K. Gaokar.

1979 Krishna Agarwal.

1980 Janardan Rai Nagar.

1981 Chunnibhai R. Bhatt, Gujarat.

1982   N. Bhadraiah, former President of the Karnataka State Adult Education Council.

1983   Bombay City Social Education Committee.

1984   Mushtaq Ahmad.

1985   Madhuri R. Shah, former Chairman of the University Grants Commission.

1986   Prof. N.G. Ranga.

1987   Prof. Ram Lal Parikh of Gujarat Vidyapith.

1988   Bhai Bhagwan, former Director of Adult Education Rajasthan Vidyapith.

1991   K.L. Jakir, Haryana.

1992   Dr. Adisheshaiya (former Vice-Chancellor, Madras University) and Prof. V.B. Mohanti.

1993   Dr. V.S. Mathur.

1994   Sadasiva Pillai and Emaben Desai.

1995   Satya Narayan Parikh.

1996   Tarlok Singh.

1997-98 Dr. D.P. Patnaik.

1999   Dr. Laxmidhar Misra.

2001   Dr. L.D. Mishra

2002   Prof. N.K. Ambast

2003   Prof. B.S. Garg

FILMS

International

Knight Commander's Cross of the Order of Merit (Germany): Billy Wilder, film director.

61ST CANNES FILM FESTIVAL AWARDS (2008)

Best Film – *The Class* (Laurent Cantet).

Grand prize of Jury (Runner-up)– *Gomorrah* (Matteo Garrone).

Jury Prize – *Il Divo* (Paolo Sorrentino).

Best Short Film – *Megatron* (Marian Crisan).

Best Actor – Benicio del Toro in *Che* directed by Steven Soderbergh.

Best Actress – Sandra Corveloni in *Linha de Passe* directed by Walter Salles and Daniela Thomas.

Best Director – Nuri Bilge Ceylan for *Three Monkeys (Üç Maymun)*.

Best Screenplay – Luc & Jean-Pierre Dardenne for *Lorna's Silence (Le Silence de Lorna)*.

Golden Camera (first-time director) – Steve McQueen (Britain) for *Hunger*.

Special 61st Anniversary Prizes – Catherine Deneuve (France) and Clint Eastwood (United States).

OTHER AWARDS

65th Venice Film Festival 2008: Golden Lion Award for lifetime achievement – Ermanno Olmi (Italian Director)

Golden Lion Award (2008): *The Wrestler:* Darren Aronofsky (Director).

Golden Conch Award (Mumbai Intl. Film Festival):*Goddesses,*a Tamil documentary by the Chennai-based film maker Leena Manimekalai has won the award for the best documentary film at the 10th Mumbai International Film Festival (MIFF), 2008. This is the time a Tamil film has won in the international category.

IFFK-2007 Awards –

NETPAC Award for the Best Malayalam Film goes to: *Ore Kadal.*

NETPAC Award for the Best Asian Film in competition goes to: *Getting Home.*

Fipresci Award for the Best Malayalam Film goes to: *Ore Kadal.*

Fipresci Award for the Best Film in competition goes to: *Sleepwalking Land.*

12th IFFK awards a special jury prize to the director : Mr. Abdullah Oguz of the Turkish film *Bliss.*

Rajatha Chakoram and cash prize of Rs 3 lakhs for the Best Debut Film of a director goes to : Lucia Puenzo from Argentina for her film *XXY.*

Rajatha Chakoram and cash prize of Rs 2 lakhs for the Best director goes to: Mr.Mania Akbari from Iran for her film *10+4*

Suvarna Chakoram and cash prize of Rs 10 lakhs for the best film will be shared equally between *XXY* directed by Lucia Puenzo and *10+4* directed by Mania Akbari.

FIPRESCI Prize (2008): *Gabbla (Inland):* Tariq Teguia (Director).

IFFI (2007): Golden Peacock Awards – Lin Chih Ju for the Taiwanese film *The Wall.* He gets a cash award of Rs 10 lakhs and a certificate.

INTERNATIONAL INDIAN FILM AWARDS (2008)

Best Picture – *Chak De India*

Best Direction – Shimit Amin (*Chak De India*)

Best Actor – Shah Rukh Khan (*Chak De India*)

Best Actress – Kareena Kapoor (*Jab We Met*)

Best Supporting Actor– Irfan Khan (*Life in a...Metro*)

Best Supporting Actress – Konkona Sen Sharma (*Life in a...Metro*)

Best Comic Role – Govinda (*Partner*)

Music Director – A R Rehman (*Barso re* in *Guru*)

Best Lyricist – Javed Akhtar (*Main Agar Kahoon* in *Om Shanti Om*)

Best Male Playback Singer – Shaan (*Jab Se Tere Naina* in *Saawariya*)

Best Female Playback Singer – Shreya Ghoshal (*Barso re* in *Guru*)

NATIONAL FILM AWARDS (1953-2006)

Year	Film	Language	Director
1953	Shyamchi Aai	Marathi	P.K. Atre
1954	Mirza Ghalib	Hindi	Sohrab Modi
1955	Pather Panchali	Bengali	Satyajit Ray
1956	Kabooliwala	Bengali	Tapan Sinha
1957	Do Ankhen Barah Hath	Hindi	V. Shantaram
1958	Sagar Sangame	Bengali	Debaki Kumar Bose
1959	Apur Sansar	Bengali	Satyajit Ray
1960	Anuradha	Hindi	Hrishikesh Mukherjee
1961	Bhagini Nivedita	Bengali	Bijoy Bose
1962	Dada Thakur	Bengali	Sudheer Mukherjee
1963	Shehar Aur Sapna	Hindi	K.A. Abbas
1964	Charulata	Bengali	Satyajit Ray
1965	Chemmeen	Malayalam	Ramu Kasiat
1966	Teesri Kasam	Hindi	Basu Bhattacharya
1967	Hatey Bazarey	Bengali	Tapan Sinha
1968	Goopy Gyne Bagha Byne	Bengali	Satyajit Ray
1969	Bhuvan Shome	Hindi	Mrinal Sen
1970	Samskara	Kannada	Pattabhirama Reddy
1971	Seemabaddha	Bengali	Satyajit Ray
1972	Swayamvaram	Malayalam	Adoor Gopalakrishnan
1973	Nirmalyam	Malayalam	M.T. Vasudevan Nair
1974	Chorus	Bengali	Mrinal Sen
1975	Chomana Dudi	Kannada	B.V. Karanth
1976	Mrigayaa	Hindi	Mrinal Sen
1977	Ghatashraddha	Kannada	Girish Kasaravalli
1978	(No Award)		
1979	Shodh	Hindi	Biplab Ray Choudhary
1980	Akaler Sandhane	Bengali	Mrinal Sen
1981	Dakhal	Bengali	Ghautam Ghosh
1982	Chokh	Bengali	Utpalendu Chakraborty
1983	Adi Sankaracharya	Sanskrit	G. V. Iyer
1984	Damul	Hindi	Prakash Jha

Year	Film	Language	Director
1985	Chidambaram	Malayalam	G. Aravindam
1986	Thabarana Kathe	Kannada	Girish Kasaravalli
1987	Halodhia Choraye Baodhan Khai	Assamese	Jahnu Bawa
1988	Piravi	Malayalam	Shaji N. Karun
1989	Bagh Bahadur	Hindi	Buddhadeb Dasgupta
1990	Marupakkam	Tamil	K.S. Sethumadhavan
1991	Agantuk	Bengali	Satyajit Ray
1992	Bhagavad Gita	Sanskrit	G. V. Iyer
1993	Charachar	Bengali	Buddhadeb Dasgupta
1994	Uneeshe April	Bengali	Rituparno Ghosh
1995	Kathapurushan	Malayalam	Adoor Gopalakrishnan
1996	Lal Darja	Bengali	Buddhadeb Dasgupta
1997	Thai Saheb	Kannada	Girish Kasaravalli
1998	Samar	Hindi	Shyam Benegal
1999	Vanaprastham	Malayalam	Shaji N. Karun
2000	Shantham	Malayalam	Jayaraj
2001	Dweepa	Kannada	Girish Kasarvauli
2002	Mondo Meyer Upakhyan	Bengali	Buddhadeb Dasgupta
2003	Shwass	Marathi	Sandeep Sawant
2004	Page 3	(Hindi/English)	Madhur Bhandarkar
2005	Kaalpurush--Memories in the Mist	Bengali	Buddhadeb Dasgupta
2006	Pulijanmam	Malayalam	Priyanandan

FILMFARE AWARDS 2008

Best Feature Film – *Taare Zameen Par.*

Best Actor – Shahrukh Khan (*Chak De India*).

Best Actress – Kareena Kapoor (*Jab We Met*).

Best Director – Amir Khan (*Taare Zameen Par*).

Best Supporting Actor – Irfan Khan (*Life in a...Metro*).

Best Supporting Actress – Konkona Sen Sharma (*Life in a...Metro*).

Lifetime Achievement Award – Rishi Kapoor.

Best Actor Critics Award – Darsheel Safary for *Taare Zameen Par.*

ACADEMY AWARDS (OSCARS)
1927-2007

1927-28	Wings		1961	West Side Story
1928-29	Broadway Melody		1962	Lawrence of Arabia
1929-30	All Quiet on the Western Front		1963	Tom Jones
1930-31	Cimarron		1964	My Fair Lady
1931-32	Grand Hotel		1965	The Sound of Music
1932-33	Cavalcade		1966	A Man for All Seasons
1934	It Happened One Night		1967	In the Heat of the Night
1935	Mutiny on the Bounty		1968	Oliver
1936	The Great Ziegfeld		1969	Midnight Cowboy
1937	The Life of Emile Zola		1970	Patton
1938	You Can't Take It With You		1971	The French Connection
1939	Gone With the Wind		1972	The Godfather
1940	Rebecca		1973	The Sting
1941	How Green Was My Valley		1974	The Godfather, Part II
1942	Mrs. Miniver		1975	One Flew Over the Cuckoo's Nest
1943	Casablanca		1976	Rocky
1944	Going My Way		1977	Annie Hall
1945	The Last Weekend		1978	The Deer Hunter
1946	The Best Years of Our Lives		1979	Kramer vs. Kramer
1947	Gentleman's Agreement		1980	Ordinary People
1948	Hamlet		1981	Chariots of Fire
1949	All the King's Men		1982	Gandhi
1950	All About Eve		1983	Terms of Endearment
1951	An American in Paris		1984	Amadeus
1952	The Greatest Show on Earth		1985	Out of Africa
1953	From Here to Eternity		1986	Platoon
1954	On the Waterfront		1987	The Last Emperor
1955	Marty		1988	Rain Man
1956	Around the World in 80 Days		1989	Driving Miss Daisy
1957	The Bridge on the River Kwai		1990	Dances with Wolves
1958	Gigi		1991	The Silence of the Lambs
1959	Ben-Hur		1992	Unforgiven
1960	The Apartment		1993	Schindler's List

1994	Forest Gump		2001	A Beautiful Mind
1995	Braveheart		2002	Chicago
1996	The English Patient		2003	The Lord of the Rings: The Return of King
1997	Titanic		2004	Million Dollar Baby
1998	Shakespeare in Love		2005	Crash
1999	American Beauty		2006	The Departed
2000	Gladiator		2007	No Country For Old Men

FILMS TO WIN THE MOST OSCARS

Film	Awards	Film	Awards
Ben-Hur (1959)	11	From Here to Eternity (1953)	8
Titanic (1997)	11	On the Waterfront (1954)	8
West Side Story (1961)	10	My Fair Lady (1964)	8
Gigi (1958)	9	Gandhi (1982)	8
The Last Emperor (1987)	9	The Godfather (1972)	8
The English Patient (1996)	9	Amadeus (1984)	8
Gone With the Wind (1939)	8*	The Lord of the Rings	11
		Plus two special awards	

80TH OSCAR AWARDS 2007
(AWARDED ON FEBRUARY 24, 2008)

Best Motion Picture: No Country for Old Men (Scott Rudin, Ethan Coen and Joel Coen, Producers).

Best Foreign Language Film: The Counterfeiters (Austria) in German.

Best Documentary Feature: Taxi to the Dark Side (Alex Gibney and Eva Orner).

Best Animated Feature Film of Year: Ratatouille (Brad Bird).

Actor in Leading Role: Daniel Day-Lewis (There Will be Blood).

Actress in Leading Role: Marion Cotillard (La Vie en Rose).

Actress in Supporting Role: Tilda Swinton (Michael Clayton).

Actor in Supporting Role: Javier Bardem (No Country for Old Men).

Original Screenplay: Diablo Cody (Juno)

Adapted Screenplay: Joel Coen & Ethan Coen (No Country for Old Men) from the novel of the same name by Cormac McCarthy.

Achievement in Directing: Joel Coen, Ethan Coen (No Country for Old Men)

Achievement in Art Direction: Dante Ferretti, Set Decoration: Francesca Lo Schiavo (Sweeney Todd The Demon Barber of Fleet Street)

Achievement in Cinematography: Robert Elswit (There Will be Blood).

Achievement in Costume Design: Alexandra Byrne (Elizabeth : The Golden Age)

Achievement in Film Editing: Christopher Rouse (The Bourne Ultimatum)

Achievement in Makeup: Didier Lavergne and Jan Archibald (La Vie en Rose)

Best Documentary Short Subject: Freeheld

Achievement in Music Written for Motion Pictures (Original Score): Dario Marianelli (Atonement)

Achievement in Music Written for Motion Pictures (Original Song): glen Hansard and Marketa Irglova for "Falling Slowly" (Once)

Best Animated Short Film: Peter and the Wolf (Suzie Templeton and Hugh Welchman)

Best Live Action Short Film: The Mozart of Pickpockets

Achievement in Sound Editing: Karen Baker Landers and Per Hallberg (The Bourne Ultimatum)

Achievement in Sound Mixing: Scott Millan, David Parker and Kirk Francis

Achievement in Visual Effects: Michael Fink, Bill Westenhofer, Ben Morris and Trevor Wood (The Golden Compass)

Academy Honorary Award: Robert F. Boyle (Art Direction)

79TH OSCAR AWARDS 2006
(AWARDED ON FEBRUARY 25, 2007)

Best Picture: The Departed (Graham King)

Achievement in Directing: Martin Scorsese (The Departed)

Best Actor: Forest Whitaker (The Last King of Scotland)

Best Actress: Helen Mirren (The Queen)

Actor in Supporting Role: Alan Arkin (Little Miss Sunshine)

Best Supporting Actress: Jennifer Hudson (Dreamgirls)

Best Animated Film: Happy Feet (Warner Bros) George Miller

Best Foreign Language Film: The Lives of Others (Germany)

Adapted Screenplay: William Monahan (The Departed)

Original Screenplay: Michael Arndt (Little Miss Sunshine)

Achievement in Art Direction: Eugenio Caballero, Pilar Ruevelta (Pan's Labyrinth)

Achievement in Cinematography: Guillermo Navarro (Pan's Labyrinth)

Achievement in Costume Designing: Milena Canonero (Marie Antoinette)

Best Documentary Feature: An Inconvenient Truth

Best Documentary Short Subject: The Blood of Yingzhou District

Achievement in Film Editing: Thelma Schoonmaker (The Departed)

Achievement in Make Up: David Marti, Montse Ribe (Pan's Labyrinth)

Achievement in Music Written for Motion Pictures: Gustavo Santaolalla (Babel)

Best Animated Short Film: The Danish Poet

Best Live Action Short Film: West Bank Story

Achievement in Sound Editing: Letters From Iwo Jima

Achievement in Sound Mixing: Dreamgirls

Achievement in Visual Effect: Pirates of the Caribbean: Dead Man's Chest

Academy Honorary Award: Ennio Morricone (Lifetime Achievement Award)

RECIPIENTS OF BHARAT RATNA

1. Dr. S. Radhakrishnan	1954	21. M.G. Ramchandran*	1988
2. C. Rajagopalachari	1954	22. Dr. B.R. Ambedkar*	1990
3. Dr. C.V. Raman	1954	23. Dr. Nelson Mandela	1990
4. Dr. Bhagwan Das	1955	24. Morarji Desai	1991
5. Dr. M. Visveswaraiya	1955	25. Rajiv Gandhi*	1991
6. Jawaharlal Nehru	1955	26. Sardar V.B. Patel*	1991
7. Govind Ballabh Pant	1957	27. M. Abdul Kalam Azad*	1992
8. Dr. D.K. Karve	1958	28. J.R.D. Tata	1992
9. Dr. B.C. Roy	1961	29. Satyajit Ray	1992
10. Purushottam Das Tandon	1961	30. Gulzari Lal Nanda*	1997
11. Dr. Rajendra Prasad	1962	31. Smt. Aruna Asaf Ali*	1997
12. Dr. Zakir Hussain	1963	32. Dr. A.P.J. Abdul Kalam	1997
13. Dr. P. V. Kane	1963	33. M.S. Subbulakshmi	1998
14. Lal Bahadur Shastri*	1966	34. C. Subramaniam	1998
15. Smt. Indira Gandhi	1971	35. Jayprakash Narayan*	1998
16. V. V. Giri	1975	36. Prof. Amartya Sen	1999
17. K. Kamraj*	1976	37. Pt. Ravi Shankar	1999
18. Mother Teresa	1980	38. Gopinath Bordoloi*	1999
19. Acharya Vinoba Bhave*	1983	39. Lata Mangeshkar	2001
20. Khan Abdul Gaffar Khan	1987	40. Ustad Bismillah Khan	2001
		41. Pandit Bhimsen Gururaj Joshi	2008

Posthumous

BOOKER PRIZE WINNERS

	Author	Name of the Book
1969	P.H. Newby	*Something to Answer For*
1970	Bernice Rubens	*The Elected Member*
1971	V.S. Naipaul	*In a Free State*

Contd...

	Author	Name of the Book
1972	John Berger	G
1973	J.G. Farrell	The Siege of Krishnapur
1974	Nadine Gordimer	The Conservationist
	Stanley Middleton	Holiday (Co-winners)
1975	Ruth Prawer Jhabwala	Heat And Dust
1976	David Storey	Saville
1977	Paul Scott	Staying On
1978	Iris Murdoch	The Sea, The Sea
1979	Penelope Fitzgerald	Offshore
1980	William Golding	Rites of Passage
1981	Salman Rushdie	Midnight's Children
1982	Thomas Keneally	Schindler's Ark
1983	J.M. Coetzee	Life and Times of Michael. K.
1984	Anita Brookner	Hotel Du Lac
1985	Keri Hulme	The Bone People
1986	Kingsley Amis	The Old Devils
1987	Penelope Lively	Moon Tiger
1988	Peter Carey	Oscar and Lucinda
1989	Kazuo Ishiguro	The Remains of the Day
1990	A.S. Byaat	Possession
1991	Ben Okri	The Famished Road
1992	Michael Ondaatjee &	The English Patient
	Barry Unsworth	Sacred Hunger
1993	Roddy Doyle	Paddy Clarke Ha Ha Ha
1994	James Kelman	How Late it Was, How Late
1995	Pat Barker	The Ghost Road
1996	Graham Swift	Last Orders
1997	Arundhati Roy	The God of Small Things
1998	Ian McEwan	Amsterdam
1999	J.M. Coetzee	Disgrace
2000	Margaret Alwood	The Blind Assassin
2001	Peter Carry	True History of the Kelly Gang
2002	Yann Martel	Life of Pi
2003	D.B.C Pierre	Vernon God little
2004	Alan Holling Thurst	The Line of Beauty
2005	John Bauille	The Sea
2006	Kiran Desai	The Inheritance of Loss
2007	Anne Enright	The Gathering
2008	Aravind Adiga	The White Tiger

NOBEL PRIZE WINNERS (1991-2008)

Physics

1991 Pierre Giles de Gennes, France.

1992 George Charpak, Poland-France.

1993 Joseph H. Taylor, Russell A. Hulse, both US.

1994 Bertram N. Brockhouse, Canada; Clifford G. Shull, US.

1995 Martin L. Perl of Stanford University and Frederick Reins of the University of California-Irvine, both US.

1996 David M. Lee, Douglas D. Osheroff and Robert C. Richardson, US.

1997 Steven Chu, William D. Phillips, both US.; Claude Cohen Tanno-udji, France.

1998 Prof. Robert B. Laughlin, Prof. Horst L. Stormer, and Prof. Daniel C. Tsui. All US.

1999 Dr. Gerardus T. Hooft and Dr. Martinun Weltman, the Netherlands.

2000 Dr. Herbert Kroemer (Germany), Zhores I. Alferov (Russia), Jack Kilby (US).

2001 Eric A. Cornell, Carl E. Wiemann and Wolfgang Ketterle, all US.

2002 One-half jointly to Raymond Davis, Jr. (US) and Masatoshi Koshiba (Japan), and one-half to Riccardo Giacconi (US).

2003 Alexei A. Abrikosov, Vitaly L. Ginzburg, Anthony J. Leggett

2004 David J. Gross, H. David Politzer, Frank Wilczek

2005 Roy. J. Glauber, John L. Hall, Theodor W. Hansch

2006 John C. Mather, George F. Smoot

2007 Albert Fert, Peter Grunberg

2008 Yoichiro Nambu, Makoto Kobayashi and Toshihide Maskawa (Japan)

Chemistry

1991 Richard R. Ernst, Switzerland.

1992 Rudolph A. Marcus, Canada-US.

1993 Kary B. Mullis, US.; Michael Smith, Britain-Canada.

1994 George A. Olah, US.

1995 Paul Crutzen, the Netherlands; Mario Molina, F. Sherwood Roland, both US.

1996 Robert Curl Jr., Richard Smalley, both US.; Sir Harold Kroto, Britain.

1997 Paul Boyer, US., John Walker, Britain; Jens Skou, D. Mark, both Denmark.

1998 Dr. Walter Kohn, Austria-US; Dr. John and Pople, Britain-US.

1999 Dr. Ahmed Zewail, Egypt.

2000 Dr. Alan Heeger, Dr. Alan Macdiarmid, Dr. Hideki Shirakawa, all US.

2001 William S. Knowles (US), Ryoji Noyori (Japan) and K. Barry Sharp (US).

2002 One-half jointly to John B. Fenn (US) and Koichi Tanaka (Japan), and one-half to Kurt Wüthrich (Switzerland).

2003 Peter Agre, Roderick MacKinnon

2004 Aaron Ciechanover, Avram Hershko, Irwin Rose

2005	Robert H. Grubbs, Richard Shrok, Yves Chauvin
2006	Roger D. Kornberg
2007	Gerhard Ertl
2008	Osamu Shimomura, Martin Chalfie, Roger Y. Tsien

Physiology or Medicine

1991	Edwin Neher, Bert Sakmann, both Germany.
1992	Edmond H. Fisher, Edwin G. Krebs, both U.S.
1993	Philip A. Sharp, U.S.; Richard J. Roberts, Britain.
1994	Alfred Q. Gilman, Martin Rodbell, both U.S.
1995	Edward Lewis, Eric Wieschaus, both U.S., Christiane Nusslein-Volhard, Germany.
1996	Peter Doherty, Australia; Rolf Zinkernagel, Switzerland.
1997	Stanley Prusner, U.S.
1998	Robert F. Furchgott, Louis J. Ignarro, Farid Murad, all U.S.
1999	Guenter Bobel, Germany.
2000	Dr. Eric Kandel, U.S., Dr. Arvid Carlsson, Sweden, Dr. Paul Greengard, U.S.
2001	Paul M. Nurse, Britain, Leland Hartwell, U.S. and Timothy Hunt, Britain.
2002	Sydney Brenner (UK), H. Robert Horvitz (US), and John E. Sulston (UK).

2003	Paul C. Lauterbur, Peter Mansfield
2004	Richard Axel, Linda B. Buck
2005	Barry J. Mashall, J. Robin Warren
2006	Andrew Z. Fire, Craig C. Mello
2007	Mario R. Capecchi, Sir Martin J Evans, Oliver Smithies
2008	Harald zur Hausen, Francoise Barre-Sinoussi, Luc Montagnier

Literature

1991	Nadine Gordimer, S. Africa.
1992	Derex Waicort, West Indies.
1993	Toni Morrison, U.S.
1994	Kenzaburo Oe, Japan.
1995	Seamus Heaney, Ireland.
1996	Wislawa Szymorska, Poland.
1997	Dario Fo, Italy.
1998	Jose Saramago, Portugal.
1999	Gunter Grass, Germany.
2000	Gao Xingjian, France.
2001	V.S. Naipaul, Britain.
2002	Imre Kertész (Hungary)
2003	J.M. Coetzee
2004	Elfriede Jelinek
2005	Harold Pinter
2006	Orhan Pamuk
2007	Doris Lessing
2008	Jean-Marie Gustave Le Clezio

Peace

1991	Aung San Suu Kyi, Myanmar.
1992	Rigoberta Menchu, Guatemala.
1993	Frederik W. de Klerk, Nelson Mandela, both South Africa.
1994	Yasser Arafat, Palestine; Shimon Peres, Yitzhak Rabin, both Israel.
1995	Joseph Rotblat, U.K.
1996	Roman Catholic Bishop Carlos Filipe Ximenes Nelo and Jose Ramos-Horta of East Timor.
1997	International Campaign to Ban Landmines (ICBL) and its coordinator Jody Williams.
1998	David Trimble, John Hume, New Zealand.
1999	Medecins Sans Frontieres (Doctors Without Borders), France.
2000	Kim Dae-Jung, President, South Korea.
2001	Kofi Annan, Ghana.
2002	Jimmy Carter, former president (US).
2003	Shirin Ebadi.
2004	Wangari Maathai.
2005	International Atomic Energy Agency and Mohamed Elbaradei.
2006	Muhammed Yunus and Grameen Bank (Bangladesh).
2007	Intergovernmental Panel on Climate Change, Albert Arnold (Al) Gore Jr.
2008	Martti Ahtisaari

Economics

1991	Ronald H. Coase, Britain-U.S.
1992	Gary S. Becker, U.S.
1993	Robert W. Fogel, Douglas C. North, both US.
1994	John C. Harsanyi, John F. Nash, both US.
1995	Robert E. Lucas Jr., US.
1996	James A. Mirrlees, UK and William Vickrey, Canada.
1997	Robert C. Merton, US and Myron S. Scholes, US.
1998	Amartya Sen, India.
1999	Prof. Robert Mondell, Canada.
2000	James J. Heckman, Daniel L. Mefadden, both US.
2001	A. Michael Spence, George A. Akerlof and Joseph E. Stiglitz, all US.
2002	Daniel Kahneman (US) and Vernon L. Smith (US).
2003	Robert F. Engle III, Clive W.J. Ganger
2004	Finn E. Kydland, Edward C. Prescott
2005	Robert J. Aumann, Thomas C. Schelling
2006	Edmund S. Phelps
2007	Leonid Hurwicz, Eric S. Maskin, Roger B. Myerson
2008	Paul Krugman

INDIAN NOBEL LAUREATES

1. Rabindranath Tagore, Literature, 1913.
2. C.V. Raman, Physics, 1930.
3. Hargobind Khorana, Medicine, 1968.
4. Mother Teresa, Peace, 1979.
5. S. Chandrasekhar, Physics, 1983.
6. Amartya Sen, 1998, Economics.

PEACE & HUMANISM
International

Charlemagne Prize 2008: Angela Merkel, Chancellor of the Federal Republic of Germany.

Gandhi Intl. Peace Award, 2008: Rev Harold Good OBE & Father Alex Reid CSSR Adam Curle (Bradford University).

MISCELLANEOUS
International

Order of British Empire: Sitar maestro Pandit Ravi Shankar, on March 27, 2001.

World Academy of Culture's prize for 2001: Arundhati Roy.

World Chess Championship 2008: Grandmaster Viswanathan Anand

ODI Player of the Year 2008 (ICC): M S Dhoni

T20 Performance of the Year 2008 (ICC): Yuvraj Singh

National

Indian Sportspersons of the Century: Dhyan Chand and P.T. Usha.

Salim Ali Intl. Award for Nature Conservation: Peter Jackson, media person and environmentalist from Britain. Rs. 1,00,000.

Indian Entrepreneur of 20th Century (FICCI): Dhirubhai Ambani.

National Award in Statistics: Prof. J.K. Ghosh, former Director of ISI. Rs. 1,00,000.

Man of the Millennium Award (Delhi Government): Urdu poet, Kaifi Azmi. Rs. 11,00,000.

Gandhi Seva Puraskar, 2000 (Gandhi Darshan Samity): Medha Patkar.

Kabir Puraskar 2008: Ghulam Ahmed Bhat, son of Mohd Akbar Bhat of Hokletri Khan Sahib, Budgam for his role in helping the victims of militancy.

Best Actress Award of the Santa Monica Film Festival, U.S.: Nandita Das (India) for her performance in *Bawandar.*

BBC Asia Award: Gulshan Grover.

People's Choice Award: Ashutosh Gowariker for his film *Lagaan.*

Gandhi International Peace Prize: Actress Shabana Azmi has been awarded the prize for the year 2006.

GENERAL KNOWLEDGE
AND
CURRENT AFFAIRS

IMPORTANT DATES (India in Space)

1975   India's entry into space age by launching 'Aryabhatta' (April 19).

1980   India launches first satellite using its own Satellite Launching Vehicle (July 18).

1981   Launching of satellite Rohini in space (May 31). Rohini burns up (June 9).

1982   INSAT-IA launched (April 10); INSAT-IA shut off due to mechanical disorder (September 6).

1983   Rohini 560 rocket with a technological payload successfully launched from Shri Harikota Range (January 13).

INSAT-1B launched into space (August 30).

1984   Prime Minister Indira Gandhi dedicates INSAT-1 system to the nation (February 11). Rakesh Sharma in space (April 2-11).

1988   With her first nuclear submarine (INS-Chakra) India joins the nuclear maritime club (February 3). India's first remote sensing satellite (IRS-IA) launched from Russia (March 17); INSAT-IC launched in space from French Guiana (July 22).

1989   Narora nuclear power station starts production (March 14); successful test of Agni (May 22); Nhava Sheva port dedicated to the nation (May 26).

1990   Successful launching of INSAT-ID (June 12); successful test of 'Akash' (August 14); Indian warship 'Andaman' sinks in the Bay of Bengal (August 21).

1991   IRS-IB launched from Baikanoor (August 29).

1992   'Prithvi' launched (May 5); SROSS C-1 launched (May 20); successful test of 'Agni' (May 29); INSAT-2A launched (July 10); test flights of 'Lakshya', the pilotless aircraft of India (September 16, 17 and 21).

1993   INSAT-2B launched by Asian Rocket from French Guiana (July 23).

1994   SROSS C-2, successfully launched (April 4); IRS-P2 successfully launched (October 15).

1995   INSAT-2C successfully launched from Kourou (French Guiana) (December 7).

IRS-IC launched (December 28).

1996   IRS-PS3 successfully launched from Shri Harikota (March 21); NAG missile test successful (August 9).

1997   INSAT-2D placed in orbit (June 4); IRS-ID successfully launched (September 29).

1998   India conducts three underground nuclear tests (May 11); India conducts two more nuclear tests (May 13).

1999   India successfully launched its first commercial telecom satellite INSAT-2E from Kourou (April 3); Agni-II test fired successfully (April 11).

2000   India's INSAT-3B launched from Kourou (March 22); India successfully test fires 'Dhanush', the naval version of 'Prithvi' missile (April 11).

2001 Indigenously developed Light Combat Aircraft (LCA) successfully test flown (January 4); GSLV-D1 fails to take off (March 28); India successfully launched GSLV-D1 from Shri Harikota (April 18).

2002 INSAT-3C launched successfully by Arianespace (January), PSLV-C4 launched KALPANA-1 (September).

2003 GSLV-D2, The second developmental launch of GSLV with GSAT-2 successfully (May).

2004 First operational flight of GSLV (F1) successfully launched EDUSAT (September).

2004 India launched World's first Education Satellite on 20th Sept. 2004 from Satish Dhawan Space Centre at Sriharikota, a tiny island in the Bay of Bengal.

2005 Launch of CARTOSAT & HAMSAT by PSLV-C6 from the second launch pad (Universal Launch Pad) (May).

2006 INSAT-4A Launched successfully, planned launch of CARTOSAT-2, SRE & LAPAN-TUBSAT; Indian Remote Sensing Satellite, IRS-1C, Completes Ten Years (Sunday, January 15, 2006)

2007 GSLV-F04 Launch Successful - Places INSAT-4CR in Orbit (Sunday, September 2, 2007)

2008 CARTOSAT-2A and IMS-1 Cameras Switched on (Thursday, May 1, 2008) Indian Space Research Organisation PSLV-C11 Successfully Launches Chandrayaan-1 (Wednesday, October 22, 2008)

WORLD RELIGIONS

Religion	World Population	Religion	World Population
Christians	2,039 million	Atheists	103 million
Roman Catholics	1,098,366,000	Sikhs	23.8 million
Protestants	590 million	Jews	18 million
Orthodox	250 million	Spiritists	12.6 million
Anglicans	73 million	Baha'is	7.4 million
Muslims	1,226 million	Confucians	6.3 million
Hindus	828 million	Jains	4.3 million
Non-religious	1 billion	Shintoists	4 million
Chinese folk religionists	390 million	Other religionists	1.1 million
Buddhists	376 million	Zoroastrians	2.7 million
Ethnic religionists	150 million	Mandeans	50,000 to 70,000

WORLD LANGUAGES

Language	Speakers (in Million) 2001	Principal Areas	Language	Speakers (in Million) 2001	Principal Areas
Chinese, Mandarin	885	China, Taiwan	Marathi	71	Maharashtra
Hindi	496	North India	Chinese, Cantonese	54.8	China
English	514	UK, USA, Canada Ireland, Australia, New Zealand	Chinese, Wu	87	China
			Vietnamese	86	Vietnam
			Javanese	76	Java (Indonesia)
Spanish	322	Spain, Latin America	Italian	73	Italy
Arabic	256	West Asia, N. Africa	Turkish	100	Turkey
			Tagalog	22	Philippines
Bengali	215	India, Bangladesh	Thai	60	Thailand
Portuguese	194	Portugal, Brazil	Chinese, Min	46	Taiwan, China, Malaysia
Malay-Indonesian	176	Malaysia, Indonesia			
Russian	275	Russia, The CIS	Swahili	45	East Africa
French	129	France, Belgium, Canada, Switzerland	Ukrainian	39	Ukraine, Russia, Poland
			Kannada	44	Karnataka
German	123	Germany, Austria, Switzerland	Polish	46	Poland
			Gujarati	46	Gujarat
Japanese	130	Japan	Hausa	40	Nigeria, Cameroon
Urdu	104	India, Pakistan	Farsi (Persian)	110	Iran
Punjabi	104	India, Pakistan	Malayalam	36	Kerala
Korean	71	North & South Korea, China, Japan	Burmese	42	Burma (Myanmar)
			Oriya	32	Orissa
			Sunda	27	Indonesia
Telugu	80	Andhra Pradesh	Romanian	24-26	Romania
Tamil	77	Tamil Nadu Sri Lanka, Malaysia	Yoruba	21	Nigeria

Contd...

Language	Speakers (in Million) 2001	Principal Areas
Amharic	27	Ethiopia
Dutch-Flemish	22	Netherlands
Serbo-Croatian	17	Croatia, Serbia
Pashtu	21-27	Afghanistan, Pakistan
Sindhi	21	Pakistan, India
Igbo	18	Nigeria
Uzbek	20	Uzbekistan
Nepali	17	Nepal, NE India, Bhutan
Hungarian	14	Hungary
Cebuano	30	Bohol Sea, Philippines
Fula	13	Cameroon, Nigeria
Sinhalese	15	Sri Lanka

Language	Speakers (in Million) 2001	Principal Areas
Czech	12	Czech Republic
Greek	12	Greece
Azeri	21-33	Azerbaijan
Kurdish	26	Iran, Iraq, Turkey
Assamese	15	Assam, Bangladesh
Byelorussian	9.1	Belarus
Catalan	12	Spain, France, Andorra
Madurese	14	Madura, Indonesia
Malagasy	17	Mag Madagascar
Nyanja	9.7	Malawi, Zambia, Zimbabwe
Oromo	24	W. Ethiopia, N. Kenya

WOMEN RULERS

No.	Name	Country	Year	Post
1.	Sirimavo Bandaranaike	Sri Lanka	1960	Prime Minister
2.	Indira Gandhi	India	1966	Prime Minister
3.	Golda Meir	Israel	1969	Prime Minister
4.	Maria Isabel Peron	Argentina	1974	President
5.	Margaret Hilda Thatcher	Britain	1979	Prime Minister
6.	Lydia Gveiler Tejada	Bolivia	1979	President
7.	Mary Eugenia Charles	Dominica	1980	Prime Minister
8.	Vigidis Flinnbogadottir	Iceland	1980	President

Contd...

No.	Name	Country	Year	Post
9.	Gro Hardem Brudtland	Norway	1981	Prime Minister
10.	Corazon Aquino	Philippines	1986	President
11.	Maria Liberia Peters Antilles	Netherlands	1988	Prime Minister
12.	Benazir Bhutto	Pakistan	1988	Prime Minister
13.	Mary Robinson	Ireland	1990	President
14.	Herta Praulopp	Haiti	1990	President
15.	Kazimiera Prunskiene	Lithuania	1990	Prime Minister
16.	Violeta Barrios De Chamorro	Nicaragua	1990	President
17.	Khaleeda Zia	Bangladesh	1991	Prime Minister
18.	Edith Cresson	France	1991	Prime Minister
19.	Hanna Suchocka	Poland	1992	Prime Minister
20.	Kim Campbell	Canada	1993	Prime Minister
21.	Tansu Ciller	Turkey	1993	Prime Minister
22.	Chandrika Kumaratunge	Sri Lanka	1994	President, Prime Minister
23.	Chaudet Verle	Haiti	1995	Prime Minister
24.	Sheikh Hasina	Bangladesh	1996	Prime Minister
25.	Ruth Perry	Liberia	1996	President
26.	Rosalia Arteaga	Ecuador	1997	President
27.	Pamela Gordon	Bermuda	1997	Prime Minister
28.	Mary McAleese	Ireland	1997	President
29.	Janet Jagan	Guyana	1997	Prime Minister
30.	Jenny Shipley	New Zealand	1997	Prime Minister
31.	Ruth Dreifuss	Switzerland	1999	President
32.	Mireya Moscoso	Panama	1999	President
33.	Vaira Vike Freiberga	Latvia	1999	President

Contd...

No.	Name	Country	Year	Post
34.	Helen Clarke	New Zealand	1999	Prime Minister
35.	Tarja Halonen	Finland	2000	President
36.	(Dame) Silvia Cartwright	New Zealand	2001	Governor-General
37.	Megawati Sukarnoputri	Indonesia	2001	President
38.	Madior Boye	Senegal	2001	Prime Minister
39.	Sian Seerpoohl Elias	New Zealand	2001	Acting Governor-General
40.	Gloria Macapagal-Arroyo	Philippines	2001	President
41.	Mirna Louisa-Godett	Netherlands	2003-04	Prime Minister
42.	Beatriz Merino (6 months)	Peru	2003	Prime Minister
43.	Yulia Timoshenko	Ukraine	2005	Prime Minister
44.	Angela Merkel	Germany	2005	Chancellor
45.	Michaelle Jean	Canada	2005	Governor General
46.	Portia Simpson Miller	Jamaica	2006	Prime Minister
47.	Ellen Johnson Sirleaf	Liberia	2006	President
48.	Michelle Bachelet	Chile	2006	President

BEAUTY QUEENS, 1951-2008
Miss Universe

Name	Year	Country	Name	Year	Country
Armi Kuusela	1952	Finland	Luz Marina Zuluaga	1958	Columbia
Christiane Martel	1953	France	Akiko Kojima	1959	Japan
Miriam Stevenson	1954	USA	Lina Bement	1960	USA
Hellevi Rombin	1955	Sweden	Marlene Schmidt	1961	Germany
Carol Morris	1956	USA	Norma Nolan	1962	Argentina
Gladys Zender	1957	Peru	Idea Maria Vargas	1963	Brazil

Contd...

Name	Year	Country	Name	Year	Country
Corinna Tsopei	1964	Greece	Cecilia Bolocco	1987	Chile
Apsara Hongsakula	1965	Thailand	Pomtip Nakhirunkanok	1988	Thailand
Margareta Arvindsson	1966	Sweden	Angela Visser	1989	Holland
Sylvia Hitchcock	1967	USA	Mona Grudt	1990	Norway
Martha Vasconcellos	1968	Brazil	Lupita Jones	1991	Mexico
Gloria Diaz	1969	Philippines	Michelle McLean	1992	Namibia
Marisol Malaret	1970	Puerto Rico	Dayanara Torres	1993	Puerto Rico
Georgia Risk	1971	Lebanon	Sushmita Sen	1994	India
Kerry Anne Wells	1972	Australia	Chelsi Smith	1995	USA
Margarita Moran	1973	Philippines	Alicia Machado	1996	Venezuela
Amparo Munoz	1974	Spain	Brook Lee	1997	USA
Anne Marie Puhtamo	1975	Finland	Wendy Fitzwilliam	1998	Trinidad
Rina McSinger	1976	Israel	Mpule Kwelagobe	1999	Botswana
Janelle Commissiong	1977	Trinidad	Lara Dutta	2000	India
Margaret Gardiner	1978	South Africa	Denise Quinones	2001	Puerto Rico
Maritza Sayalero	1979	Venezuela	Justine Pasek*	2002	Panama
Shawn Wcatjcrlu	1980	USA	Amelia Vega	2003	Dominican Republic
Irene Sacz	1981	Venezuela			
Karen Baldwin	1982	Canada	Jennifer Hawkins	2004	USA
Lorraine Downes	1983	New Zealand	Natalie Glebova	2005	Canada
			Zuleyka Rivera	2006	Puerto Rico
Yvonne Ryding	1984	Sweden	Riyo Mori	2007	Japan
Deborah Carthy-Dcu	1985	Puerto Rico	Dayana Mendoza	2008	Venezuela
Barbara Teyde	1986	Venezuela			

(*The original winner, Oxana Fedorova of Russia, was later stripped of the title for refusing to fulfil her commitments as a title winner.)

Miss World

Name	Year	Country	Name	Year	Country
Kerstin Ilaakonson	1951	Sweden	Wilnelia Merced Cruz	1975	Puerto Rico
Mary Louise Flodin	1952	Sweden	Cynthia Breakspcarc	1976	Jamaica
Denise Perrier	1953	France	Mary Ann Stavin	1977	Sweden
Antigonc Constanda	1954	Egypt	Silvana Rosa Clarence	1978	Argentina
Carmen Zubillaga	1955	Venezuela	Gina Swainson	1979	Bermuda
Petra Schurmann	1956	Germany	Gabriella Brum	1980	Germany
Marita Lindahl	1957	Finland	Carmen Leon Crespo	1981	Venezuela
Penelope Anne Coelen	1958	South Africa	Mariascla Lcbron	1982	Dominican Republic
Corinne Rottschafer	1959	Netherlands	Sarah-Jane Hutt	1983	UK
Norma. Cappagli	1960	Argentina	Astrid C. Irrazabal	1984	Venezuela
Rosemarie Frankland	1961	UK	Holmfriour Karlsdottir	1985	Iceland
Catharina Lodders	1962	Netherlands	Giselle Laronde	1986	Trinidad & Tobago
Carole Joan Crawford	1963	Jamaica	Ulla Weigerstorfer	1987	Austria
Ann Sidney	1964	UK	Linda Petursdottir	1988	Iceland
Lesley Langley	1965	UK	Aneta-Beata Kreglicka	1989	Poland
Reita Faria	1966	India	Gina Marie Tolleson	1990	USA
Madeline Hartog Bell	1967	Peru	Ninibeth Jimenez	1991	Venezuela
Penelope Plummer	1968	Australia	Julia Kourotchkina	1992	Russia
Eva von R. Staier	1969	Austria	Lisa Hanna	1993	Jamaica
Jennifer Hosten	1970	Grenada	Aishwarya Rai	1994	India
Lucia Tavares Petterle	1971	Brazil	Jacqueline Marcano	1995	Venezuela
Belinda Roma Green	1972	Australia	Irene Skliva	1996	Greece
Marjorie Wallace	1973	USA	Diana Hayden	1997	India
Helen Morgan	1974	UK			

Contd...

Name	Year	Country
Linor Abargil	1998	Israel
Yukta Mookhey	1999	India
Priyanka Chopra	2000	India
Agbani Darego	2001	Nigeria
Azra Akin	2002	Turkey
Rosanna Davison	2003	Ireland

Name	Year	Country
Maria Julia Mantilla Garcia	2004	Peru
Unnur Birna Vilhjalmsdottir	2005	Iceland
Tatana Kucharova	2006	Czech Republic
Zhang Zilin	2007	China

Mrs World

Name	Year	Country
Aditi Govitrikar	2001	India
Nicole Brink	2002	USA
Suzanna Vicheinrut	2003-04	Thailand
Sima Bakhar	2005	Israel

Name	Year	Country
Sofia Arzhakvskaya	2006	Russia
Diana Tucker	2007	USA
Nataliie Shmarenko Kamaliya	2008	Ukraine

FIRST IN INDIA

The first woman to climb Mount Everest	Bachendri Pal
The first woman to climb Mount Everest twice	Santosh Yadav
The first President of the Indian Republic	Dr. Rajendra Prasad
The first Prime Minister of free India	Pt. Jawaharlal Nehru
The first woman Prime Minister of India	Mrs. Indira Gandhi
The first Indian Air Force Officer to get the Param Vir Chakra	Nirmal Jit Sekhon (posthumous)
The first Indian to win the Nobel Prize	Rabindranath Tagore
The first President of the Indian National Congress	W.C. Banerjee
The first Muslim President of India	Dr. Zakir Hussain
The first Indian lady to become Miss World	Reita Faria

Contd...

FIRST IN INDIA

The first woman Ambassador of India	C.B. Muthamma
The first woman President of the United Nations General Assembly	Mrs. Vijayalakshmi Pandit (1953-54)
The first woman President of the Indian National Congress	Mrs. Annie Besant
First woman Governor of a Province in free India	Mrs. Sarojini Naidu
The first woman Chief Minister of an Indian State	Mrs. Sucheta Kriplani (C.M. of U.P.)
The first Indian woman to become Speaker of a State Assembly in India	Shanno Devi (Haryana Assembly)
The first Governor-General of free India	Lord Mountbatten
The first and the last Indian to be the Governor-General of India	C. Rajagopalachari
The first British Governor-General	Warren Hastings
The first Indian Commander-in-Chief of India	General Cariappa
The first man to introduce a Printing Press in India	James Hickey
The first Indian member of the Viceroy's Executive Council	S.P. Sinha
The first Indian to join the I.C.S.	Satyendranath Tagore
The first Field Marshal of India	S.H.F.J. Manekshaw
The first Indian to get the Nobel Prize for Physics	C.V. Raman
The first President of India who died in office	Dr. Zakir Hussain
The first Prime Minister of India who was defeated in a General Election	Indira Gandhi
India's first man in space	Squadron Leader Rakesh Sharma
The first woman of Indian origin in space	Kalpana Chawla
The first PM who resigned before completing the full term because his party was reduced to a minority owing to large-scale defections	Morarji Desai

Contd...

FIRST IN INDIA

The first Prime Minister who was assassinated while in office	Indira Gandhi
The first Indian artificial satellite to go into space	Aryabhatta
The first woman Judge in the Supreme Court	Mrs. Meera Sahib Fatima Bibi
The first woman Chief Justice of a High Court	Mrs. Leela Seth
The first Indian Surgeon to be admitted to the Royal Australasian College of Surgeons	Dr. Inderjeet Singh Virdi
The first woman pilot in the Indian Air Force	Harita Kaur Dayal
The first Indian woman to bag a medal in Weightlifting at the Olympic Games	Karnam Malleshwari
The first Indian-American citizen to be elected to the American Senate in November 2000	Satvir Chaudhary
The first woman President of India	Mrs. Pratibha Patil

PLACES & NAMES AFFILIATED WITH PERSONALITIES AND EVENTS

Places	Personalities	Places	Personalities
Bardoli	Sardar Patel	Lumbini	Buddha
Chittor	Rana Pratap	Macedonia	Alexander the Great
Corsica	Napoleon Bonaparte	Mecca	Prophet Mohammed
Fatehpur Sikri	Akbar the Great	Pearl Harbour	Japan's attack on the U.S.A. during World War II (1941)
Haldighati	Rana Pratap		
Hiroshima	Dropping of first Atom Bomb	Pawnar Ashram	Acharya Vinoba Bhave
Jallianwala Bagh	Massacre of Indians by the British on April 13, 1919	Pondicherry	Aurobindo Ghosh
		Porbunder	Mahatma Gandhi
Jerusalem	Jesus Christ	Rajghat	Mahatma Gandhi
Kapilvastu	Buddha	Srirangapattam	Tipu Sultan

Contd...

Places	Personalities	Places	Personalities
Shantiniketan	Rabindranath Tagore	Grand Old Man of Britain	William Gladstone
Shaktisthal	Indira Gandhi	Grand Old Man of India	Dadabhai Naoroji
Shantivan	Jawaharlal Nehru	Gurudev	Rabindranath Tagore
Talwandi	Guru Nanak		
Trafalgar	Horatio Nelson	Guruji	M.S. Golwalkar
Vrindavan (U.P.)	Lord Krishna	Ike	Dwight Eisenhower
Vijai Ghat (Delhi)	Lal Bahadur Shastri	The Iron Duke	Duke of Wellington
Veer Bhumi	Rajiv Gandhi	J.P.	Jayaprakash Narayan
Waterloo	Napoleon, Duke of Wellington	Lady with the Lamp	Florence Nightingale
Bangabandhu	Sheikh Mujibur Rehman	Lal, Bal, Pal	Lala Lajpat Rai, Bal Gangadhar Tilak, Bipin Chandra Pal
Bapu	Mahatma Gandhi		
Bard of Avon	William Shakespeare	Lion of Punjab (Sher-e-Punjab)	Lala Lajpat Rai
Chacha	Jawaharlal Nehru	Little Corporal	Napoleon
C.R.	C. Rajagopalachari	Lokmanya	Bal Gangadhar Tilak
Deenbandhu	C.F. Andrews	Man of Destiny	Napoleon
Desert Fox	General Erwin Rommel	Mahamanya	Pt. Madan Mohan Malaviya
Il Duce	Benito Mussolini		
Deshbandhu	C.R. Das	Mahatma	M.K. Gandhi
The Enlightened One	Gautam Buddha	Maiden Queen	Elizabeth I
Father of English Poetry	Geoffrey Chaucer	Man of Blood and Iron	Otto von Bismarck
Father of the Nation	Mahatma Gandhi	Man of Iron	Sardar Patel
Fuehrer	Adolf Hitler	Strong Man of India	Sardar Patel
G.B.S.	George Bernard Shaw	Man of Peace	Lal Bahadur Shastri

Contd...

Places	Personalities	Places	Personalities
Maid of Orleans	Joan of Arc	Quaid-e-Azam	Mohammad Ali Jinnah
M.G.R.	M.G. Ramchandran	Uncle Ho	Dr. Ho Chi Minh
Netaji	Subhash Chandra Bose	Wizard of the North	Sir Walter Scott
		Wizard of Hockey	Dhyan Chand
Nightingale of India	Sarojini Naidu	Sunny	Sunil Gavaskar
Punjab Kesri	Lala Lajpat Rai	Master Blaster	Sachin Tendulkar

NAMES OF PARLIAMENT OF DIFFERENT COUNTRIES

Country	Parliament	Country	Parliament
Afghanistan	Shora	Malaysia	Majlis
Britain	Parliament	Mongolia	Khural
Denmark	Folketing	Nepal	Rashtriya Panchayat
Germany	Bundestag	Netherlands	States General
Norway	Storting	Poland	Scym
India	Parliament (Sansad)	Spain	Crotes
Iran	Majlis	Sweden	Riksdag
Ireland	Dail Eireann	Taiwan	Yuan
USA	Congress	Japan	Diet

NATIONAL EMBLEMS OF DIFFERENT COUNTRIES

Country	Emblem	Country	Emblem
Australia	Kangaroo	Ireland	Shamrock
Canada	White Lily	Japan	Chrysanthemum
Denmark	Beach	Pakistan	Crescent
France	Lily	Spain	Eagle
Germany	Corn Flower	U.K.	Rose
Iran	Rose	U.S.A.	Golden Red
Italy	White Lily		

HIGHEST MILITARY DECORATIONS OF VARIOUS COUNTRIES

India – Param Vir Chakra.

Italy – Medal for Valour.

Germany – Iron Cross.

Japan – Order of the Rising Sun.

Great Britain – Victoria Cross.

Russia – Order of the Patriotic War.

USA – Victory Medal.

France – Croix de Guerra.

Belgium – Military Cross.

ALTERNATIVE OR NEW NAMES OF COUNTRIES/CITIES

Country/City	New Name/Alternative Name	Country/City	New Name/Alternative Name
Abyssinia	Ethiopia	Christina	Oslo
Allahabad	Prayagraj	Congo (Belgian)	Zaire
Angora	Ankara	Constantinople	Istanbul
Aurangabad	Sambhaji Nagar	Dacca	Dhaka
Bachuanaland	Botswana	Dahomey	Benin
Baroda	Vadodra	Dutch East Indies	Indonesia
Basutoland	Lesotho	Dutch Guiana	Surinam
Batavia	Djakarta	Ellice Island	Tuvalu
Benaras	Varanasi	Formosa	Taiwan
Bhatinda	Bathinda	Gold Coast	Ghana
Bombay	Mumbai	Holland	The Netherlands
British Guiana	Guyana	Honduras	Belize
Burma	Myanmar	India	Bharat
Calcutta	Kolkata	Ivory Coast	Cote D'Ivoire
Calicut	Kozhikode	Japan	Nippon
Cape Canaveral	Cape Kennedy	Jubbulpore	Jabalpur
Ceylon	Sri Lanka	Jullunder	Jalandhar

Contd...

Country/ City	New Name/ Alternative Name	Country/ City	New Name/ Alternative Name
Leopoldville	Kinshasa	Rangoon	Yangon
Madagascar	Malagasy	Republic of Ireland	Eire
Madras	Chennai	Rhodesia	Zimbabwe
Malaya	Malaysia	Saigon	Ho Chi Minh City
Manchukuo	Manchuria	Salisbury	Harare
Mesopotamia	Iraq	Sandwich Islands	Hawaiian Islands
Nayasaland	Malawi	Siam	Thailand
New Guinea	West Irian	Simla	Shimla
New Hebrides	Vanuatu	South-west Africa	Namibia
North Borneo	Sabah	Spanish Guinea	Equatorial Guinea
Northern Rhodesia	Zambia	Stalingrad	Volgograd
Nyasaland	Malawi	Tanganyika and Zanzibar	Tanzania
Ooty	Udhagamandalam	Tanjore	Thanjavur
Palghat	Palakkad	Trichur	Thrissur
Panjim	Panaji	Trivandrum	Thiruvananthapuram
Peking	Beijing	United Arab Republic	Arab Republic of Egypt
Persia	Iran	United Provinces	Uttar Pradesh
Petrograd	Leningrad	Upper Volta	Burkina Faso
Poona	Pune	Vizagapatam	Vishakhapatnam
Pretoria	Tshwane	Zaire	Republic of Congo
Quilon	Kollam		

FIRST IN DIFFERENT FIELDS

First in Space

The first cosmonaut to spend about 17½ days in a space endurance flight.

Adrin Nikolayev and Vitaly Sevastyanosov in Soyuz-9 (June 1, 1970)

The first person to land on the moon.

Neil A. Armstrong and Edwin E. Aldrin Jr. of USA. Armstrong was the first to set foot on the moon followed by Aldrin, July 21, 1969.

The first man to enter space.

Major Yuri Gagarin (USSR)

The first woman cosmonaut of the world.

Valentina Tereshkova

The first American astronaut to float in space.

Edward White

The first unmanned spaceship to have soft landed and lifted off from the moon and returned to the earth.

Luna-16 (USSR) September 21, 1970

The first manned space vehicle to land on the moon.

Lunar Exploration Module nicknamed 'Eagle'

The first spaceship which carried three American astronauts to land two of them on the moon.

Apollo-11

The first country to send man to the moon.

USA

The first space vehicle to orbit the moon.

Luna-10 (USSR)

The first unmanned moon buggy to explore the surface of the moon.

Lunakhod-1 (USSR)

The first space rocket brought back to earth after orbiting the moon.

Zond-5

The first crew transfer between orbiting spaceships.

Soyuz T-15 with Mir Space Station

The first mission of a link-up in space by manned spaceships of USA and the Soviet Union.

Apollo-Soyuz Test Project Mission (launched on July 15 and linked up in space on July 17, 1975)

India's first scientific satellite.

Aryabhatta

Contd...

The first man to fly into space belonging to a country other than USSR or the USA.	Vladimir Remek (Czechoslovakia)
USSR's first spaceship with an international crew on board.	Soyuz-28
The first country to send a nuclear-powered spacecraft to explore Jupiter.	USA
The first Indian to go into space.	Sq. Ldr. Rakesh Sharma
The first country to launch an earth satellite or artificial baby moon.	USSR
The first Russian cosmonaut to make two space flights.	Late Col. Vladimir Komarov
The first American astronaut to make two space flights.	Gordon Cooper
The first country to launch a cosmic space rocket towards the moon.	USSR
The first space rocket to hit the moon.	Lunik II
The first spaceship in the world to sample the moon's crust.	Surveyor-3 (USA)
The first space vehicle to soft land on the Moon.	Luna 9 (USSR)
The first manned spaceship to perform the longest stay in space (11 days).	Apollo-7 (USA)
The first manned spaceship to perform a space flight round the moon.	Apollo-8 (USA)
The first American manned spaceship to perform a crew transfer in space.	Apollo-9 (USA)
The first woman of Indian origin in space.	Kalpana Chawla
The first residents on the International Space Station.	Bill Shepherd (USA), Yuri Gidzenko and Sergei Krikalev (Russia)
The first tourist in space.	Dennis Tito (USA), on April 28, 2001
The 1st Female Space tourist	Anousheh Ansari (Iranian-American)

First in Sports

The first Indian woman to swim across the English Channel.	Aarati Saha-Gupta
The first Indian man to swim across the English Channel.	Mihir Sen
The first person to ski down Mount Everest.	Yuichiro Miura of Japan
The first Indian to win the World Billiards Trophy.	Wilson Jones
The first black player to win the Wimbledon men's singles title.	Arthur Ashe (U.S., 1975)
The first Indian woman to climb Mount Everest.	Bachhendri Pal
The first Indian Chess Grandmaster.	Viswanathan Anand
The first man to win 4 Olympic Gold Medals.	Alvin Kranzein (USA) in 1900
The first tennis player who won the Wimbledon championship for five years consecutively.	Bjorn Borg
The first batsman to score three Test centuries in three successive Tests on debut.	Mohammed Azharuddin
World's first cricketer to score more than 10,000 runs in his Test career.	Sunil Gavaskar. He is also the record holder for most centuries (34) in Test cricket; now surpassed by Allan Border of Australia with more than 11,000 runs.
The first batsman in the world to score centuries against all the other 8 Test playing nations.	Steve Waugh (Australia)
The first country whose cricket team won 12 Test matches in a row.	Australia
The first Asian to win Volvo Masters at Sotogrande, Spain on 28th October 2006.	Jeev Milkha Singh

Contd...

The first Indian woman to win women singles final of Philippines Open 2006 in Manila (Philippines)	Saina Nehwal
40th ODI century during tri-series cricket tournament in Kuala Lumpur (Malaysia) on Sept. 14, 2006	Sachin Tendulkar
Ranked at No. 2 position in FIDE on Sept. 30, 2006	Vishwanathan Anand
The world record for most 'caught and bowled' (25).	Anil Kumble
The country's highest wicket take with 501 wickets on 12th March 2006	Anil Kumble

First Expeditioners

The first person to reach the North Pole by overland journey.	Robert Peary
The first person to reach the South Pole.	Roald Amundsen
The first person to climb Mount Everest.	Sherpa Tenzing (19th May, 1953)
The first person to sail round the world.	Ferdinand Magellan
The first woman to conquer Mount Everest.	Mrs. Junko Tabei (Japan)
The first man to have climbed Mount Everest twice.	Nawang Gombu
The first vessel ever to reach the North Pole by sailing through the thick Arctic ice.	Soviet Arktika (atomic-powered ice-breaker)
The leader of the expedition 'Ocean to Sky'.	Sir Edmund Hillary
The first two mountaineers who reached the summit of Everest without using oxygen.	Peter Habeler (Austria) and Reinhold Messner (Italy)
The first person to reach the North Pole by a 7-dog sledge.	Naomi Uemura (Japan)
The leader of the first Indian Antarctic Expedition.	Z.A. Kasim
The first Pakistani to scale Mount Everest.	Nazir Sabir

First/Last Heads of State

The first woman Prime Minister of a country.	Mrs. Sirimavo Bandaranaike (Sri Lanka)
The first President of the USA.	George Washington
The first President of the Chinese Republic.	Sun Yat Sen
The first Governor-General of Pakistan.	Mohammed Ali Jinnah
The last King of France.	Napolean III

First Visitors and Invaders

The first European to visit China.	Marco Polo
The first Chinese pilgrim to visit India.	Fa Hian
The first European invader on Indian soil.	Alexander the Great

Politics

The first U.S. President to resign.	Richard Nixon
The first woman ambassador of Britain.	Anne Warburton
The first woman Prime Minister of a European country.	Margaret Thatcher
The first woman Prime Minister of France.	Mrs. Edith Cressan
The first Prime Minister of Pakistan who was deposed and exiled.	Nawaz Sharif

THE LARGEST, LONGEST, BIGGEST, HIGHEST, SMALLEST IN THE WORLD

Aerodrome, highest—La Paz (Bolivia) (4,080 metres)

Archipelago, largest—Indonesia

Largest Railway Bridge—Long Bridge, Louisiana, USA (7 km)

Bird, largest—Ostrich

Bird, smallest—Humming-bird

Building, tallest—Sears Tower in Chicago (443 metres high with 110 storeys)

Canal, longest irrigational—Thekalakumsky Canal (1,200 km)

Canal, longest (joining two oceans)—Suez Canal (168 km)

City, biggest in area—Mount Isa (40,978 sq. kms) (Queensland-Australia)

City, highest—Van Chuan (China), (5,100 metres high)

City, most expensive—Tokyo

Capital, highest—La Paz (Bolivia) (3,632 metres high)

Continent, biggest—Asia (44,000,000 sq. kms.)

Contd...

Continent, smallest—Australia (7,704,441 sq. kms.)

Country, biggest—Russia (17,075,000 sq. kms.)

Delta, largest—Sunderbans (West Bengal)

Desert, biggest—The Great Sahara

Dam, world's highest gravity—Rogunskaya (Tajikistan)

Dam, largest—Grand Coulee Dam (USA)

Diamond, largest—The Cullinan (over 1½ lb.)

Electorate, largest—India (about 60 crores)

Epic, biggest—Mahabharat

Genius, world's greatest—Leonardo da Vinci, painter, sculptor, architect, engineer, scientist etc.

Irrigation scheme, world's biggest—Lloyd Barrage, Sukkhur (Pakistan)

Island, biggest in the world—Greenland

Island Sea, largest—Mediterranean Sea

Mountain Peak, world's highest—Mount Everest (Nepal, 8,848 metres)

Lake, deepest—Baikal (Russia, 1,940 metres)

Museum, world's biggest—British Museum (London)

Ocean, biggest—Pacific Ocean

Park, biggest—Yellowstone National Park (USA)

Peninsula, largest—Arabia (32,50,000 sq. kms)

Palace, biggest—Vatican (Italy)

Planet, largest—Jupiter

Planet, smallest—Pluto

Plateau, highest—Pamir

Population, largest—China (1,285 million)

Radio Telescope, largest—New Mexico (USA)

Railway Platform, longest—Kharagpur, India (833 metres)

River, world's longest—Nile (6,648 Kms)

Region, highest—Tibet (4,875 metres)

Region, world's coldest—Verkhoyansk (Siberia)

Stamp, world's first—Penny Black (Britain)

The richest country in the world (in terms of Gross National Product per inhabitant)—Switzerland (per capita income US$ 28,760)

Tramway, world's first—New York, 1832

Tunnel, longest—Laerdal Tunnel (Norway, 24.5 km)

Thoroughfare, world's largest—Broadway (New York)

Volcano, highest—Cotopaxi (Andes, Ecuador)

Volcano, largest—Mauna Loa (Hawaii)

Wall, world's largest—The Great Wall of China

Contd...

Waterfall, world's highest—Angel Falls (Venezuela, 979 metres)

Water body, lowest—Dead Sea (around 1,300 feet below sea-level)

Zoo, largest in the world—Kruger National Park, South Africa

An observatory situated at the highest place in the world—Indian Astronomical Observatory, situated at Hanle, Ladakh

LARGEST, SMALLEST, HIGHEST AND LONGEST IN INDIA

Biggest Hotel—The Oberoi on the shore of the Arabian Sea in South Mumbai

Highest Mountain Peak—K2 (8,611 metres)

Largest Populated City—Mumbai (1.26 crores)

Longest River (in India)—Ganga (2,510 km)

Highest Waterfall—Gersoppa Waterfall (Jog Falls) Karnataka, (830 ft.)

Largest Lake—Wular Lake, Kashmir

Largest State (area)—Rajasthan (342,239 sq. kms.)

Largest State (population)—Uttar Pradesh (166,052,859)

Highest Population Density—West Bengal (904 persons per sq. kms)

Longest River Bridge—Mahatma Gandhi Setu, Patna (5.75 kms. long)

Highest Gateway—Buland Darwaja, 54 metres (Fatehpur Sikri, Agra)

Wettest place/heaviest rainfall—Mausinram (Meghalaya)

Tallest Statue—Statue of Gomateshwar, Karnataka (47 metres high)

Largest Tunnel—Jawahar Tunnel (J&K, 1½ km, Banihal Pass)

Largest Museum—Indian Museum, Kolkata

Largest Zoo—Zoological Gardens, Alipur, Kolkata

Largest Forest State—Assam

Largest Road—Grand Trunk Road (2,400 kms)

Largest Delta—Sunderbans Delta (12,872 sq. kms)

Largest Cave Temple—Ellora (Kailash Temples, Maharashtra)

Largest Cantilever Span Bridge—Howrah Bridge (Kolkata)

Highest Tower—Qutub Minar, Delhi

Largest Dome—Gol Gumbaz, Bijapur (Karnataka)

Largest Mosque—Jama Masjid, Delhi

Highest Straight Gravity Dam—Bhakra Dam

Smallest State (area)—Goa (3,702 sq. kms.)

Smallest State (population)—Sikkim (540,493)

Contd...

Largest Desert—Thar (Rajasthan)

Largest Man-made Lake—Govind Sagar (Bhakra)

Largest Corridor—Rameswaram Temple Corridor (121 metres long)

Largest Animal Fair—Sonepur Fair, Bihar

Airport—Largest: King Khalid International Airport outside Riyadh (Saudi Arabia) Highest: Bangda Airport, Tibet (now China)

Animal—Tallest on land – Giraffe, Largest land Animal – African Bush Elephant, Fastest land Animal – Cheetah (Leopard)

Bank—Largest – Deutsche Bank AG, Frankfurt (Germany)

Bay—Largest – Hudson Bay (Northern Canada)

Building—Tallest – Taipei 101, Tallest Office Building – Petronas Twin Towers, Kuala Lumpur (Malaysia)

Canals—Longest in Ancient World – Grand Canal of China (From Beijing to Haugzhou), Busiest Ship Canal – Kiel Canal linking North Sea with the Baltic Sea in Germany, Longest Irrigation Canal: Karakumsky Canal from Haun-Khan to Ashkhabad, Trukmenistan

Castle—Largest (Inhabited) – Windsor Castle (Windsor, Berks)

Church—Largest – Ohlsdorf Basilisca of St. Peter in Vatican City, Rome (Italy)

Dams—Most Massive – Itaipu Dam on Parana River on the boundary between Brazil & Paraguay

Forest—Largest – Coniferous forest of Northern Hemisphere(CIS)

Gorge—Largest – Grand Canyon (On the Colorado, river in north-central Arizona (USA),

Hydroelectric Plant—Biggest – Itaipu (Brazil)

Lagoon—Largest – Lagoa Des Patos (Brazil)

Lakes—Largest – Caspian Sea (in Azerbaijan, Russia, Kazakhstan, Turkmenistan and Iran)

Largest Freshwater—Lake Superior (N. America)

Ocean—Deepest – Pacific Ocean (deepest part – Mariana Trench)

Tunnel—Longest (Railway) – Seikan Rail Tunnel below the sea bed of the Tsugaru Strait between Tappi Saki, Honshu & Fukushima, Hokkaido, Japan (53.85 km)

Longest & Largest Canal Tunnel—Le Rove Tunnel on the Canal de Masseille au Rhone in the south of France (7, 120 m long, 22 m wide & 11.4m high)

OFFICIAL BOOKS

Green Book - Italy, Persia	Grey Book - Japan, Belgium
White Book - Germany, Portugal, China	Yellow Book - France
Blue Book - Britain	Orange Book - Netherlands

ANSWERS

1. Penguin. The greatest enemy of its eggs is the skua, a bird of the Arctic region.

2. Animates can breathe and multiply; in-animates cannot.

3. Dolphin.

4. Sea Horse.

5. 3×39,841 km. In this distance, one can go round the earth thrice.

6. They migrate in search of food because in cold regions no food is available for these birds in winters.

7. Lichen. This small plant is an example of the symbiosis of algae and fungi.

8. "Stomata" is the plural of "stoma". These words are used for the tiny pores, often numerous, present on leaves which are necessary for them to breathe.

9. Her lifespan is 3 to 4 years and she lays approximately 2,000 eggs in a day.

10. From sea vegetation; this is approximately 70% of the total oxygen.

11. It is used for the study and research of deeper levels of the sea.

12. Black Holes are hypothetical heavenly objects whose gravity is supposed to be so great that not even light can escape from it. Anything that falls into a Black Hole would not be seen again. Black Holes are thought to form when massive stars shrink at the ends of their lives. Matter is then squeezed to infinite density within the Hole.

13. The BARC (Bhabha Atomic Research Centre).

14. Challenger. This research ship carried out physical, chemical, biological and geological surveys of the depths of the oceans from December, 1872 to May, 1876. It completed a journey of 1,27,500 kms; fathomed the ocean at 492 places; measured the oceanic temperatures at 263 places; also found its salt contents and discovered 4,717 species of marine life.

15. On January 1, 1996, the National Nautical Science Institute was established, headquartered in Goa.

16. Oxyn is a substance present in plants which helps them grow; but in sunlight, Oxyn loses its potency. Hence, that side of the tree or plant which is in light grows slower than the other side. Consequently, the stem bends towards light.

17. A horse is measured by an accounting unit called 'hands'. The height of a horse is measured up to its withers.

18. Zebra.

19. Venus is known as the 'Morning Star'.

20. Anaconda is the biggest, longest and most massive water-snake, which is non-poisonous.

21. By the end of the first year, it increases to 32, by the second year 512 and by the end of the third year, this number reaches 8,000.

22. The longest and strongest bone in the human body is the femur. It is 27.5 per cent of a person's total height. Out of the three bones in the human ear, the middle one "stapes" is the smallest. It is 2.6 to 3.4 millimetres long and weighs only 2.0 to 4.3 grams.

23. This is a technique by which an X-ray of the brain or spine is obtained by filling in gas in those parts (of the brain or spine of which the X-ray is to be taken) that have liquid in them. The X-ray so obtained shows the cavities of the spot.

24. AIDS stands for Acquired Immuno Deficiency Syndrome. It is a viral disease – acquired through HIV or Human Immunodeficiency Virus – in which all immunity of the body is sapped. A person suffering from it falls a victim to various diseases easily. Sexual intercourse with a person suffering from this ailment or blood transfusion from an HIV-infected person causes this disease. No effective remedy has been found for it so far.

25. It is used to prevent tuberculosis (T.B.).

26. The four blood groups are – A, B, AB, O. Persons in the AB group can give blood to any of the four.

27. Approximately 8% of the total weight of the body (or its twelfth part).

28. A Geostationary satellite rotates round the earth with the same speed at which the earth rotates round its own axis. It rotates round the earth 35,000 kms above the earth. That is why it appears static at a certain point.

29. Rohini-75. It was launched from Thumba on 20th November, 1967 for observation of the earth. Indigenously made by a team of Indian space scientists, its diameter was only 75 centimetres.

30. Sriharikota is a small island covering an area of 13,000 hectares. It is 100 kms from Chennai city and is situated in Andhra Pradesh. It is India's launching station from where Rohini and S.L.V. were launched.

31. OTEC (Ocean Thermal Energy Conversion) is a technique by which electricity is generated from the different temperatures existing in the sea or ocean water. France, USA and other countries have been experimenting with this since 1920 but have not yet achieved a major breakthrough. In India too, we are trying to generate ocean electricity at the OTEC power-station near Lakshadweep Island.

32. The first hydro-electric project on a tiny river near Darjeeling was established in 1897. But on a bigger scale, it was the Shivsamudram Project of 1902 which was in the then Mysore state. Its capacity was 4,500 kilowatts.

33. 'PURNIMA' denotes 'Plutonium Reactor for Neutronic Investigations in Multiplying Assemblies'. This reactor was made at the Bhabha Atomic Research Centre for the study of neutrons.

34. In Italy. In 1904 an Italian, Count Pierre, effectively and successfully generated electricity from hot-water springs to produce a current enough to light 5 bulbs.

35. Horsepower is a unit used for measuring power. It is an accounting unit which is equivalent to 550 foot-pounds per second. It is equivalent to 746 watts. This name was given by James Watt in the 18th century when the horse was a symbol of strength. James Watt calculated that a strong horse could work 32,400 foot-pounds in one minute. Later he and one of his associates, Bolton, calculated it to be 33,000 foot-pounds by rounding the figure. An average horsepower is 20 times more than a man's average working capacity.

36. Mach number is the ratio between the speed of a thing and the speed of sound in identical circumstances. (In the context of air, one Mach is equal to 1,224 kilometres per minute.)

37. A technique by which cloth or paper is pressed between rollers to make the surface smooth. Usually this is used in paper and cloth industries.

38. An electronic device consisting of a small piece of semiconducting solid (usually germanium or silicon) to which contact is made at appropriate places by three wires. The three parts resemble in function (not construction) the cathode, anode, and grid of a thermionic valve. Transistors are compact and economical. The device was invented by Bardeen, Brattain and Shockley, in 1948.

39. Methyl Isocynate. But phosgene was the cause of maximum deaths.

40. The technique of generating electricity by light-energy. It has semiconductors like silicon, germanium and others. These elements absorb the light-energy and consequently electric potential is generated.

41. The mixture of yttrium, berium, gelium and oxygen.

42. The air is saturated with steam before rains. Consequently, sweat cannot evaporate.

43. When wet, the pores between the threads of cloth are filled with water drops. Light reflects from these drops and the colour acquires a deeper hue because the colour affects our eyes.

44. John Fitch in 1787.

45. INSAT-1B is a satellite launched by the Indian Space Programme. This satellite was launched into space by the American space shuttle 'Challenger' in 1983. It started working on 15th October, 1983. It beams television pictures, sends weather charts and is useful for telecommunication as well.

46. Chalk is calcium carbonate and lime is calcium hydroxide.

47. Communications satellites are those man-made satellites with the help of which far-off places are connected with telephone, television and radio. These are rotating round the earth at a height of 36,000 kms. The rotation speed of these artificial satellites match the speed of the earth's rotation round its axis. This is the reason why they appear static. Arthur C. Clarke was the first to imagine a device like this. Clarke is a science fiction writer.

48. LUNA-II, a Russian rocket, landed on the moon on 12th September, 1959.

49. Jules Verne, the 19th century science fiction writer, who gave an imaginary account of flying up to the moon and returning to the earth (in 1865). It was in 1969 that man succeeded in landing on the moon in reality.

50. Robert Godard was an American space-scientist. He developed the first moon rocket in 1929. However, it was not a successful attempt. By 1941, he had already designed rockets like V-2.

51. Escape Velocity is that speed which the earth or other planets require for breaking away from the gravitational pull of a planet. In order to break away from the earth, the minimum necessary speed is 40,000 kilometres per hour.

52. The flow of electrons. These are discharged by the electrode cathode through an electronic valve. Cathode rays travel very fast but are affected by magnets.

53. When cooled at very low temperatures, i.e. –260°C, metals lose their electrical resistance. This loss of electrical resistance is known as super-conductivity.

54. Yes. Pumice-stone.

55. Bhasker, who had named his work 'Leelavati', after his daughter, Leelavati.

56. Adeshir Karsetji. He was nominated to the Royal Society of London as a Fellow in 1847.

57. Dr. Meghnad Saha was a world-famous physicist. He was the founder of The Institute of Nuclear Physics and represented India at the Soviet Academy of Sciences. He was nominated as F.R.S. in 1927. In 1949,

Ans. 48

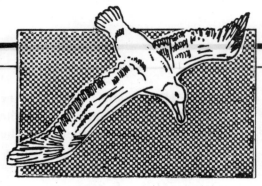

he established an institute which is now named after him as The Saha Institute of Nuclear Physics.

58. Dr. Homi Jahangir Bhabha was a gifted physicist. He discovered the Meson. He was the first to start generation of atomic energy in India. He is accredited with having established The Atomic Energy Commission in August 1948 and the Atomic Energy Institute in Bombay (now Mumbai) in 1957. This institute is now named Bhabha Atomic Research Centre (BARC).

59. By producing Ultrasonic Waves. These are high frequency sound waves which are not otherwise audible.

60. Albatross. Its wings spread 3.6 metres or 12 feet.

61. Salt-water fish drink water whereas fresh-water fish never do. The salt-water fish have to drink continuously because their body contents contain fewer salts than the water around them. The water they drink comes out of their mouth and skin. In order to compensate this loss, they have to drink water, otherwise they will not survive.

On the other hand, fresh-water fish have more salt content in their body than the contents in the water surrounding them. If they drink water, it may be retained in their body, which may be fatal. That is why they do not drink water. Whatever water enters their body through their skin is eliminated through urine.

62. John Napier of Scotland. He was a priest but mathematics was his hobby.

63. The Fibonacci Sequence was first invented by the 12th century mathematician Leonardo Fibonacci of Italy. This is a number system in which a number is exactly the sum of the last two numbers. Some mathematicians start this system from zero and others from one. Some of its initial numbers are – 0, 3, 5, 8, 13; 21, 34, 55....

64. Mahaviracharya was a 9th century mathematician. He was a Jain. His famous book is *Ganit Saar Sangraha.*

65. *Elements.*

66. The Barnali Dynasty from Antwerp in Belgium is famous for having produced eight great mathematicians in the 17th and 18th centuries. They were Jacob, Johan I, Danium, Nicolas I, Nicolas II, Johan II, Johan III, and Jacob II.

67. Jupiter. It is 1,300 times bigger than the Earth and is 483 million miles away from the sun.

68. The observatories built by Raja Sawai Jai Singh (second) of Jaipur (1686-1743). One of the observatories is in Delhi and the other is in Jaipur.

At Jantar-Mantar, the planets and stars are studied with the help of huge structures made of bricks, lime and stone.

69. Zepolarni in Russia on January 1, 1985. Its depth is 12,500 metres.

70. Novya Jemya in USSR where a 62-90 megaton atomic explosion was carried out on 30th October, 1961.

71. On Antarctica, where the speed is more than 300 kms per hour.

72. A man-made satellite which revolves round the earth and sends weather reports. Some of the satellites, apart from sending weather reports, are very useful for telecommunications also. The first satellite was the US-made Vanguard-II, but it was not too successful. The first successful satellite was Tiros-I, made in 1960.

73. When mercury is mixed with any other metal.

74. Carbon, Hydrogen and Oxygen.

75. Vinegar.

76. Saturated salt water.

77. In liquid Ammonia.

78. Yolk of egg has sulphur. When in contact with silver, this produces silver sulphite, which changes the colour of the silver spoon.

79. Mercury.

80. It is the gravitational field which is spreading. This force is produced due to matter distribution forces. These waves can be speculated with the help of the General Theory of Relativity. These waves travel with the speed of light-waves (3,00,000 kms per second) and exert pressure on the materials present in their path. These are also called gravitational radiation.

81. In cold places like Ladakh, the atmosphere is not dense, consequently, sun-rays reach the earth without any obstruction and the sun is bright and the sunlight is hot and sharp. But since the atmosphere is not dense, the heat of the sun is not absorbed and the air under shade remains cool.

82. When boiling water is poured into a glass, its outer surface does not undergo any change, whereas its inner part expands due to the heat. Because of this sudden expansion, the glass breaks.

83. When we are chewing a hard piece of bread, the crunching noise travels outward and reaches people around us through the air which carries sound. But since we are chewing it, the sound travels through our teeth to the brain via nerves. This noise takes place only in our ears and changes into a harsh sound. That is the reason why it does not disturb people around us.

84. Yes. If a singer produces a sound which in its vibrations is commensurate with the size of a glass item nearby, the dimensions of the vibrations of the sound in the thing increase manifold and a glass item may break into fragments.

85. Chromosomes are the structures contained within the nucleus of every animal and plant cell by which genetic information is transmitted. The chromosome number in body cells is constant in each species of plant and animal. For example, in man it is 46.

86. It is a genetic disease caused by chromosome aberration. It is produced by the presence of extra chromosomes (number 21), and is known as Down's Syndrome or '21 Trisome Syndrome'.

87. Haemophilia is a genetic disease associated with X-chromosomes. Its effect gets exhibited only in males even if the disease is transmitted from one generation to the next by females.

The blood of the patient affected by this disease is deficient in 'factor VIII'. It does not produce thromboplastin and hence the blood does not coagulate.

In case a patient affected by this disease gets a cut on any part of the body resulting in bleeding, it continues for hours and in some cases for days. The cut can become fatal.

The only treatment for this disease is the transfusion of blood containing factor VIII.

88. Enrico Fermi in 1942.

89. Dr. John H. Gibbon invented the heart-lung machine in 1953.

90. 1,862°F.

91. Sir Robert A. Watson-Watt.

92. Thomas Alva Edison invented it in 1913.

93. An American engineer, A.H. Gose, in 1913.

94. Willis H. Carrier in 1911.

95. Karl Benz of Germany in 1885.

96. In 1882, Schuyler S. Wheeler invented it.

97. An optical instrument for viewing objects at a distance with both eyes is called a binocular. It consists of an object glass and an eye lens, with two intermediates to bring the object into an erect position. A lens brings it near to us, and the magnifier enlarges it for our inspection.

98. Because the air is of more uniform density, and there are fewer currents of air of equal temperature to interrupt the sound waves. Besides this, dense air can propagate sound-waves more readily than rarer air.

99. Igor Sikorsky in 1939.

100. A galaxy or Milky Way is a cluster of numerous stars that are held by each others' gravitational force. There are millions of galaxies in the cosmos. They are so large that their expanse can be measured only in light-years. They are in three shapes – spiral, elliptical and irregular.

101. National Physical Laboratory, New Delhi; The Indian Institute of Science, Bangalore; and The Tata Institute of Fundamental Research, Mumbai.

102. Those matters which behave like non-conductors when the heat is low and like conductors when the heat is high. These are sensitive to rays of light and can be controlled either by adding electrons to their atoms or by removing them. Semiconductors conduct badly because they have very few free electrons, many thousand times fewer than metal. Germanium, silicon, selenium and lead sulphite are some common substances called semiconductors.

Semiconductors are used in transistors.

103. In broad-gauge, it is 1.67 metres (5.6 feet) and in narrow-gauge, it is 75 centimetres (2.6 feet).

104. Demerara is a town in Guyana known for its sugarcane. A kind of 'Brown Sugar' produced there is known after the name of the town.

105. The two wheels in a watch have two jewels each whereas its rolling-pin has only one jewel. That is why the number of jewels in a watch is always odd.

106. Both are alloys. In Sterling Silver, the content of silver is 92.5% and copper is only 7.5%. In German Silver, the proportion of copper, nickel and zinc is in the ratio of 5:2:2.

107. In Great Britain. Known for its huge telescope with the help of which numerous astronomical research projects have been completed.

108. Proxima Centauri, which is 4.22 light-years away. It is faintly visible. Alpha Centauri is the only star which can be seen with naked eyes. It is 4.35 light-years away.

109. No. Because the inclination of the earth's axis changes every 26,000 years, different stars come to be known as pole stars. 3,000 years before the birth of Christ, Alpha Draconis was the Pole Star. Now it is Polarus-B. In 7,500 A.D., Alpha Saphari will be the Pole Star. In 14,000 A.D., this status will go to Velga.

Ans. 100

110. Pulsars are stars which show fluctuations in their luminosity. They are also called 'Pulsating Stars' or 'Cepheid'. They shine very brightly sometimes and at other times lose their brightness. They also contract and expand in the same fashion.

111. On a clear night without clouds, dust or fog we can see as many as 7,000 stars. These belong to our galaxy alone.

112. Alpha Canis Majoris. It is 8.7 light-years away.

113. 499 seconds i.e. 8 minutes 19 seconds.

114. The Platypus lays eggs but like mammals, it feeds its young ones with its milk.

115. Sooty Tern, a bird which can fly continuously for 3 to 4 years.

116. Blue Whale. So far the largest one trapped has been 33.58 metres long, caught near South Georgia in 1904.

117. Blue Whale. A 12-month-old young one can weigh up to 26 tons.

118. Col. Yuri Gagarin of the then USSR, who took off in a 4.65-ton space vehicle Vostok (East) on April 12, 1961 to complete a single orbit of the Earth in 1 hour 48 minutes.

119. The Nobel Prize was first given on December 10, 1901 on the first death anniversary of Sir Alfred Nobel.

120. Rene Descartes, the French mathematician of the 17th century.

121. North Pole is not situated on land but in the Arctic Ocean. The Arctic Ocean is frozen all the year round and this ice is always moving clockwise. That is why it is necessary to use a compass to find the north.

122. Samuel Colt, in 1835.

123. Christopher Sydney Cockrel. He patented it on 12th December, 1955.

124. It was first conceived in 1790 by Thomas Saint, but in its modern form, it was made by Elias in 1867.

125. Water tension causes bubbles to burst as soon as they are formed. But soap makes water tenacious and prevents the bubbles from bursting as soon as they are formed. A large area of water has greater surface tension.

126. During his space flight, Colonel Glen had spotted countless small luminous particles in the sky on a dark night. It was called the Glen Effect after him. This luminosity is of yellowish green hue.

127. Valentina Vladimirova Tereshkova of the then USSR, who started her space voyage on 16th June, 1963 in Vostok-VI and landed back on earth on 19th June, 1963.

128. Edwin Aldrin.

129. These tower-like structures, which can be as tall as 20 feet, are made by termites in Africa near the equator. It takes approximately eight years for a full termite camp to build it.

130. Messier-31 of the Andromeda Nebula. It is 2,120,000 light-years away from the earth.

131. A combination of positron, anti-proton and antineutrons. According to scientists, billions of years ago when the universe was being formed, matter and anti-matter collided causing the extinction of anti-matter.

132. Nuclear Magnetic Resonance.

133. It is a unit to measure the intensity of sound.

134. He was awarded the Nobel Prize for Physics in 1922. His full name was Niels Henrik David Bohr. A Danish Nuclear Physicist whose research into the structure of the atom gave him great authority in the world of theoretical physics, with Rutherford, he applied the Quantum Theory to the study of the atomic process.

135. Max Karl Ernest Ludwig Planck of Germany.

136. Because of a mirage. In the polar regions, many a time on the light and hot layers of air, a thin layer of cold but heavy air is spread. The presence of these phenomena works like a lens.

There is total internal reflection which produces images. The rising sun seen before the actual sunrise is nothing but its virtual image or reflection.

137. Red.

138. Small drops of water always tend to be round because of a phenomena called surface tension, which occurs because the molecules in water attract each other. Surface tension is only strong enough to pull small droplets into balls.

139. Nobel Laureate.

140. Richard Trevithick, a Cornish mine manager's son, invented the road-locomotive, putting upon the highway on Christmas Eve, 1801, the first steam-propelled vehicle for passengers. It was, however, George Stephenson who made the first steam engine in 1825.

141. In 1940 the Nobel Prize was not awarded because of the outbreak of World War II and the invasion of Sweden. It was restored in 1943.

142. This is nature's way of controlling their population. Lemmings breed rapidly and their population becomes overwhelming within a short time. When unable to sustain themselves in

Ans. 140

their area, they spread towards fields and gardens and flood markets and homes in order to find food. They attack eatables, fruits, vegetables, plants and leaves, whatever they find. But the self-regulating process of nature works in such a way that when in overwhelming numbers, they start moving towards the sea in large groups. Many feeble ones die en route while the others just jump into the sea and drown.

143. European eel. This fish, which looks like a snake, is born in the sea, but moves towards the rivers and reaches lakes and pools through underground water-springs. It prefers the quiet waters.

144. To spawn. The salmon swims against the current to reach the source of a river from the sea, lays eggs and dies there.

145. August Piccard and Captain Walsh. Piccard, a Swiss physicist, is noted for his balloon ascent in the stratosphere. Jacques Piccard, his son, made a descent in 1960 of over 7 miles in the Marianna Trench in the Western Pacific in a Bathyscaphe designed and built by him.

146. A unit of measure for distance on the sea/ocean. One nautical mile is 1,853 metres or 1.85 kilometres. If measured in feet, it comes to 6,080, while ordinarily a mile comes to 5,280 feet.

147. It was a nuclear submarine which reached the North Pole through the frozen ocean by travelling below the snow and ice.

148. Roald Amundsen.

149. A unit to measure the depth of water. One fathom is equal to 6 feet.

150. Cyclotron is used to split atoms.

151. Laser rays. They are more powerful than a thousand suns.

152. 0°Kelvin to 0.00003° (i.e. –273.15° Celsius). It was recorded by Prof. Ono and his companions in Tokyo in 1983.

153. A molecule which is made of anti-protons, antineutrons and positrons.

154. Saturn's satellite called Titan, but it has methane gas only.

155. Supernovae are stars which explode and when they explode their brightness increases suddenly by 10 to 20 magnitudes or more and then fades into normal brightness.

156. Quasi Stellar Radio Sources are those stars which emit radio waves. First identified in 1960-62, they have small size and enormous energy output.

These are at vast distances. Many are strong sources of radio waves and fluctuate in intensity. Their nature and cosmology presented a major astronomical problem in the 1960s.

157. Venus. As compared to the earth, it weighs 0.81 times and its size is 0.88 times. It completes its revolution around the sun in 225 days.

158. Soyuz T-II which joined Salyut-7 in space.

159. This is a wonderful phenomenon of nature. Seen at high latitudes (in North and South poles). As seen in the Northern hemisphere, it is called Aurora Borealis and in the Southern hemisphere, it is known as Aurora Australis. Auroral display may take several forms e.g. a faint glow, a diffused ribbon of light, great folded waving curtain-like draperies, the whole sky may be a grand panoply of light. The aurora is a kind of light essentially different from that of the rainbow, which is a partly subjective phenomenon. Each observer sees his own rainbow, while light is sunlight refracted and reflected by many raindrops. The raindrops that produce his rainbow depend on his position as well as on the direction of the sun. The aurora, on the contrary, is a light as objective as that of a candle. It is a self-luminescence of the air in particular regions of the atmosphere that lie far above the clouds.

160. Sodium silicate.

161. A fat person, because he displaces more water than a slim person and can learn it speedily.

162. No river comes out of it because it is not the source of any river but the name of the research centre set up at the Antarctic by the Indian expedition in 1982.

163. Dr. Shanti Swarup Bhatnagar. C.S.I.R. was established in 1942.

164. In January 1784 by Sir William Jones in Calcutta (now called Kolkata).

165. Le Bureau International Des Poids Me'vres, Paris. .

166. Virus Research Centre, Pune. It was jointly established by the Indian Council of Medical Research and the Rock-feller Foundation.

167. In 1898 in Kodaikanal (Tamil Nadu). It was a part of the Madras Observatory established in 1792.

168. Ahmedabad, Gujarat. It was established to study occupational diseases and find their remedies.

169. In 1911; it was known as Indian Research Fund Association. In its present form, it was set up in 1949.

170. Indian Agricultural Research Institute, Delhi.

171. The penny-farthing is an old-fashioned bicycle with a big front wheel and a small rear one. Its front wheel is four

times bigger than the hind wheel. Just like the difference between the value of two British coins – the Penny and Farthing.

172. When the sprays of a fountain rise upward with force, the air around them loses its pressure. A ball placed on a fountain continues to dance and does not come out of it because when it tries to move out of the water, the air presses it inward and the ball continues dancing.

173. The atmosphere around the earth has the colour spectrum out of which only the blue colour is scattered and the rest are removed. Because of the blue spectrum, the sky and the sea look blue.

174. When the flame of a candle burns, the air around it becomes light due to heat and rises upwards. This air lifts up the flame of the candle and, hence, it always burns upward.

175. James Watt was at the Glasgow University (1736). In 1765, he made revolutionary changes in the steam engine, thus enhancing its capacity. His steam engine became so famous that he has since been associated as its inventor.

176. Boiling point 101.4°C and freezing point 3.8°C.

177. Celsius is another name for Centigrade.

178. Strong alkali, also called sodium hydroxide (NaOH).

179. Crooks was the inventor of sunglasses. His main purpose was to protect the eyes from ultraviolet rays of the sun.

180. Zinc sulphate or $ZnSO_4.7H_2O$.

181. Brass – Copper and Zinc; Bronze – Copper and Tin; Mild Steel – Iron and some percentage of Carbon; German Silver – Copper, Zinc and Nickel; White Gold – Gold and Silver.

182. Yes. If his throat is kept wet he will not feel thirsty even if the water level in the body is low. We feel thirsty when our throat dries. The work of keeping the balance of water in the body is performed by an organ just above the spine, right in the middle of the brain, called Hypothalamus.

183. Yes. Sugar contains carbon, hydrogen and oxygen. Water contains hydrogen and oxygen, and charcoal is carbon.

184. Yes. Approximately 22%.

185. They eat seeds and plants which contain little water. So, they assimilate hydrogen from these seeds and get oxygen from the air. A mixing of the two fulfils their water requirement as these two elements produce water.

186. We sweat and lose much water. If we stay in the shade we will not lose water through perspiration. We will then require less quantity of water.

187. An average male has 75% water in his body. The percentage of water differs with different people. For example, a

thin person has less than 75% water in his body. In women the quantity is 52%.

188. 97%.

189. Sea water contains 3.5% of salts while the human body can tolerate only 0.9% salt content. If the salt content in the body increases, our kidneys can remove them, but for this they require more intake of water and they have to work hard. The human body can take and tolerate up to 2.2% extra salt. But when man drinks sea water, which has 3.5% salt, the body loses much water in its efforts to take out the extra salt. In the process, man feels thirsty and can die of thirst.

190. It is a waxy element known for its fragrance. It oozes out of the intestines of the Sperm Whale and is found floating on the sea.

191. For its Civet, which is like the musk in fragrance.

192. The musk deer. This animal is an inhabitant of the higher reaches of the Himalayas and is found in Nepal, Tibet, Kashmir, Himachal Pradesh and in some parts of North and Central Asia. Its abode is at places which are 2,500 to 4,000 metres high.

193. These were made out of sap collected from rubber plants. In fact, it was Joseph Priestly who coined the name 'rubber', since it could rub out pencil marks.

194. Approximately 2%.

195. No. The normal adult brain is 1,400 cubic centimetres in volume while its weight is 1.08 –1.4 kilograms.

196. Helium. At –269°C.

197. Einstein was working on the problem of unifying all the fundamental forces of nature. This theory, which is still incomplete, is called the Unified Field Theory.

198. Hydrogenated oils are those liquid oils which have been made solid by hydrogen in the presence of a catalyst. The 'Vanaspati' oils we get in the market are those oils.

199. It is a strong westerly wind blowing in the Southern hemisphere at 40 to 50 degree longitudes. This area has no land and as such it is free of any obstruction and the wind can blow without any hindrance. These winds make a shrill sound as if shrieking.

200. Nobel laureate Fritz Haber of Germany. His aim was to make Germany debt-free. This experiment turned out to be a failure because the expenditure involved in extracting gold was many times higher than the market rate of gold.

201. At the bottom of the ocean there are polymetallic nodules which are shaped like potatoes. It is contended that they have some metals like manganese, iron, nickel, cobalt, etc. in large quantities. Scientists are planning to take out these metals from the nodules.

202. India is the only developing country being permitted by the UNO to take out polymetallic nodules from the bottom of the Indian Ocean.

203. Dr. Salim Ali was a famous ornithologist. He studied in detail the birds of India and Pakistan and suggested measures to protect them. His contribution to the preservation of the environment is also noteworthy.

204. Approximately 4 kilowatt. In one year it comes to 6×10^{17} kilowatt.

205. Dr. Chandra Shekhar Venkatraman received the Nobel Prize for Physics in 1930. He is known for his theory of the 'Raman Effect'

206. In 1895 by Wilhelm Konrad Roentgen.

207. Kymograph.

208. Srinivas Ramanujan.

209. Leevanhauk. He was a Dutch scientist of the 17th century.

210. Ozone layers are 25 kilometres above the earth in the stratosphere. These layers filter out the harmful and cancerous ultraviolet rays of the sun and do not let them reach the earth.

211. The ozone layer is gradually disappearing because of atmospheric pollution, and the presence of chlorofluorocarbons in the air.

212. Dynamo is an apparatus which changes mechanical energy into electrical energy. It is also known as a generator. On the other hand, the electric motor converts electric energy into mechanical energy.

213. It is a method of correcting and finding out faults in a computer and its working.

214. When iron or steel is given a zinc layer, it is known as 'galvanising'. It protects iron from rusting.

215. An electric current can go round the earth 11 times in one second.

216. Dr. P.K. Sen of the K.E.M. Hospital, Mumbai, in February 1968.

217. Computerised Axiel Tomography. Used for finding out faults by the use of screening.

218. A method of taking out liquid or cells from the body for examination and detection of diseases like cancer.

219. Enophelis Culisiphez and Enophelis Stephensai are the two types of mosquitoes, which are found in urban and rural areas.

220. In 1842, the American doctor Crawford Long used ether for it.

221. Loss of 2% of water does not harm the body in any way, except that one feels thirsty. If the skin develops wrinkles, then the loss is 5%, tongue and palate dry up, and one gets hallucinations. Loss of 15% causes death.

222. Melvin Kelvin. He received the Nobel Prize in 1961 for his theory that carbon dioxide can be turned into sugar with the help of A.T.P. Energy.

223. Madame Curie. She was awarded the Nobel Prize twice, a rare achievement, in 1903 for Physics and in 1911 for Chemistry.

224. Dr. Norman Ernest Borlog, a Mexican scientist. He has developed a variety of wheat which, though dwarf, gives immense yield. These seeds and the hybrids made from them have helped our farmers in increasing their wheat production.

225. Only 0.2% of the total solar energy that falls on the earth. They turn it into food.

226. The layer of air between the two shirts does not allow the body heat to escape. This layer between the two shirts works as a non-conductor and consequently we feel warm.

227. The larger the bell the more the energy produced when struck. As a result of this, the sound produced is louder.

228. Approximately four times faster in water than in air. The speed of sound is 300 metres per second; in fresh water it is 1,420 metres per second and in salt water it is 1,500 metres per second.

229. 0.621 miles.

230. M. Visvesarayya.

231. Al-Beruni was a 11th century astronomer who was also an authority on many other faculties – Mathematics, Astrology, Geography and Chemistry. His full name was Abu Rehman Al-Beruni. He came from Iran, visited India, and wrote about his travels here in 20 volumes. As per his account, the land mass we call India was an ocean once.

232. Ernest Rutherford. Although he was awarded the Nobel Prize for Chemistry in 1908 for his research in the chemical faculties of radioactive substances, his most notable contribution has been in the field of research leading to changing one element into another. In 1919, he changed nitrogen into oxygen by showering nitrogen atoms with alpha particles.

233. Titanium, discovered by Gregor. Titanium has substituted steel in engineering.

Ans. 223

234. The sudden change occurring in the gene of a living being is called mutation. It takes place when hereditary characteristics undergo changes.

235. Producing the desirable gene which can be transmitted into a living being through genome, to change its hereditary mental and physical characteristics and to give it those characteristics which we desire. With these experiments, man may be able to produce new types of living beings by transmitting the new genes in them.

236. Ehren Bergs.

237. Vegetation can make their own food and survive while animals totally depend upon vegetation for their food.

238. Bamboo. It grows at the rate of 40 cms per day.

239. In order to shake off lice and other parasites feeding on them.

240. Received the Nobel Prize in 1930. Born on November 7, 1888 at Trichanapalli in South India.

241. During day time, the density of the atmosphere is reduced considerably due to the heat of the sun which obstructs the free flow of radio-waves. But after sunset, it increases and the waves start flowing unhindered. Consequently, the radio sound is audible without any disturbances.

242. Since the wavelength of the rays of red colour is strong, its dispersion is minimum and so it is visible even in bad weather.

243. The density of river water is lesser than the density of sea-water. It is, therefore, easier to swim in the ocean or sea than in a river, because there is less resistance in the sea.

244. Because the heat of the earth cannot escape into the upper region of air, but is pent-up by the clouds, and confined to the surface of the earth. This pent-up heat raises the temperature of the air around us. Hence, we feel suffocated and hot.

245. When thrown, the ball, because of its inertia, runs in the same direction and with the same speed as does the train and keeps pace with us. That is why we can catch it.

246. When small pieces of camphor are immersed in clear water, they go down to the bottom of the container and start dissolving. Since these pieces are unequal in size, some, i.e., the smaller ones, dissolve faster than the bigger ones. Moreover, the tension of clear water is always more than that of a solution. So, the two contradictory factors start working – less and more tension. The camphor pieces are then attracted towards the part with more tension and appear to be dancing.

247. Carotenoid and Anthocynin. Carotenoid gives them colours like yellow and tomato-red with different shades and hues. Carotenoid also makes the yolk of the egg yellow and accounts for the yellowness of butter; it is also responsible for Vitamin 'A' in them. On the other hand, Anthocynin gives them colours like light pink, green, violet and mauve.

248. On the coastal areas of Peru (South America). It has more than one crore birds of different varieties. It harbours mainly the booby and cormorant birds. They feed on the sweet-water fish of the Hambolt current. The droppings of these birds, called Guano, is one of the best Nitrogen fertilisers.

249. Chlorophyll is a green pigment in plants and trees which helps them in producing their own food. Apart from chlorophyll, flowers and fruits have a large number of other colours and colouring substances. The purpose of these colours is to attract insects and birds to them for pollination.

250. The first zoo in the world was opened in Vienna, the capital of Austria and was known as Schonbrunn. King Francis I of Austria got it built for the entertainment of Queen Maria in 1752.

Today this zoo has all modern facilities but the initial structure and layout have been kept intact.

251. Arctic Tern. These birds travel 16,000 kilometres to reach the Antarctic region when winter sets in on the Arctic region. Some of these Terns reach the islands in the Antarctic while some divert their flight towards Africa, Europe and Asia.

252. About 300 species of birds visit India every year when they migrate in winters.

253. Etienne Lenoir, the French engineer, invented it in 1860.

254. James T. King, the American engineer, in 1851.

255. Jacob Perkins, in 1834.

256. British scientist Thomas Savery invented the steam engine in 1698. And in 1712, another British scientist Thomas Newcomen came up with the piston-fired steam engine.

257. Blaise Pascal, the French scientist, in 1642.

258. The Montgolfier brothers – G.E. and E.M. Montgolfier made a gas balloon in 1783.

Ans. 251

259. Charles Babbage of England in 1822.

260. Michael Faraday in 1822.

261. Lever, Inclined Plane, Wheel and Axle, Pulley, Wedge and Screw.

262. Fredrick G. Banting, Best and John J.R. Macleod, in 1922. In 1923 Banting and Macleod were awarded the Nobel Prize for medicine.

263. Through its skull bones which catch the vibrations and carry them to the brain.

264. Lysergic Acid Diethylamide. A very low quantity (as low as 1/3,00,000 ounce) can intoxicate a person. He sees everything colourful, even everyday things appear either too beautiful or too dreadful to him, he plays with his shadow and considers himself immortal.

265. Alcohol.

266. No. Instead of stimulating the brain as caffeine does, it dulls it.

267. He got the Nobel Prize for his work on Quantum Theory.

268. Louis Pasteur of France.

269. For the invention of Penicillin.

270. Archaeopteryx – a Jurassic era bird, with a long bony tail. It could not fly because its wings could not bear the weight of its body.

271. Reserpine, Chlorpromazine and Meprobamate.

272. The Universal Fastener Company was the first to make Zips. Louis Walker established it. It was, however, in 1891 that Whitcomb Judson had displayed successfully the working of zips.

273. Iron. Of all the metals used in the world, iron is used the most, i.e., 90% of the total metals used.

274. Hugo de Vreez.

275. Wilson's comet. It was first spotted on August 5, 1986 at Caltek Observatory. When photographs of Halley's comet were taken, this new comet was first spotted by a student, Christon Wilson and has been named after him.

276. Acetic acid.

277. Around the coast, where the difference between the high and low tides is 15 feet or more. In India, the coastal area of Bhavnagar in Gujarat is fit for this project as the difference between the tides is around 28 feet. Likewise, on Hooghly River in Kolkata, Sunderbans area, Navlaxmi in Kutch and in the bay of Khambat.

278. These are instituted in honour of Dr. Shanti Swarup Bhatnagar, the founder-director of C.S.I.R. There are seven prizes awarded in the fields of Physics,

Chemistry, Biology, Engineering, Medicine, Mathematics and other sciences, for outstanding contribution. Each award has a cash prize of 20,000 rupees.

279. Fuel cell is an electronic apparatus used for converting fuel into electric energy. William Grove is accredited with having developed it in 1839. It is used particularly for spacecrafts.

280. Kenneth Arnold, a US businessman and pilot, was flying his plane from Chehalis to Yakima, when he sighted a peculiar formation of nine objects near Mount Rainier. Later, while reporting the incident, he referred to them appearing as 'saucers skipping on water'. That is how the term 'flying saucer' was coined. Sceptics feel that what Arnold had seen was a peculiar formation of clouds.

281. Cubic Boron Nitride. It was made by the American General Company in 1957. In common language it is called 'Borazon'. According to Moh's scale, it is as hard as diamond, i.e., 10. It can scratch a diamond as any other diamond may, but it can tolerate more heat than diamond. It is used as an abrasive.

282. Yes. The sand absorbs 90% of solar energy whereas moist earth absorbs only 40%.

283. Desert releases 90% of the heat absorbed during day time and sends it up in the atmosphere while moist earth can send only 50% of the heat absorbed. Since more heat is freed, the desert becomes cooler at night than during day time.

284. Bactrian.

285. About three thousand cocoons are boiled and destroyed.

286. Giraffe.

287. 64 pounds, 490 pounds and 15 pounds.

288. On the Theory of Numbers and the Theory of Partition.

289. 0.405 hectare.

290. Richter Scale.

291. In the form of glycogen.

292. Werner von Siemens on May 31, 1879.

293. Because of Carotenoid pigment.

294. Enzymes are proteins and their main function is to catalyse the various body functions.

295. About 50 kilograms.

Ans. 286

296. The harem of a male Elephant Seal contains about 300 females. Elephant Seals are found in the Antarctic region.

297. Five.

298. No. It is not bald but the hair atop its head are white, which makes it look bald. Hence the name.

299. Yes. An overdose of Vitamin 'A' causes drowsiness, headache and lethargy. It also causes peeling of the skin and nausea.

300. Thirteen – A, C, D, E, K and the eight varieties of B-Complex.

301. Seventeen types. They are calcium, chlorine, iron, magnesium, phosphorus, potassium, sodium, sulphur, chromium, cobalt, copper, fluorine, iodine, magnesium, molibdenum, celeum and the salts of zinc.

302. When gold is made into an alloy by a mixture of some other metal, its value is lessened. Carat is counted by measuring the percentage of metal mixed in it. 24-carat gold is pure. 14-carat means 14 parts pure gold with 10 parts of other metal, which could be silver, nickel, copper or zinc.

303. A surgeon of the 3rd – 4th century, his contribution to various branches of surgery has been remarkable. His work is known as 'Sushrut Samhita'.

304. A renowned physician of ancient India. Born 100 years after Christ, he composed the 'Charak Samhita'.

305. The annual deforestation rate is approximately 13 lakh hectares.

306. Uranus – 84 years, Neptune – 165 years and Pluto 248 years.

307. Yes. It takes 25 years to complete one rotation.

308. As a diver dives deeper down, the pressure on his body increases, with the result that the various gases in the body start diluting in blood. When he starts coming up, the pressure decreases and the gases leave the blood in bubbles. This is painful and may cause death.

When the diver comes up slowly, the gases get time to come out through the lungs, which is a natural process.

309. Approximately 6 litres.

310. Approximately 30 metres (100 ft).

311. By melting snow. They dig small pits 15 centimetres deep and fill them with sea-water. The first layer formed on water has very little salt in it. They take out this snow-crust, melt it and obtain drinking water.

312. According to Plate Tectonics Theory, the lithosphere of the earth is made of 13 thin plates, which are hard and close

together. These are – Indian plate, Philippines plate, Pacific plate, Juan de Fuca plate, North American plate, Cocos plate, Caribbean plate, South American plate, African plate, Arabian plate, Eurasian plate, Anatolian plate and Antarctic plate. When these plates collide, earthquakes occur.

313. An intoxicant made of Morphine. Chemically, it is Diacetymorphine.

314. 'Unknown'.

315. At high altitudes, the air is dry and cannot stop the ultraviolet rays of the sun.

316. Approximately 2°C at every 300 metres.

317. Voyager-II.

318. (a) Stegosaurus (b) Tirenosaurus (c) Placiosaurus.

319. In Japan, as it is on the border of the most active earthquake plate, according to the Plate Tectonics Theory.

320. Dr. S.Z. Kadim. First Indian expedition was organised in December, 1981.

321. Faulting, folding and volcanic burst.

322. Because of moisture, light, heat and oxygen, there is auto-oxidation.

323. Approximately 6,00,00,00,00,00,000.

324. That characteristic of computers and robots which makes them reason and behave like humans.

325. Cybernatics is a process by which animate beings and machines (like computers) control their movements and inner actions. In cybernatics, a comparative study of the movements and control systems of automatic machines and the brain is made. It was started by Professor Nobert Wiener of Massachusetts Institute of Technology, USA.

326. That heat which maintains an equilibrium between liquid oxygen and its vapour. The boiling point of liquid oxygen is –182.96°C.

327. A colour which can lend its hue to other colours. Every coloured thing is not a dye.

328. About 16 km above the earth.

329. 4.546 litres.

330. 1 quintal is 100 kilograms.

    10 quintals is 1 metric ton or 1,000 kilograms.

331. By Galileo in 1609. In Italy.

332. Hydrometer. When in use, the density of the acids change due to chemical reactions, and the batteries exhaust. They need recharging.

333. 600 volts that can even make a horse benumbed.

334. Yes. It has citric acid.

335. Chlorine.

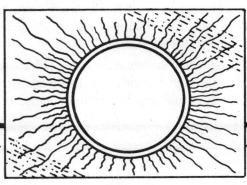

Ans. 315

336. Alcohol, because mercury freezes in temperatures at −40°C, while alcohol remains in liquid form even at −114°C.

337. That opening of a lens through which light reaches the film.

338. L = 50; M = 1000 and D = 500.

339. In a vacuum there is complete silence always, because sound cannot travel at all without molecules.

340. First – bronze; second – brass.

341. A plastic sheet is placed between two glass sheets and the three sheets are joined by the application of heat. This is how safety glass is made. Used for the windscreens of vehicles, in case of accidents the glass cracks but does not break.

342. Wilbur Wright was elder. He died before Orville of typhoid.

343. 72.

344. Charles Babbage.

345. James Watt, who invented the steam engine.

346. Mercury.

347. Magnesium in Chlorophyll and iron in Haemoglobin.

348. This speed is approximately 325 kms per hour.

349. Anything of the size of 100 microns kept at a distance of 25 cms away from the eye. (One micron = 0.001 millimetres = 0.003937 inches.)

350. Electric current is the flow of electrons through a conductor. Electrons flow from the negative to the positive but appear as if the electric current in the conductor is flowing from the positive to the negative. Electronics is the science of the behaviour and control of free electrons. Electrons are expelled from solids by light, heat, electric fields and other influences.

It is interesting to note that while all electric appliances are electric, all electronic appliances are not electronic.

351. It is one of the most natural plastics that ever existed. Arboform is the name of the material developed by Jurgen Pfizer and Helmut Nagele that consists entirely of renewable raw materials. The basic component is lignin. To make it, lignin is mixed with hemp. This mixture is heated resulting into hollow moulds and hardened into fixed shapes.

352. A nanoparticle is a minute particle whose size is measured in nanometer (nm), that is, a billionth of a metre.

353. A light-year is the distance covered by light in one year in vacuum travelling at a speed of 299,792.5 km per second.

354. The Milky Way is our home galaxy. A peculiar feature of this galaxy is a bright band of light that runs almost in a perfect circle.

355. The world record for the longest stay in space (366 days) was achieved by two Soviet cosmonauts aboard the Mir Space-Station followed by the US Skylab Mission in 1973-74 for 83 days.

356. A space-station is a place where people can live and work in space for long periods while orbiting the Earth and at a height of about 300 to 480 kilometres. The Soviet Union launched the first space-station, Salyut I, on April 19, 1971. Three cosmonauts – Georgi T. Dobrovolsky, Victor I. Patsayev, and Vladislav N. Volkov – linked their Soyuz II spacecraft with Salyut I. They spent 23 days aboard the space-station.

357. The Lithosphere is the top crust of the Earth on which our continents and ocean basins rest. It is thickest in the continental regions (40 km) and thinner in the oceans (10-12 km).

358. The Richter Scale is a logarithmic scale devised in 1935 by geophysicist Charles Richter, for representing the energy released by earthquakes. A figure of 2 or less is barely perceptible, while an earthquake measuring over 5 may be destructive.

359. Australia, measuring 7,704,441 sq km, located in the Indian Ocean.

360. 206 bones.

361. The face has 14 bones.

362. 20 teeth.

363. Marasmus.

364. An HIV-infected mother can infect the child in her womb through her blood.

The unborn baby is more at risk if the mother is in a later stage of AIDS, or she has been recently infected. Transmission can also occur at the time of birth when the baby is exposed to the mother's blood. Theoretically, transmission of the disease can also occur through breast milk.

365. The Celsius scale, the Fahrenheit scale and the Kelvin scale.

366. Dr. M.C. Modi.

367. A rotating wheel which can revolve round its fixed axis or its centre of gravity freely. It is used particularly in ships, aeroplanes and missiles, so they go ahead on their prefixed paths.

368. James Watt.

369. Centre for Development of Telematics.

370. Coal.

371. Ceres.

372. C.V. Raman.

373. Mango.

374. Apsara.

375. A butterfly.

376. Because of the century's last solar eclipse.

377. 90 years.

378. 16 hours.

379. Archimedes, the great scientist and mathematician born in 287 BC in Sicily, is said to have uttered these words.

380. On July 20, 1969 when Neil Armstrong and Edwin Aldrin landed on the moon for the first time.

381. King Louis XV of France.

382. Stories based on Lord Buddha's previous birth.

383. The Zend Avesta.

384. Nero.

385. Chanakya, the Prime Minister of Chandragupta Maurya, is known as Kautilya. His contribution to the establishment of the Mauryan Empire was very significant.

386. Raja Ram Mohan Roy.

387. Dr. Annie Besant.

388. Vikramaditya ruled from 375 AD to 413 AD. Fa-Hien visited India during his reign.

389. Hsuan Tsang.

390. 4th August, 1914 to 11th November, 1918.

391. Karl Marx from Germany, who was born in 1818 and died in 1883.

392. Madan Mohan Malviya is accredited with publishing various newspapers. In 1907, he started a weekly "Abhyu-daya", which was converted into a daily in 1915. In 1910, he started a monthly "Maryada" and in 1921, "Kisan".

In the field of English journalism, he launched an English daily "Leader" on 24th October, 1909 which contributed significantly to the freedom movement along with "Abhyudaya".

Mr. Malviya was also the chairman of the Board of Directors of The Hindustan Times from 1924 to 1946.

393. South Korea.

394. Sher Shah Suri.

395. Nine times between December, 1921 and June, 1945. His last imprisonment was the longest (1,041 days).

396. On 1st November, 1954.

397. Noor Jehan.

398. In 1431, when she was only 19.

399. During the Calcutta (now called Kolkata) session of December 1911. Later, on 24th January, 1950 it was accepted as the National Anthem.

400. After the death of Chandragupta Maurya in 297 BC, his son Bindusar ascended the throne and ruled for 25 years. Ashoka, Bindusar's son, became the king after his death.

401. Sir Thomas Roe visited India in 1615. King James I was the King of England then.

402. From A.D. 78.

403. Jesus Christ was born in Bethlehem and Mohammed in Mecca.

404. The Gestapo. This is an abbreviation of Geheime Staatspolizei (German for the Secret State Police).

405. After the Battle of Waterloo fought between the Duke of Wellington and Napolean in June 1915.

406. The devastation caused by the Persian Emperor Nadir Shah in 1739, which continued for 9 hours. The streets of Delhi were littered with dead bodies and the drains were overflowing with blood.

407. Mrs. Sarojini Naidu.

408. Qutubuddin Aibak constructed it in 1199.

409. Megasthenese visited India and stayed in Patliputra, the capital of Chandragupta Maurya, for 7 years.

410. Total number 24. They are known as Tirthankars.

411. Jodhabai.

412. Muhiyuddin Mohammed Aurangzeb Alamgir, and Khurram Shihabuddin Mohammed Shah Jehan.

413. Great Britain. He is known for being the youngest king ever to ascend the British throne, when he was only nine months old.

414. Gregorian. It was made by Pope Gregory XIII of Italy in 1582.

415. Thirteen.

416. Eleven. One of them was the Marquis of Cornwallis who came twice as the Viceroy at two different times—once for 12 years and a second time for 2 years only.

417. Diwan-e-Khas, Red Fort, Delhi.

418. In 1558. She ruled over England up to 1603, till her death.

419. Daulatabad, also known as Devgiri.

420. Mrs. Indira Gandhi became the Prime Minister on this date for the first time.

421. George Washington (1732-99), who became the first President of the United States of America on April 30, 1789.

422. Swami Dayanand Saraswati.

423. From October 1924 to May 1927. In January 1941 he disappeared from Calcutta.

424. Adolf Hitler.

425. France.

426. Queen Victoria of the British Empire ruled for 63 years and 216 days.

427. From 1939 to 1945.

428. Emperor Ashoka.

429. Pune, in the compound of the Aga Khan Palace. Before Baa's death, Gandhiji's secretary, Mahadev Desai, was cremated there.

430. Abraham Lincoln. Lawyer by profession.

Ans. 430

431. Vasco da Gama, who started his journey from Lisbon in July 1497 and reached Calicut on 23rd May, 1498.

432. Fourteen years old.

433. Allan Octavian Hume founded the Indian National Congress.

434. On 23rd June, 1757, in a village in the North of Calcutta, between Robert Clive and Nawab Shirazuddaulah of Bengal. Clive defeated the Nawab within a couple of hours because the Nawab's Commander-in-Chief defected.

435. Sharda Act. It was passed in 1929 by the Indian Legislative Assembly. According to a major amendment of 1978, the marriageable age is 21 for men, 18 for women.

436. The Taj Mahal. Shah Jehan got it built in the memory of his wife Mumtaz Mahal. Shah Jehan was married to Mumtaz Mahal in 1612. She died at the age of 39 in 1631.

437. On May 1, 1960. Prior to this, both the states were a part of Bombay Presidency. Later, they were separated on language basis. Bombay (now called Mumbai) became the capital of Maharashtra. Initially, Ahmedabad was the capital of Gujarat, but it was later shifted to Gandhi Nagar.

438. In December 1991.

439. Dauphin Louis Antoine. As King Louis XIX, he ascended the throne only for 15 minutes.

440. Student (Celibate Brahmacharya) up to 25 years; 25 to 50, Householder (Grihastha); 50 to 75, Contemplation (Vanprastha); and 75 onwards Recluse (Sanyas).

441. The Chancellor.

442. 552.

443. Justice M. Hidayatulla, who was elected the Vice-President in 1979.

444. In 1959. Now settled in Dharamsala (Himachal Pradesh).

445. Satyendranath Tagore, Rabindranath Tagore's elder brother.

446. The Presidentship of the Indian National Congress.

447. His father's name was Shahji Bhonsle. Those who influenced him were Swami Samarth Ramdas, his Guru, and his mother Jeeja Bai.

448. Nero was the fifth and last Roman Emperor from Julius Caesar's dynasty.

His full name was Lucius Domitius Ahenobarbus.

449. From Venice (Italy) to Beijing (China), then known as Cathay.

450. Four years.

451. Bahadur Shah Zafar. He was born in 1775 and died in Rangoon in 1862.

452. An Italian explorer, Amerigo reached a new continent by the sea in 1497. This new continent was named America after him.

453. Humayun died on 24th January, 1556, from serious injuries suffered when he fell from the stairs in the Old Delhi Fort.

454. Altutmish.

455. In 1954.

456. Clement Atlee.

457. Iraq.

458. Gulzari Lal Nanda.

459. At the Summit held in Tashkent, Indian Prime Minister Lal Bahadur Shastri and Pakistan President Ayub Khan tried to reach a solution to the Kashmir problem. Lal Bahadur Shastri died in Tashkent after this Summit.

460. Andhra Pradesh. It became a state in 1953. Prior to this, it was a part of the Madras Province.

461. In December 1911 by King George V at the Delhi Darbar.

462. November 1, 1966 when Punjab was divided. Chandigarh has remained a common capital for both.

463. King Edward VIII, the son of George V.

464. In 1952.

465. Mrs. Sirimavo Bandaranaike, who became the Prime Minister of Sri Lanka in 1960.

466. Between 246 and 210 BC.

467. Andaman Islands. After 1857, prisoners serving life imprisonment were sent there.

468. Hua Kuo-Feng, who had also held the office of the Prime Minister after Chou En-Lai.

469. Father Shuddhodan, mother Mahamaya. His mother expired within 7 days of his birth. He was brought up by his stepmother, Prajapati Gomati.

470. Born in 1627, died in 1680 at the age of 53 years.

Ans. 451

471. 1025 AD. Ghazni was a tiny but powerful kingdom in Afghanistan.

472. 4th July, 1776 when America was declared independent.

473. In 623 BC in Lumbini (Kapilvastu), which is in Nepal.

474. In 1800. DC stands for District of Columbia.

475. Narendra Nath was known later as Vivekananda. He founded the Ramakrishna Mission at Vellur in 1892.

476. In 1526—between Babar and Ibrahim Lodi. In 1556—between Akbar's Commander-in-Chief Bairam Khan and Hemu. In 1761—between Ahmed Shah Abdali and the Marathas.

477. Chakravarti Rajagopalachari.

478. Dadabhai Naoroji. He presided over the Congress session thrice—in 1886, 1893, 1903.

479. Lal-Bal-Pal. They are Lala Lajpat Rai, Bal Gangadhar Tilak and Bipin Chandra Pal.

480. Lord Curzon.

481. In 1930. The then British Prime Minister Ramsay McDonald presided over it.

482. On 13th April, 1919.

483. In 1885, the first session was held in Bombay (now Mumbai), under the chairmanship of Byomesh Chandra Bannerjee. This session was to be held at Poona but due to the outbreak of cholera, the venue was changed.

484. News reached quickly because it was conveyed by carrier pigeons. By the time the fastest messenger could reach England by road or the fastest ship, it was already a known fact in England that Napolean was defeated.

485. It has been estimated to be one billion, 3,849 million dollars.

486. His father was Jehangir, mother, a Rajput princess, Bhanumati; she was popularly known as Jagat Gusain. Shah Jehan got his brothers Khusro and Shahryar assassinated and grabbed the throne.

487. Moolshanker. He was born in 1824 at Morvi (Gujarat).

488. Magellan. He started on his adventure in 1519.

489. Nalanda was an ancient university of the 7th century AD. It was situated near Rajgir in the southern part of modern Bihar and was known as the centre of Buddhist religion and philosophy. The remains of this university are still found near Borgaon.

490. Between 10th century AD and 11th century AD.

491. The Eastern coast of India spread between the Mahanadi and Godavari rivers. This part falls in the State of Orissa of today.

492. In 1857, with the establishment of universities at Calcutta (now Kolkata), Benares and Madras (now Chennai). Benares Hindu University at Varanasi and Delhi University were established in 1915 and 1922 respectively.

493. Acharya Vinoba Bhave started the Bhoodan Yagya.

494. Subhash Chandra Bose was born on 23rd January, 1890 at Cuttack. Mother Prabhavati Devi and father Janaki Nath.

495. He jumped out of Hazaribagh jail on November 9, 1942. Incidentally, it was Diwali day. His companions were Yogendra Shukla, Ramanand Misra, Suraj Narayan Singh, Shaligram Singh and Gulab Chand, five in all.

496. Madeleine Slade, born in 1892 in England.

497. Taxila is located 35 kilometres north-west of Rawalpindi (now in Pakistan). Today, there is a railway station near the site, named Sarai Kalan.

498. It was framed by the Law Commission appointed during the Governor-Generalship of Lord William Bentick and was enforced in 1860.

499. In 1889, during a world fair in Paris, Alexander Gustav Eiffel made a minaret which remained the centre of attraction ever since. This tower was completed on 31st March, 1889.

500. The Constituent Assembly adopted it on 22nd July, 1947.

501. Tipu was born on 20th November, 1750 at Devnahini in Karnataka. His mother's name was Fakhrunnisa.

502. Miss Nobel came into contact with Swami Vivekananda and was highly impressed by him. She got initiated as Swami Vivekananda's disciple and came to be known as Sister Nivedita.

503. Gopal Krishna Gokhale established it in 1905.

504. Jatindra Nath Das, born in 1904, who was imprisoned for the Lahore Conspiracy Case. He died in jail on 13th September, 1929 during his 63 days' hunger-strike.

505. At Sikandara near Agra.

506. Childhood name Manu. Nana Sahib Peshwa of Bithoor nicknamed her 'Chhabili'.

Ans. 503

507. Australia is an island as well as a continent.

508. This is the world's longest formation of coral. It is 2,012 km long and is spread on the shores of Queensland in Australia.

509. Greenland.

510. Yang-Tse river.

511. The Dutch are from the Netherlands, also known as Holland. Its capital is Amsterdam.

512. Sinhalas and Tamils.

513. Titicaca is the lake situated at the highest point, which is 12,500 ft. above mean sea level, and the Dead Sea is the lowest, being 1,292 ft. below mean sea level. (Dead Sea, though named so, is not a sea, but a lake.)

514. Silvassa is the capityal city.

515. In Venice, there are 177 canals. If their length is jointly calculated, it will be 28 miles, although this city is only 2 miles in length and 1 mile in breadth.

516. Lusaka is the capital of Zambia.

517. Tashkent is the capital of Uzbekistan.

518. 5½ hours.

519. Beaufort Scale.

520. Laos and Thailand.

521. Kilimanjaro. It is 6,012 metres high.

522. Cape Comorin.

523. Uttar Pradesh.

524. Diameter is 12,681 km and circumference 39,841 km.

525. Hanoi is the capital of Vietnam.

526. Budapest, the capital of Hungary. On the right bank of river Danube is Buda and on the left is Pest.

527. 21st June.

528. Turkey. Its Istanbul side is in Europe.

529. Latex.

530. Alaska and Hawaii. They were granted statehood in 1959.

531. Spain.

532. East Timor.

533. A city in the northern territory of Australia.

534. Sierra Leone is located in Africa. The name means 'Mountain of the Lion'.

535. Sir Jamshedji Tata.

536. Tripura, which is surrounded by Bangladesh.

537. 564 kilometres (350 miles).

538. New Delhi was officially inaugurated in 1931.

539. Opened in 1869, De Lesseps, the French engineer, is credited with having made this canal, which joins the Mediterranean and the Red Sea.

540. Dispur is the capital of Assam.

541. One hectare (10,000 square metres) is approximately 2.471 acres.

542. Nippon. In Japanese, it means "land of the rising sun".

543. On river Sutlej.

544. Kanchenjunga at 8,598 metres.

545. The International line between India and China.

546. Ganges, Gomati, Chambal and Tapti.

547. Found in Arizona (USA) and Sonora (Mexico), these cactii of Seguaro species are the biggest in the world. They can be as tall as 16 metres.

548. The Ajanta Caves.

549. Cairo, the capital of Egypt.

550. Raipur is the capital of Chhattisgarh.

551. Rajasthan.

552. In Mongolia and Rajasthan (India).

553. In the USA there are towns with these names.

554. Four minutes backwards.

555. Ranchi is the capital of Jharkhand.

556. Walloons are the French-speaking residents of Belgium who are different from the Flemish-speaking people.

557. In summer season, in the Polar region, the sun seen at night is called the midnight sun. In the Arctic, there is sunlight all twenty-four hours from 21st March to 23rd September, and in the Antarctic from 23rd September to 21st March. As one travels from the North Pole towards the South Pole or vice-versa, the duration of the midnight sun decreases.

The midnight sun can be seen in North Scandinavia, Northern Russia, Alaska, North Canada and Greenland. This phenomenon occurs due to the inclination of the Earth on its axis.

558. Delhi was declared a Union Territory on November 1, 1956.

559. Five movements. 1. Its rotation round the sun. 2. While it is revolving round

Ans. 548

itself, there occurs a movement because of the gravitational attraction of the cosmic bodies, particularly, the sun and the moon. 3. Its movement when it rotates round itself. 4. Because of the sun's movement in the Milky Way at the rate of 240 kms per second. 5. Movement because after every 26,000 years, the axis of the Earth changes its leanings.

560. Chandigarh is the capital of Punjab as well as Haryana.

561. Mohs scale is a measurement used to gauge the hardness of minerals. It was invented by a German mineralogist Friedrich Mohs (1773-1839).

562. Those natural chemical substances which can be found in rocks or under the crust of the earth, alone or mixed with other inorganic/mineral substances. According to some scientists, non-carbonic products are minerals.

563. Gondwanaland was that part of the earth which comprised today's continents of Africa, Australia, Antarctica, South America and the southern part (Deccan) of India. Approximately 12 crore years ago, this mass of land, which was combined, started segregating and formed into the present-day continents.

564. Tithis Sea.

565. A black Basalt lava of fine particles. Millions of years ago, the eruption of volcanoes in the southern part of our sub-continent formed the land full of Basalt lava. With the passage of time, gradually, it turned into the black cotton soil of the south. Basalt is an African word. It is an igneous rock composed essentially of plagioclase and pro-pyroxene and commonly olivine and magnetic or titaniferous iron.

566. Radcliffe line.

567. Sahara desert of North Africa, which is spread over an area of about 56,00,000 sq. kilometres.

568. Sicily.

569. Canada. Its area is 99,76,139 sq. kms.

570. Zagreb.

571. Portugal.

572. The crater of Mount Oso of Japan (height 1,590 metres), which is spread 27 kms from South to North and 16 kms from East to West. The diameter of this crater is 114 kms.

573. Canberra.

574. St. Petersburg.

575. Approximately one-fifth of the land.

576. Malaysia and Indonesia.

577. Largest sea is the China Sea and the largest ocean is the Pacific Ocean.

578. Hawaii.

579. Eucalyptus regans is the fastest growing tree, which grows up to 30 metres in 7 years. It is found mainly in Zimbabwe.

580. Bhilai in Madhya Pradesh – USSR aided; Rourkela in Orissa – West Germany aided; and Durgapur in West Bengal – UK aided.

581. Built in 1869, its length is 162.5 kilometres, breadth 60-65.5 metres, depth 10 metres.

582. Chhattisgarh, Orissa, Maharashtra, Karnataka and Tamil Nadu.

583. Coal is divided into four categories according to its carbon contents. First, Anthracite. It has more than 92% carbon. Second, Bituminous. It has approximately 70% carbon. Third, Peat. It has 50 to 60% carbon. Fourth, Lignite. It has only 40% carbon.

584. The credit for having discovered Australia goes to the English navigator Captain James Cook, who reached there in 1770, although prior to him William Johnson had reached the continent in 1606.

585. River Sindhu.

586. Sunderbans. It is situated between West Bengal (India) and Bangladesh. This delta, formed by the Ganges and Brahmaputra rivers, has an area of 75,000 sq. kilometres.

587. Mount Godwin Austen and Kanchenjunga or K2.

588. Riyadh (Royal) and Jeddah (Administrative).

589. Lake Victoria.

590. Its previous name was Siam.

591. Khetri in Rajasthan.

592. Caspian Sea is the largest lake in the world. The largest lake in India is Wular Lake in Kashmir.

593. Previously known as Hailey National Park, it was named Jim Corbett National Park in 1957 to commemorate Edward James Corbett.

594. Total islands 224, out of which 205 are Andaman and 19 are Nicobar islands.

595. Highest literacy is in Kerala, lowest is in Jammu & Kashmir.

596. Haryana got its statehood on 1st November, 1966. It was then the 17th State of India.

597. Arunachal Pradesh was known as NEFA (North-East Frontier Province). It was given the new name Arunachal Pradesh on 20th June, 1972.

598. Construction of Panama Canal was completed in 1914. Its length is 81.6 kilometres, breadth 91.4 to 304.8 metres and depth 12.5 to 25.9 metres.

599. Japan has 3,900 islands, the main among them being Honshu, Kyushu, Hokkaido and Shikoku.

600. Si-kiang, Hwang-ho, Yangtze.

601. Pretoria (Administrative), Cape Town (Legislative) and Bloemfontein (Judicial).

602. The Republic of San Marino, founded in 301 AD. The capital city is also called San Marino.

603. 1. USA, 2. Russia, 3. China.

604. Rabi crop is sown in October-November and harvested in March-April.

605. Main crops of Kharif are Paddy, Jowar, Bajra, Cotton, Sugarcane and Ground-nut. These are sown in May-June and harvested in September-December.

606. In 1935.

607. Durand line.

608. Vatican City. Its area is only 0.272 sq. kilometres.

609. On river Danube.

610. Brazil, which supplies three-fourths of the world demand.

611. Rajasthan. Its area is 342,239 sq. kilometres.

612. Myanmar (formerly Burma).

613. Spanish.

614. On river Chambal.

615. Reykjavik.

616. Bangladesh is the largest jute-producing country in the world.

617. St. Lawrence River.

618. Cuttack.

619. Telugu.

620. Hudson River.

621. The largest country is Russia.

622. Egypt, Syria, Lebanon and Jordan.

623. Uttaranchal. The capital city is Dehra Dun.

624. Rial-Iran and Saudi Arabia; Lira-Italy; Franc-France; Yen-Japan.

625. Isotherms.

626. Switzerland.

627. Panna in Madhya Pradesh.

628. The coastal area of the Dead Sea, which is about 400 metres below mean sea level.

629. Dhaka, Bangladesh. The country has over 200,000 mosques.

630. Between Saudi Arabia and Egypt.

631. Sikkim became India's 22nd State in 1975.

632. Chhattisgarh, Uttaranchal and Jharkhand.

633. Kolkata, Mumbai and Chennai.

CURRENCIES OF DIFFERENT COUNTRIES

Country	Currency	Country	Currency
Afghanistan	Afghani	Jamaica	Dollar
Albania	Lek	Japan	Yen
Argentina	Peso	Jordan	Dinar
Austria	Schilling	Korea (South)	Won
Australia	Australian Dollar	Korea (North)	Won
Brazil	Cruzado	Kuwait	Dinar
Bulgaria	Lev	Lebanon	Pound
Canada	Canadian Dollar	Libya	Dinar
Chile	Escuda	Malaysia	Ringgit
China	Yuan	Mexico	Peso
Columbia	Peso	Morocco	Dirham
Congo	CFA Franc	Myanmar	Kyat
Costa Rica	Colon	Nepal	Rupee
Cuba	Peso	Netherlands	Guilder
Czech Republic	Koruna	New Zealand	Dollar
Denmark	Krone	Norway	Krone
Egypt	Pound	Peru	Sol
El Salvador	Colon	Philippines	Peso
Ethiopia	Birr	Poland	Zloty
Finland	Markka	Portugal	Escudo
France	Franc	Romania	Leo
Germany	Deutsche Mark	Russia	Rouble
Ghana	Cedi	Singapore	Singapore Dollar
Greece	Drachma	South Africa	Rand
Guatemala	Quetzal	Spain	Peseta
Guyana	Dollar	Sri Lanka	Rupee
Iceland	Krona	Switzerland	New Franc
Indonesia	Rupiah	Sweden	Krona
India	Rupee	Thailand	Baht
Iraq	Dinar	Turkey	Lira
Iran	Rial	UK	Pound
Ireland	Pound	USA	Dollar
Israel	Shekel	Vietnam	Dong
Italy	Lira	Yugoslavia	Dinar

634. Rigveda, Yajurveda, Samveda and Atharvaveda. The oldest of them is Rigveda.

635. Kamalapati Tripathi, who received the Mangala Prasad Award.

636. Seven chapters. They are serially as follows—Balkand, Ayodhyakand, Aranyakand, Kishkindhakand, Sunderkand, Lankakand, and Uttarkand.

637. Bilhan.

638. *Padmavati.*

639. Famous astronomer Arya Bhatt (476-499); he wrote it when he was barely 23 years old.

640. Firdausi.

641. Panini.

642. Saiyad Ibrahim.

643. Vincent Van Gogh.

644. Banabhatt.

645. *Brihad Samhita.*

646. Chaitanya's real name was Vishvambhar. He was also known as Nimayi and Gaurang. Born in Navdweep, in Bengal, in 1486 on a 'Purnima' day, his father was Jagan Nath Mishra and mother Shachi. His first wife was Laxmi. After her death, he married Vishnu Priya, a girl from a wealthy family.

647. Plato, born in 427 BC.

648. Goswami Tulsidas.

649. Hariaudh. Full name—Ayodhya Singh Upadhyaya.

650. Dr. Radhakrishnan.

651. Bal Gangadhar Tilak.

652. Narayan Shridhar Bendre and Katangari Krishna Hebbar are renowned painters.

653. *Bharat Bharati.*

654. *Raj Tarangini.* In it, the history of Kashmir is given in verse form, from its beginning to the 12th century.

655. Jayadev.

656. In 1913 for *Gitanjali.*

657. Rajrishi Purshottam Das Tandon.

658. Dr. Dharmavir Bharti.

659. Mohan Rakesh.

660. William Shakespeare.

661. Thomas Hardy—1840-1928.

662. George Eliot was a British novelist (1819-1880). 'His' real name was Mary Ann Evans!

663. It is a novel written by Charles Dickens. Oliver Twist is its hero on whose name the book is titled.

664. In Budapest. Her father was Sardar Umrao Singh Majithia and her mother was a Hungarian, Marie Antoniette Gottesmann. They were married in Lahore on 4th February, 1912.

665. *Nandan.* Its editor is Jaya Prakash Bharti.

666. *Samaj Kalyan.* Editor, Pradeep Pant.

667. Sant Gyaneshwar had two brothers Nivrutti Nath and Sopan Dev; and a sister, Mukta Bai. His famous Marathi work is *Gyaneshwari,* a commentary on the Gita.

668. Both the books were written by John Milton. They were published within four years of each other. (One was published in 1667 and the other in 1671.)

669. Sir Arthur Conan Doyle.

670. Julius Caesar, the great Roman Emperor, said these words after his victory.

671. Bhaskaracharya, born in 1114.

672. Samuel Langhorne Clemens.

673. Kalidas. *Raghuvansha, Ritusamhar, Meghdoot* and *Kumarsambhav* are in verse form; the rest are plays.

674. Aphrodite.

675. Popularly known as Hans, he is famous for his fairy tales for children. He belonged to Denmark. Born in 1805, he died in 1875.

676. Pen name.

677. Nicholas Blake.

678. Henri Dunant, the founder-father of the Red Cross, in 1862.

679. The author was Devaki Nandan Khatri. The novel was *Bhootnath,* which his son Durga Prasad Khatri completed.

680. Children's Book Trust of India, established in 1957 by the well-known cartoonist Shanker Pillai.

681. All India Fine Arts and Crafts Society— AIFACS, situated in Delhi. It was established in 1928.

682. It is an honour given for special achievement in the field of literature; it confers a cash prize of one and a half lakh rupees.

683. Vishnu Sharma in 200 BC.

684. *The Old Man and The Sea.*

685. Maulana Abul Kalam Azad, the famous freedom fighter and India's first Education Minister.

686. Sir Winston Churchill in 1953.

687. Gajanan Madhav 'Mukti Bodh'; Pandeya Bechan Sharma 'Ugra'; Raghupati Sahay 'Firaq'.

688. Amrita Pritam.

Ans. 663

689. G. Shankar Kurup, the Malayalam writer, received it in 1965.

690. Mirza Asadulla Beg. Ghalib was married to the daughter of the celebrated court-poet Mirza Illahi Baksh. The alliance increased his acquaintances and he got access to the Delhi Court.

691. Muhammad Iqbal.

692. Pearl Sydenstricker Buck, known as Pearl S. Buck.

693. *With No Regrets.*

694. *Malayala Manorama.*

695. Georges Simenon was a Belgian crime writer who created Inspector Maigret of the French Surete, who appeared in a series of detective novels.

696. E.M. Forster.

697. Abul Fazal, born in 1551, wrote it. Fazal died in 1602.

698. Lewis Caroll. His real name was Charles Lutwidge Dodgson. Birth 1832, death 1898.

699. Books such as—*Mother*, *Comrade*, *Lower Depths.*

700. The title of the book is *City of Joy* and its author is Dominique Lapierre.

701. Hank Ketcham.

702. Goethe (birth 1749, death 1832).

703. Alexander Dumas.

704. Dharmavir Bharti, who also edited the well-known Hindi Weekly *Dharmayug.*

705. In 1956.

706. The first line is written by Tulsidas, the second by Abdul Rahim Khankhana.

707. Shani. The novel was *Kala Jal*.

708. *The Tempest.*

709. Gauri Pant.

710. John Keats, P.B. Shelley and Lord Byron respectively.

711. Ann Taylor (born in 1782, died in 1866).

712. Fedor Dostoevsky.

713. Ernest Hemingway, who was born on July 21, 1899.

714. Virginia Stephen (born in 1822).

715. O.K. is a short form of the American slang "Ol Korrect", which in itself means "All Correct".

716. In *Anand Math,* a novel written by Bankim Chandra Chatterjee.

717. Rudyard Kipling.

718. Ian Fleming.

719. Italian author Giovanni Boccaccio.

720. Hans Christian Anderson. He was from Denmark. Born in 1805, he remained a bachelor all his life and wrote for children. Died in 1875.

721. Esperanto is a language developed by L.L. Zamenhof from Poland. His pen name was Esperanto. He hoped to make it an international language, unifying the world.

722. Vijay Tendulkar.

723. The Bronte sisters were Charlotte, Emily and Anne Bronte.

724. Mrs. Nayantara Sehgal, the daughter of Mrs. Vijayalakshmi Pandit (born in 1927, Allahabad).

725. Harivanshrai Bachchan.

726. Padma Sachdev.

727. Rajendra Singh Bedi.

728. Within his lifespan of 56 years, he wrote 51 novels. His first novel was *Ghat ka Patthar* and the last one *Gunah ka Rishta*.

729. About 1,652.

730. *Pride and Prejudice.*

731. *The Hindustan Times*. It was started on 24th September 1924. It has a circulation of 8,78,320.

732. Sahitya Akademi Award was given for *Sanskriti ke Char Adhyaya* and Jnanpeeth Award for *Urvashi*.

733. Farishwar Nath Renu. His story on which *Teesri Kasam* was based, was entitled *Teesri Kasam* alias 'Mare Gaye Gulfam.'

734. *Rang Mein Bhang*, published in 1910.

735. Pratap Narayan Mishra.

736. *Young India.*

737. Vinayak Rao Bhave.

738. Kabir Das, the saint-poet and social reformer. Born in 1399, died in 1495.

739. Ras Khan.

740. Maithili Sharan Gupt.

741. Poet Bhushan.

742. Abul Fatah Umar Bin Ibrahim Al Khayyami.

743. William Wordsworth was a poet of nature. He is known as the first poet of the Romantic movement in English literature. Dorothy was his sister, who nursed him to health after the setback he received in France when the French Revolution turned bloody.

744. P.B. Shelley wrote these in his poem 'Ode to the Skylark'.

745. Premendra Mitra (born in 1905 in Varanasi).

746. Elizabeth Barrett Browning.

747. P.B. Shelley.

748. English author John Bunyan (1628-1688).

749. In 1885.

750. Respondez S'il Vous Plais—a French expression meaning 'Reply please'.

751. "Cotta" means "baked". Terracotta is an Italian word which means the 'baked soil'.

752. Albert Camus (1913-1960).

753. Arundhati Roy for her first and only novel, *The God of Small Things*.

754. The magazine was entitled *Vigyan Lok*. Its editor, then, was R.D. Vidyarthi.

755. From Gita Press, Gorakhpur.

756. Saki's real name was Hector Hugh Munro (1870-1916).

757. Ernest Hemingway.

758. Gopal Das Niraj.

759. Shrikant Verma, who got the Akademi award in 1987, posthumously. He died in 1986.

760. 'Montessori' derives its name from Maria Montessori, an Italian educationist. Dr. Montessori was born on 31st August, 1870. She was a doctor by profession, but was engaged all through her life in child-welfare activities.

761. R.K. Narayan (1906-2001), who wrote *Malgudi Days*.

762. These are the words of Lokmanya Bal Gangadhar Tilak.

763. *Pravda* is a prominent newspaper of Russia.

764. The Padma Bhushan.

765. Pheroze Rangoonwalla.

766. Harriet Elizabeth Stowe.

767. In Dogri.

768. Orwell's real name was Eric Arthur Blair.

769. Kamban transcribed the Tamil Ramayana and it is, therefore, called 'Kamb Ramayana'.

770. *Taar Saptak*. It was edited by the late Agyeya.

771. The first newspaper *Hickey's Gazette* was published from Calcutta in 1779.

772. Two—Indian Federation of Working Journalists (IFWJ), and National Union of Journalists (NUJ). Out of the two, IFWJ was established first.

773. *One More Over.*

774. Samuel Beckett (1906-1989).

775. Samuel Johnson (1709-1784).

776. Suryakant Tripathi 'Nirala'. Birth 1899, death 1961.

777. Ismat Chugtai.

778. The celebrated female journalist is Promila Kalhan.

779. Prem Chand. Real name, Dhanpat Rai.

780. Scottish lawyer James Boswell (1740-1795), who achieved fame with his biography on Johnson.

781. Composition in light.

782. *Tamas* has been written by Bhishma Sahni. The TV serial was directed by Govind Nihalani.

783. Dale Carnegie (1888-1955), who wrote the best-seller, *How to Win Friends and Influence People.*

784. March 1877, between England and Australia at Melbourne.

785. In Bombay (now Mumbai) in 1721.

786. In 1926.

787. Calcutta Cricket Club, established in 1792.

788. In 1744.

789. The length of the pitch is still 22 yards.

790. In 1928-29. The first President was R.E. Grantgowen.

791. Birth: 10th September, 1872, death: 2nd April, 1933.

792. A Parsee team toured England in 1896. In 1889-90, a team under the captaincy of G.F. Vernon came to India.

793. In the history of Test cricket, the first century was scored by an Australian player Charles Bannerman in the first-ever Test.

794. Sir W.G. Grace in 1880.

795. In 1934-35. Bombay defeated North India.

796. Ranji Trophy.

797. Trevor Chappell of Australia. This delivery has since been banned.

798. In 1932 against England. C.K. Naidu captained the Indian team and D.R. Jardin captained the team of England.

799. In 1951-52, under the captaincy of Vijay Hazare, at Madras.

800. Sunil Manohar Gavaskar, who captained the team in 47 Tests.

801. Iftikhar Ali Khan Pataudi (senior) who played in the 1936 Olympics in Berlin under the captaincy of the hockey wizard Dhyan Chand.

802. 52 Tests, 80 innings, not out 10 times, total score 6,996, number of centuries 29, average 99.94.

803. Imperial Tobacco Company Trophy.

804. Wicket-keeper Budhi Kundaran.

805. Salim Durrani in 1961.

806. 1930-31.

807. In New Delhi in 1966.

808. In 1951, at Delhi and in 1962, at Jakarta.

809. Maharaja K.S. Ranjit Singhji (Ranji) in 1896-97.

810. V.V.S. Laxman, 281 runs at the Eden Gardens against Australia on March 15, 2001.

811. Lala Amarnath, Deepak Shodhan, A.G. Kripal Singh, Abbas Ali Baig, Hanumant Singh, G.R. Viswanath, Surinder Amarnath and Mohammed Azharuddin.

812. Mohammed Azharuddin of India.

813. Mumbai — Bombay Gymkhana, Brabourne Stadium and Wankhede Stadium.

814. No. The ball is to be caught with the hands only.

815. No. It is necessary that the ball should hit the stumps after hitting a player.

816. When a batsman is out, his replacement should reach the wicket within two minutes. In case of a delay, the incoming batsman can be declared 'time out' by the umpire.

817. The World Cup Tournament started in England in 1975.

818. Rangaswamy Cup.

819. A bowler is on the verge of delivering the ball; at the bowler's end the batsman leaves the crease for a run, and in the meantime the bowler hits the wicket with the ball. The batsman is supposed to be "crease out". This was done for the first time in cricket history by Veenu Mankad.

820. Durand Cup Tournament, which was started by Sir Mortimer Durand in 1888, at Shimla.

821. 'The Big Three' in Indian Football means the first three important tournaments viz.—Durand Cup (started in 1888), Rover's Cup (started in 1891) and IFA Shield (started in 1893).

822. In 1940, the Calcutta Mohammedan Sporting defeated the Royal Warwickshire Regiment in the finals by 3-1 goals.

823. Football was included in the Paris Olympics, held in 1900.

824. Sunil Gavaskar.

825. Sailen Manna in 1951 and Suvimal 'Chunni' Goswami in 1962.

826. This cup was started in the year 1930 and was named after Jules Rimet, the French Football administrator and the founder of FIFA. The Cup was awarded to the World Champions. Since 1974, however, the World Champions are awarded the FIFA Cup.

827. Louis Lawrence of France. On 13th July, 1930, playing against Mexico at Montevido in Uruguay, Louis scored the first-ever goal in a World Cup Tournament. This match was won by France 4-1.

828. Diano Joff, captain of the Italian team, was 40 when he won the World Cup in 1982 for his country.

829. Pele of Brazil.

830. In 66 AD Roman Emperor Nero participated in every event. All other contestants, terrified of the emperor, accepted defeat and let him win all the events.

831. In the 1966 finals, Geoff Hurts of England made three goals against West Germany. England won the match 4-2.

832. It was with Pt. Nehru's efforts that the Asian Games were first instituted in

Ans. 825

1951 and were held in New Delhi. These are organised once in four years.

833. A Marathon race covers approximately 42 km (26 miles and 385 yards). The race was first included in the Olympics in 1896 at Athens.

834. In the 1958 Tokyo Asiad.

835. Pakistan was the first winner on the basis of goal average against India. In the 1986 Seoul Asiad, South Korea, the host country defeated Pakistan 2-1 and won the Gold.

836. Bangkok. In 1966, 1970 and 1978.

837. Milkha Singh, for having completed the 400 metres race in a record time of 45.6 seconds during the Jakarta Asiad in 1962. Earlier, he had won the 400 metres race in 1958 by 47.0 seconds.

838. Courtney Walsh (West Indies).

839. In 1951, after having won the 100 and 200 metres races, he became famous as the best runner in Asia.

840. In 1896, at Athens, Greece.

841. Baron Pierre de Coubertin of France.

842. Since the 1928 Amsterdam Olympics.

843. Total eight. 1928: Amsterdam, 1932: Los Angeles, 1936: Berlin, 1948: London, 1952: Helsinki, 1956: Melbourne, 1964: Tokyo and 1980: Moscow.

844. Goran Ivanisevic of Croatia, who won the tournament in 2001.

845. P.K. Banerjee in 1961.

846. (i) Football (ii) Cricket (iii) Chess (iv) Table Tennis (v) Badminton.

847. Prakash Padukone in 1980.

848. India has either won these Tests or drawn them, but has never been defeated in these Tests.

849. (i) Cricket (ii) Football (iii) Billiards. This is given to the winner of the world cup (iv) Football (v) This cup is awarded to the winning team/country in Tennis. (vi) These are awarded in Badminton. Winning countries in men's events are awarded the Thomas Cup and in the women's events, the Uber Cup.

850. Major Dhyan Chand.

851. Arti Saha and Arti Pradhan. Arti Pradhan, a 13-year-old girl, performed this feat in 1987.

852. Pullela Gopichand. P. Gopichand capped his spectacular run at the All England Badminton Championship with a straight games victory over Chinese Chen Hong in the final on March 11, 2001 at Birmingham to become the only second Indian to win the Men's Singles title. Gopichand, 27, who did not drop a single game throughout the tournament, won 15-12, 15-6 in less than an hour to emulate the legendary Prakash Padukone, who had won in 1980.

853. There are four major competitions in Tennis: Wimbledon, US Open, Australian Open and French Open. A winner of all the four events is known as a 'Grand Slam' winner (both men and women). Previously, to bag the Grand Slam title, a player had to win all the four competitions in a calendar year.

854. Leander Paes and Mahesh Bhupathi reached all the four Grand Slam finals in 1999 and won the French Open and Wimbledon.

855. Ramanathan Krishnan reached the semi-finals twice in 1960 and then in 1961.

856. In 1900. India is participating since 1921.

857. In 1884, Maud Watson.

858. (i) Hungary – Football (ii) USSR – Tennis (iii) Indonesia – Badminton (iv) Pakistan – Hockey (v) Pakistan – Squash (vi) England – Cricket.

859. Ravi Shastri.

860. (i) Athletics 800 mts. (ii) Cricket (iii) Tennis.

861. Sonny Liston.

862. In 1877.

863. Fencing.

864. Antonio Abbertondo of Argentina crossed the channel to and fro in 1961 in 43 hours 10 minutes. He took rest for four minutes only.

865. Saint Louis; Antwerp; Los Angeles; Helsinki.

866. Because it was first played at the Badminton Hall in Glouscestershire.

867. Pakistan.

868. Edson Arantes De Nascimento Pele. He played for Brazil in the 1958, 1962, 1966 and 1970 World Cups. Except for 1966, Brazil won the World Cup thrice. In the final round, Pele had 12 goals to his credit.

869. (i) Five (ii) Only six players on the snow at a given time (iii) Seven (iv) Four.

870. The team from Greece.

Ans. 855

871. From left to right, upper rings—blue, black and red. Lower rings—yellow and green.

872. Sardar Nihal Singh (1908).

873. Gaus Mohammed (1939).

874. Kapil Dev.

875. 19 against England; 4 against India; 4 against South Africa; 2 against West Indies.

876. Tug-of-War.

877. Tennis.

878. 242, out of which 101 were scored by Dhyan Chand.

879. Sandeep Patil created the world record by hitting six fours in one over.

880. Donald Budge.

881. 1,000 runs on 25th January, 1973 and 5,000 on 20th September, 1979.

882. Dennis Amiss of England who scored 141 runs at Old Trafford, Manchester against Australia.

883. Kiran Bedi nee Kiran Peshavaria.

884. Charles Bannerman of Australia was the batsman and Alfred Shaw of England was the first bowler.

885. In 1936 for men, in 1976 for women.

886. Joe David. Since 1927, when this championship was first organised, till 1946, David won it 15 times.

887. Umpire Swarup Kishan, who was awarded the Padmashree in 1986.

888. Bachendri Pal.

889. Syed Modi was born on 31st December 1962. Eight times National Champion, this outstanding player was murdered in Lucknow on 28th July, 1988.

890. Sachin Tendulkar. He has scored more than 10,000 runs.

891. In the following races: 100 metres, 400 metres, 400 metres hurdle race and 4 × 100 metres relay race.

892. Harbhajan Singh. He achieved this feat against Australia at Eden Gardens (Kolkata).

893. Anil Kumble in 1998.

894. Chetan Sharma (1987), against New Zealand.

895. Steve Waugh (Australia).

896. He was associated with cricket. Nadkarni created a world record by sending down 22 maiden overs against England in the Madras Test in 1964. His full name was Rameshchandra Gangaram 'Bapu' Nadkarni.

897. Karnam Malleswari.

898. 270 against England at Melbourne in 1936-37.

899. *Raja Harish Chandra* was the first silent film made in Hindi. It was screened in 1913.

900. *Don Juan* in 1927. Producer: Warner Brothers.

901. The dubbing was done in Indra Bansal's voice.

902. Ram Chandra Dwivedi alias 'Pradeep'.

903. Amusingly, the credit for being the first 'heroine' in a Hindi movie goes to a man named Salunke, who had played Taramati in *Raja Harish Chandra*!

904. Anand Rao Painter of Kolhapur had made a movie camera with an old cinema projector. A comic film was made with it in 1918.

905. In 1932, a Hindi movie *Ayodhya ka Raja* was also made in Marathi as *Ayodhya cha Raja.*

906. Elphinstone Picture Palace, built in 1907 by J.F. Madan in Bombay.

907. Sir Charlie Spencer Chaplin.

908. Devika Rani.

909. Kundan Lal Saigal.

910. Mrs. Pratima Puri. Later she became a known face on TV.

911. Kamla, who was the heroine of *Bhasmasur Mohini* made in 1913.

912. Ferozeshah Mistry, who composed music for *Alam Ara.*

913. Dadasaheb Phalke was the producer of the first silent film *Raja Harish Chandra*. The film was made in 1912 and released on 3rd May, 1913.

914. In 1938, it was used for the first time in India by Wadia Movietone during film production.

915. *Kalpana* in 1948.

916. On 24th January, 1952 in Bombay. It was held for 15 days.

917. Fatima A. Rashida.

918. The Padmashree was awarded in 1958. His first film *Pather Panchali* was completed in 1955.

919. *Hamari Beti*, 1951.

920. Entered filmdom in 1952. Born on October 8, 1933, Raj Kumar came on the screen with his first film *Rangili.*

921. Dilip Kumar, 11th December, 1922, Dev Anand, 26th September, 1923, Raj Kapoor, 14th December, 1924.

922. At Kolkata, in 1975.

923. *Around the World* made by Pachhi, in 1967.

Ans. 910

924. The first black and White cinemascope film was *Kagaz ke Phool,* made in 1959. The first coloured one in cinemascope was *Pyar ki Pyas* made in 1961.

925. Lata Mangeshkar.

926. 24.

927. Sunil Dutt. His first appearance was in *Railway Platform.* He was also an announcer on AIR.

928. Yes. It was an English film *Melody of Love,* screened in Calcutta in 1929.

929. On 7th July, 1896 at the Watson Hotel of Bombay, *Marvel of Century* was shown.

930. Peenaz Masani.

931. Hero, Richard Burton, heroine, Elizabeth Taylor. The director was Joseph Mankiewiez.

932. Baby Aradhana.

933. The late Shyamji-Ghanshyamji.

934. Devika Rani married the Russian painter/artist Svetoslav Roerich.

935. Child actress Gita Khanna.

936. Ashok Kumar in the film *Achhut Kanya.*

937. *Aan* of Mehboob Productions.

938. *Sholay,* which ran at Minerva Talkies, Bombay for six uninterrupted years, an all-time record.

939. *Indra Sabha* made in 1932. It has 71 songs.

940. In California (USA). Hollywood is known as the capital city of the film world.

941. Marilyn Monroe.

942. *Kalpana* directed by Uday Shankar.

943. M.F. Husain. (Full name Maqbul Fida Husain.)

944. Shubhangi Khote, who became famous with Mehmood as a woman comedian. Populary known as Shubha Khote, her first film was *Seema.*

945. In Paris, in 1902.

946. Walt Disney, the father of animated films.

947. Character-actor Janki Das. He won the half-a-mile Cycling Championship in Sydney, Australia on 13th January, 1938.

948. *Dharti ke Lal.*

949. *Adi Shankaracharya.*

950. Established in 1955. First film made was *Jaldeep,* 1956.

951. Zakaria Khan and his son, Amjad Khan.

952. Basu Bhattacharya's first film was *Teesri Kasam*, released in 1966 and Basu Chatterjee's first film was *Saara Aakash* released in 1969.

953. Sudhir Pandey has shown his acting talent in the TV serials *Buniyad* and *Manoranjan*.

954. *Hamrahi*. Its Bengali version was *Udayer Pathe*.

955. Raj Kapoor's *Jagte Raho* received this award.

956. These were—*Balam*, *Ayodhya cha Raja*, *Joymati*, *Kapal Kundala*, *Ishk-e-Punjab* and *Ekta* respectively.

957. Born on 11th October, 1942 in Allahabad (UP). His first film was *Saat Hindustani*.

958. Dr. Jayant Narlikar.

959. Baldevraj Vilayatiram Chopra.

960. Khwaja Ahmed Abbas.

961. Akhlak Mohammad Khan Shahryar.

962. In 1928.

963. Ronald Reagan.

964. September 1959, in Delhi.

965. The Radio City Music Hall in New York. Capacity 5,882.

966. Deepti Naval.

967. Yash Chopra. It was the first film he directed.

968. It is based on Shrilal Shukla's novel *Raag Darbari*. He received the Sahitya Akademi award for it in 1969.

969. Greta Garbo, whose real name was Greta Gustafsson.

970. *Roti* (old).

971. Kamini Kaushal.

972. Jai Raj.

973. *Valmiki Pratima*.

974. Hermann Hesse is the author of *Siddhartha*. The leading cast in the film was Shashi Kapoor and Simi Garewal.

975. *Do Ankhen Barah Haath*.

976. *Mr. Sampat*.

977. *Cinema Girl*.

978. Shyam Benegal.

979. *Baghdad ka Chor*.

980. *Prithvi Vallabh*.

981. Rishabh Charan Jain.

982. Don Bragg, a US citizen, who had performed the role of Tarzan, also participated in the Pole Vault competition in the 1960 Olympics at Rome; he won a medal.

983. R.C. Boral.

984. Lata Mangeshkar, Asha Bhonsle, Meena Mangeshkar and Usha Mangeshkar.

Ans. 953

985. Ecology is the branch of science which deals with the relationships of life forms with each other and with their surroundings.

986. In 1866, Ernst Haeckel coined the term 'ecology'.

987. Ecosystem is defined as a group of living things which live together in a certain environment in a particular area.

988. By ecological balance, we mean the ability of nature to sustain the environment and its diverse life forms through a system of checks and balances.

989. The four elements of an ecosystem are:
   (a) The non-living environment
   (b) Producers (green plants)
   (c) Consumers
   (d) Decomposers.

990. Omnivores are living beings which eat both plants and animals. Human beings, rats, pigs, bears and certain birds are omnivores.

991. The interconnected food chains in an ecosystem are called food webs.

992. Saprophytes are living beings that feed on dead or decayed organic matter. Most saprophytes are fungi and bacteria which contain no chlorophyll.

993. A biome is a broad natural assemblage of plants and animals shaped by common patterns of vegetations and climate. Some examples of biomes are forest biomes, desert biomes, grassland biomes or tundra biomes.

994. Biosphere is a term used to describe that part of the earth (land and water) and the thin layer of air above its surface that supports life.

995. Tundra, coniferous forest, deciduous forest, grasslands and savannas, chaparral, tropical rain forest and deserts.

996. The system in which all organisms are identified by a two-part Latinised name is called binomial system of nomenclature. We also call it the Linnaean system as it was devised by the biologist Carolus Linnaeus (1707-1778). The first name is capitalised and identifies the genus—the second identifies the species within the genus.

997. It is the process by which living beings change with new environmental conditions.

998. It is an area in which animals and plants having similar habits and needs live together.

999. Creatures living in or on the soil. Earthworms, centipedes, snails and the like.

1000. Animals living on trees, such as monkeys, langurs, macaques and the like.

1001. A natural means of disguise used by creatures to hide or escape from enemies.

1002. Aestivation is a state of inactivity and reduced metabolic activity similar to hibernation, that occurs during the summer in species like lungfish and snails.

1003. Animals or plants which live at the bottom of the sea or other water bodies are called benthos.

1004. Planktons are small, often microscopic, plant and animal life living in water.

1005. Man appeared on earth about a million years ago.

1006. Charles Darwin (1809-1882).

1007. It is located in the Mojave Desert near Dagget, California. It produces 675 MW of electricity, enough for one million people.

1008. It is the power obtained from the energy stored in the nuclei of atoms.

1009. It is the region of air close to the earth extending up to 10 km in which temperature decreases with height. It contains water vapour, dust particles, oxygen, nitrogen, carbon dioxide, clouds etc.

1010. It is the region above the troposphere, extending from 10 to 40 km, wherein the temperature is constant. Its upper part contains ozone which absorbs most of the ultraviolet radiation of the sun.

1011. It is the region above the stratosphere and below the thermosphere, extending between about 50 km and 80 km above the ground.

1012. It is the layer in the earth's atmosphere above the mesosphere and below the exosphere.

1013. It is the uppermost layer in the earth's atmosphere, beginning at about 700 km. Hydrogen is its main constituent.

1014. Creatures capable of living both in water and on land are called amphibians. Examples include frogs, toads, and salamanders.

1015. Those countries of Africa, Asia and Latin America (around 120) which are still undergoing industrial development as a result of major political changes caused by the break-up of the European overseas empires. The USA and the erstwhile USSR (now Russia) form the First World. The industrial European States together with Canada and Japan form the Second World. The Three Worlds Theory was allegedly first formulated by Mao Zedong.

Ans. 1006

1016. Titicaca (in South America).

1017. Ghawar Field (Saudi Arabia).

1018. The Experimental Breeder Reactor (EBR), Idaho, USA.

1019. The world's largest nuclear power station with 10 reactors and an output of 9,096 MW is the station in Fukshima, Japan.

1020. Smog is a mixture of pollutants that causes a fog-like haze over a city. In 1905, H.A. de Vocux coined the term 'smog'.

1021. Aerosols are dispersions of solid or liquid particles in a gaseous medium, for example: smoke, dust, artificial sprays etc.

1022. Tokyo, the capital of Japan.

1023. It is a scale used to detect acidity.

1024. As a result of a fire at a chemical storage warehouse near Bessel, Switzerland, spilled chemicals killed thousands of fish and eels in the Rhine River.

1025. The Dharavi slum near the Santa Cruz Airport, Mumbai.

1026. It is an agricultural practice whereby a pulse crop is grown in between two serial crops.

1027. Madame Curie. She was a Polish scientist, who won the Nobel Prize in 1903 and 1911.

1028. On 6th August, 1945 an atom bomb named "Little Boy" was dropped on Hiroshima.

1029. The second atom bomb was dropped on Nagasaki on 9th August, 1945.

1030. It is a small hydrogen bomb that kills by radiation without destroying buildings and other structures.

1031. The lowest level of sound, barely audible to human ears.

1032. An orbit at a height of 850 km from earth.

1033. To reduce the emissions of greenhouse gases.

1034. Industrial and automobile exhaust fumes contain chemicals called sulphates which react with moisture in the air to form sulphuric acid. The resulting acid rain damages trees and the environment.

1035. The culprit is plastic, a 19th century invention.

1036. The United States under George W. Bush.

1037. Since plastics cannot be broken down by micro-organisms, they are non-biodegradable.

1038. LNG stands for Liquefied Natural Gas.

1039. Coal is the fossilised remains of vast forests that existed as much as 300 million years ago.

1040. Ozone is a highly reactive pale blue gas and an allotrope of oxygen.

1041. At a height between 15 and 60 km in the upper atmosphere.

1042. The ozone layer surrounds the earth and shields it from harmful radiation of the sun. It absorbs about 99% of the sun's ultraviolet radiation. It lets infra-red radiation enter the earth's atmosphere, which is useful for warming the earth.

1043. The main culprits for destroying the ozone layer are man-made CFC (chlorofluorocarbon) gases.

1044. It was a protocol signed at Montreal, Canada in 1987 in which representatives of 46 developed countries reached an agreement to limit the use of CFCs.

1045. They are called wetlands.

1046. Silica particles in the air.

1047. It was the pneumonic form of plague which killed a quarter of the population of Europe and some 7.5 million worldwide during 1347-51.

1048. Hygroscope measures the relative humidity of the atmosphere. Anemometer measures the wind velocity and a hygrometer is used to measure the relative humidity of air.

1049. It is an instrument for measuring the turbidity of water.

1050. It is an instrument used to measure variations in gravitational force.

1051. Radioactivity is measured by a Geiger counter.

1052. Florometers are used for measuring fluid velocities.

1053. By counting the annular rings in the transverse sections of a tree stem.

1054. Tensiometer is used to measure moisture in the soil.

1055. Meteorological satellites are used for studying the weather.

1056. Radiometer is a device used for measuring the intensity of radiation.

1057. It is an instrument used to measure sea tides.

1058. Barometer is used for measuring atmospheric pressure. It was invented by an Italian physicist, Evangelista Torricelli.

1059. A rain gauge is used to measure rainfall.

1060. Radiosonde is a balloon-carried instrument package used by meteorologists to make observations of the upper atmosphere. It is used to study the weather.

1061. Super computers.

1062. It is an instrument used to measure high temperatures.

1063. A psychrometer is used for measuring relative humidity.

1064. It is a sophisticated balloon used for studying the weather.

1065. It is an instrument used to measure changes in the slope of the ground surface and indicates earthquakes or volcanic activity.

1066. Sonar is a device for locating underwater objects by the reflection of ultrasonic waves.

1067. Solarimeter is used for measuring total solar radiation per unit as received on the ground.

1068. Earthquakes are detected by seismographs. The instrument is used for recording the activity of an earthquake.

1069. The term 'Lidar' stands for light detection and ranging. It is a kind of radar wherein laser beams are used, not microwaves.

1070. Compressed Natural Gas. It is a good quality fuel for automobiles, causing less pollution.

1071. It is the latest technology for treating brackish water, sea-water and waste effluents and producing water for a wide range of applications.

1072. Nek Chand's Rock Garden is located in Chandigarh. It is an exquisite work of art made out of waste material.

1073. A mass extinction of many giant species of mammals occurred about

10,000 years ago. It is known as the 'Pleistocene Overkill.'

1074. Cheetah, polar bear, tiger, leopard, jaguar, crocodile, margay, giant panda, and a host of other creatures.

1075. The Asiatic Lion.

1076. In Dudhwa, a sanctuary in UP.

1077. In the Western Ghats of India.

1078. From the willow trees grown in Northern India, which almost exclusively supply the wood for cricket bats.

1079. An ozone hole.

1080. Explorer-I.

1081. Like coal, oil and natural gas are also fossil fuels.

1082. Shark.

1083. From the thyroid gland of the cat.

1084. Animals whose body temperature does not remain constant and changes according to the surroundings.

1085. 5th June.

1086. The danger from radioactive wastes and the likelihood of nuclear mishaps.

1087. Rising levels of greenhouse gases such as carbon dioxide and man-made CFCs (chlorofluorocarbons) are causing a steady and dangerous rise in global temperatures, leading to climatic changes. This is referred to as global warming.

1088. Global warming will expand the water in the oceans, raising water levels worldwide. The Polar ice caps, would also melt. Many islands would be submerged and low-lying areas like Bangladesh would be flooded and devastated, while coastal cities such as Mumbai, Sydney and New York would disappear.

1089. Ecomark is a labelling for environment-friendly goods which satisfies the requirements of Indian environmental standards for that product.

1090. Green colour.

1091. Dr. Salim Ali was a world-famous ornithologist from India. He wrote *The Book of Indian Birds* and *Handbook of the Birds of India and Pakistan.* These books were co-written with Sir Dillon Ripley. Dr. Salim Ali's other classic is *The Fall of a Sparrow.*

1092. The Corbett National Park in UP.

1093. Sundarlal Bahuguna, Medha Patkar and Maneka Gandhi.

1094. On 24th April, 1973 in Mandal near Gopeshwar. Goura Devi, Chandi Prasad Bhatt and Sundarlal Bahuguna have been the leaders of this movement.

1095. This is the contract between the Government of Maharashtra and the Enron Power Company, entered in 1993, for setting up a 2,015 MW power plant at Dabhol, on the Konkan coast. With the collapse of Enron, the project is no longer operational.

1096. The Narmada Project is supposed to generate 2,500 KW of power and irrigate 20 lakh hectares of land. It is a Rs 40,000-crore project which envisages the construction of 30 big, 135 medium and over 3,000 minor irrigation dams.

1097. It is a joint venture of the states of Punjab, Haryana and Rajasthan and is the largest multi-purpose dam project in India. It is built on Sutlej River. This project was completed in 1968 at the cost of Rs 235 crores.

1098. India's first remote sensing satellite (IRS-IA) was launched in March 1988.

1099. In 1986, a nuclear reactor in the power station at Chernobyl overheated during test and caught fire. More than 30 people died instantly and thousands were affected by the nuclear radiation.

1100. The Amerada Hess Refinery in St. Croix, Virgin Islands, US.

Ans. 1098

1101. The World Bank.

1102. Yellowstone National Park.

1103. London Zoo (1853).

1104. The study of birds.

1105. The study of the behaviour of animals in their natural surroundings.

1106. The study of the genesis, life and development of vegetative formations.

1107. The study of ice, snow, hail and other low temperature phenomena.

1108. December 2nd and 3rd, 1984.

1109. The Sunderbans in West Bengal.

1110. In the Sunderbans.

1111. The Red Data Book.

1112. Charles Darwin.

1113. *Nature and Resources.*

1114. The J. Paul Getty Wildlife Conservation Prize is a prestigious award given by the Worldwide Fund for Nature in recognition of global conservation efforts.

1115. Dr. Verghese Kurien, the father of India's white revolution.

1116. In Orissa.

1117. Atmosphere is the blanket of air that surrounds the earth.

1118. Solid carbon dioxide.

1119. The Indian Forest Act was passed in 1927.

1120. In 1972.

1121. The Bishnoi Movement is believed to have been started by a sage called Sambaji, 400 years ago in Rajasthan. People worship trees and resist cutting them down. Besides, they revere all creatures.

1122. An environmental movement against a 75 MW hydro-electric project on Kuthipuzha (a tributary of the Periyar River) in the dense evergreen forest region of the Western Ghats.

1123. A movement for proper rehabilitation of over 100,000 people being evicted for building a Rs 1,000-crore multi-purpose dam project over the Narmada River. The movement is led by Baba Amte and Medha Patkar. Arundhati Roy, the Booker Prize winner, is also supporting the movement.

1124. The Baliyapal Movement was against taking over of the thickly populated Baliyapal village's fertile land for testing of missiles.

1125. Iodine-131 and Strontium-90. Iodine-131 can damage white blood cells, bone marrow, spleen, lymph-nodes and cause tumours in human beings. Strontium-90 can replace calcium in plants and animals.

1126. Biosphere Reserves are multipurpose protected areas meant to preserve the genetic diversity in representative eco-systems.

1127. India has 12 Biosphere Reserves.

QUIZ BOOKS

Knowledge is Power — Arm your child with it!
• THE POWER TO WIN • THE POWER TO EXCEL • THE POWER TO COME FIRST

That's what your child will find in these Quiz books. Brilliant books packed with up-to-date information. Designed precisely to boost your child's knowledge-base. Each page alive with new facts. In an engrossing form of short Questions and Answers with explanatory Illustrations. Making it easy to read. Easy to follow.

72/-

60/-

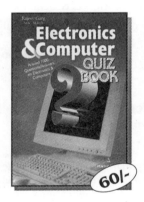

60/-

72/-

60/-

72/-

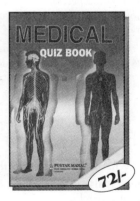

72/-

Postage: Rs. 10/- to 25/- each book

QUIZ BOOKS

Global Quiz Bank

—Gladys Ambat

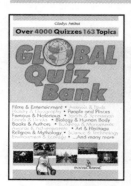

Quiz blitzkrieg are brain fitness fundas of a unique kind! The thrill to win or lose gaming session of a quiz programme can give you an optimum level of mental fitness and alertness. You simply bubble over with the sheer joy of challenge.

The book is a lively presentation for all youngsters & a pleasant leisure companion for the elders. The veteran author has put together over 4000 exciting quizzes and interesting brain-teasers to get all keyed up. While you race through every page — you could find yourself sitting on the edge of the chair. Yet, you get charged with a spirit of challenge to unearth hidden answers or solve uncharted problems by your latent thinking power. The enormous variety of startling quizzes promises to stretch your mind to new horizons of thought & learning.

This is your vantage point for self-improvement and an enriching pursuit.

The book covers: • Quiz Medley & Quickies • Palindromes & Proverbs • Villains in History & Fiction • Word Game— A Bouquet of Words • Vowel-less Words & Words of Two Letters • Sobriquets & Scrambles

The list has 163 subtitles, each crammed with many interesting quizzes and teasers. Read on and get ready for action to star in a captivating quiz gaming session.

Demy Size • Pages: 256 • Price: Rs. 96/- • Postage: Rs. 15/-

4000 Quizzes
on General Science, Physics, Chemistry and Biology

"How come he's got more marks than me when

I'm more intelligent than him ?"

It's a common sentiment expressed by many students from time to time. The answer to this is simple. Taking an exam is an art —and only he who approaches the task in a more systematic and scientific manner comes out a winner.

One common aspect of the exam-taking strategy is revision. Answering random questions about your subject can clearly demonstrates the extent of your preparation.

Now '4000 Quizzes' makes revision easier and convenient for all science students. Written by leading experts in the field, it helps students with quick revisions in one-line questions with one-word answers.

- Which of these Vitamins is soluble in water?
  A B C D E
- Which is the odd man out ?
  Gunpowder, Petrol, Phosphorous, Water, Paraffin, Alcohol
- What is the missing word?
  Hailstorms are frozen ....
- What name is given to the molten rocks that are erupted by volcanoes ?

The book is also useful for quiz-buffs and those who have an abiding interest in science. Covering every aspect of general science, physics, chemistry and biology, it works as a ready reckoner for every student of science.

Demy Size • Pages: 240 • Price: Rs. 96/- • Postage: Rs. 15/-

Popular Science & Encyclopedias

140/- each

Also available in Hindi

120/-

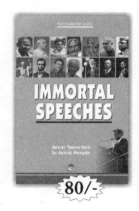

80/-

150/-

Also available in Hindi

120/-

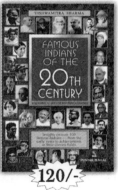

120/-

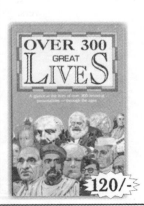

120/-

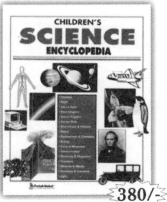

380/-

96/-

Postage:
Rs. 15/- to 30
each book.

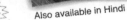